WITHDRAWN

Campaigning to the New American Electorate

# Campaigning to the New American Electorate

*Advertising to Latino Voters*

Marisa A. Abrajano

Stanford University Press
Stanford, California

Stanford University Press
Stanford, California

Printed in the United States of America on acid-free, archival-quality paper

Library of Congress Cataloging-in-Publication Data

Abrajano, Marisa, 1977–
Campaigning to the new American electorate : advertising to Latino voters / Marisa A. Abrajano.
    p.  cm.
    Includes bibliographical references and index.
    ISBN 978-0-8047-6895-5 (cloth : alk. paper) — ISBN 978-0-8047-6896-2 (pbk. : alk. paper)
    1. Advertising, Political—United States.   2. Political campaigns—United States.   3. Hispanic Americans—Politics and government.   I. Title.
JK2281.A26 2010
324.70973—dc22
                                                                        2009052985

Typeset by Motto Publishing Services in 10/14 Minion

*This book is dedicated to my parents,*
*Jess and Mary Abrajano, for all their*
*sacrifices, support, and unconditional love.*

# Contents

# Acknowledgments

THIS BOOK, A WORK IN PROGRESS since 2003, would not have been possible without encouragement, advice, and suggestions from so many individuals. I am most indebted to my graduate advisor and now collaborator, Jonathan Nagler, for the countless hours of advice and suggestions. It is really difficult to express in words my deep gratitude for all the support he has provided throughout my graduate career and postgraduate life as junior faculty. This book is truly a reflection of all the years of training and mentorship that he provided. I also thank Mike Alvarez for being such a great mentor and for his constant encouragement and motivation.

I was fortunate to receive feedback on an earlier version of this project from the political science departments at Brown University; Dartmouth College; Texas A&M University; the University of California, San Diego (UCSD); the University of Connecticut; the University of Illinois at Urbana-Champaign; The University of Texas at Austin; and the University of Washington. My colleagues at UCSD—Amy Bridges, Gary Cox, Steve Erie, Zoltan Hajnal, Thad Kousser, Mat McCubbins, Megumi Naoi, Keith Poole, Sam Popkin, and Sebastian Saiegh—have offered very helpful suggestions and support on the project over the years. I offer a most heartfelt thanks to Zoli in particular for reading the entire manuscript and providing so many thoughtful and constructive comments. I thank Gary for his assistance in the development of the policy complexity scale, and Mat for his words of encouragement during the book review and publication process. Sebastian painstakingly read the manuscript and offered endless hours of advice and support, especially in the bleakest of times. I thank also Neal Beck, Ben Bishin, Feryal Cherif,

Anna Harvey, Tomás Jiménez, Paul Kellstadt, Skip Lupia, Becky Morton, and Costas Panagopoulos for their assistance and advice in the framing and packaging of the project. Special thanks must also go to Lisa García Bedolla, who has been a great source of support during the ups and downs of the writing process.

Moreover, I owe a debt of gratitude to Steve Erie, who introduced me to Stacy Wagner and the excellent staff at Stanford University Press. It has been a pleasure to work with Stacy, and she has guided me through the book publication process in such an efficient and painless manner. I would also like to thank the two reviewers of the book who provided constructive comments. Three graduate research assistants at UCSD—Hans Hassell, Michael Rivera, and Jaime Settle—did an excellent job at coding the 2004 ads, for which I am most grateful.

Finally, my family and friends have been an ongoing source of support and encouragement throughout this whole process. To Ana, Brett, Baleen, Michelle, Nicole, Carolina, Sunny, Costas, and Caroleen, thanks so much for all your support from the very beginning. And to my parents, Jess and Mary Abrajano, and my siblings, Malou and Judd, I cannot thank you enough for all your pep talks and words of encouragement throughout the years.

Campaigning to the New American Electorate

# 1 Campaigning to a Changing American Electorate

*Hispanics are different to communicate to . . . the Hispanic community is not homogenous. . . . They are complex in their own and unique ways, less partisan, more independent. . . . I don't pretend to understand . . . but I do know enough to hire people who do.*[1]
—**Bill Knapp, 2000 Gore campaign media strategist**

IN THE SPRING OF 2000, the leaders of the Democratic Party faced a crisis that would have serious repercussions for the upcoming presidential election. The issue involved a boy by the name of Elian Gonzalez who had illegally crossed the Florida straits along with his mother and others from Cuba. Elian's mother died in the crossing, and the U.S. government was faced with a decision—send Elian back to his father in Cuba or grant him permanent residency in the U.S. so he could reside with his relatives in Florida. Vice President and Democratic presidential candidate Al Gore split with the administration and supported a congressional bill that would provide the boy with permanent residency. Gore adopted this position with the hope of securing the support of Florida's crucial voting bloc of Latinos, composed mostly of Cuban Americans but also of Central and South Americans. The Clinton administration, however, decided to go in the opposite direction. On April 13, 2000, the Department of Justice sent eight fully armed agents from the Immigration and Naturalization Service (INS) to forcibly remove Gonzalez from his great-uncle's house and return him to his father in Cuba. The handling of the Elian Gonzalez case proved to be disastrous for Gore's support among Florida Latinos.[2] It infuriated the Cuban community and, as scholars Kevin Hill and Dario Moreno (2005) note, Cuban voters used the 2000 presidential election as a referendum on the Clinton-Gore administration's handling of the affair. In light of the fallout from this incident, the Gore campaign surrendered any hope of winning the Latino vote in Miami and minimized its Spanish-language outreach efforts. This was hailed as a crucial mistake, as noted by Paulo Izquierdo, one of the consultants in charge of Gore's Spanish-language campaign: "With a true 20-20 hindsight, I'm sure it would have made a big difference . . . We think that if we had been stronger in Miami we would have won Florida. We could have picked up those thousand votes very easily" (Oberfield and Segal 2008, 297).[3]

Undoubtedly, as this sequence of events reveals, the Latino electorate and Latino outreach efforts play a critical role in the electoral success of any presidential hopeful. Bill Knapp's sentiments, however, illustrate that *what* to say to the Latinos and *how* to say it can be a challenge, particularly in the high-stakes game of presidential campaigns. The Latino population, as defined by the U.S. Census Bureau, encompasses an ethnically and culturally diverse group of individuals from Mexico and Latin America.[4] People of Latino origin also vary tremendously in their histories and backgrounds. Whereas much of the southwestern portion of the U.S. once belonged to Mexico, many Cubans immigrated to Florida seeking political asylum from the Castro regime; Puerto Ricans, meanwhile, are a unique case because, as American citizens, they can come and go as they please.[5] Individuals of Latino origin can be fifth- or sixth-generation Americans, recent immigrants, or somewhere in between. Although these are just a few of the features that contribute to the heterogeneity of the Latino population, they exemplify some of the difficulties that politicians face in courting this group of voters.

Latinos' rising prominence in American politics can primarily be attributed to their rapid demographic growth over the past three decades. Consider, for instance, the following realities—Latinos in 2009 make up 15 percent (44.3 million) of the total U.S. population, but by 2050, the U.S. Census projects that Latinos will constitute a quarter of the population. From 1990 to 2000, the Latino population increased by 57.9 percent, from 22.4 million to 35.3 million, while the rest of the U.S. population grew by only 13.2 percent during this same period (Guzman 2001). The rapid growth of the U.S. Latino population can be attributed to two factors: demographics and immigration trends. With a median age of 26.9, the Latino population is younger, on average, than the rest of the U.S. population, which has a median age of 40.1 (U.S. Census Bureau 2007). Because they tend to be younger, Latinos also tend to have higher fertility rates than the population as a whole. A steady stream of immigrants from Mexico and Central and South America over the past four decades has also contributed to the Latino boom. In 1970, only 19.9 percent of the U.S. Latino population was foreign born; by 2000, almost half of the Latino population (45.5 percent) was born outside of the U.S. (Campbell and Lennon 1999).

These demographic changes have important implications for the current and future state of American politics. First, Latinos are still politically "up for grabs"—they have yet to exhibit stable political and partisan preferences to the same degree as African Americans (Frymer 1999).[6] Although estimates of the Latino electorate's support for the Democratic presidential candidate have generally hovered around 60 percent for the past thirty years (Schmal 2004), many more Latinos than Anglos report being independents or uncertain about their partisan preferences (Hajnal and Lee 2008). Forty-seven percent of Latino respondents in the 1993–94 Multi-City Survey of Urban Inequality refused to answer the party identification question, responded that they "didn't know" which party they supported, or indicated that they had no preference for either of the two main political parties. The 2006 Latino National Survey similarly found that 16.6 percent of Latinos report being independent, 16.3 percent "don't care" about their party identification, and 20.1 percent don't know or do not consider themselves to be affiliated with a political party (Abrajano and Alvarez, forthcoming).

Recent elections have also revealed Latinos' lack of partisan rootedness. In the 1998 midterm elections, Republican candidates were able to secure more than one-third (36.3 percent) of the Latino electorate. And in the 2004 presidential election, the National Election Pool estimates that 53.3 percent of Latinos supported the Democratic candidate, John Kerry, while 44 percent cast their ballots for the Republican incumbent, George W. Bush. This marked the first time that Republicans captured 40 percent or more of the Latino vote in a presidential or midterm election.[7] Republicans interpreted this level of support as a sign that Latinos' political preferences are changing, whereas the result convinced Democrats that they cannot assume Latinos will automatically support their candidates.

Much of the Latino population is also geographically concentrated in battleground states and those with a large number of electoral college votes. In each of the five states of California, Texas, Florida, Illinois, and New York, Latinos constitute between 20 and 35 percent of the statewide population; these five states alone account for 168 total electoral college votes, which is more than half of the votes needed for victory in a presidential election. Latinos similarly make up a sizable segment of the statewide population in battleground states such as Arizona, Colorado, Nevada, and New Mexico. And in the politically important southern region of the United States, the Latino population is growing faster than in any other region of the country (Kochhar et al. 2005). For instance, Mecklenburg County, North Carolina, which includes the city of Charlotte, experienced a 500 percent increase in the size of its Latino population from 1990 to 2000 (Kochhar et al. 2005). Latinos are important political players, then, not only in the states in which they have traditionally settled (primarily in the southwestern United States) but also in nontraditional settlement areas across the nation. The geographic concentration of Latinos in key states, along with the instability of their political orientation, heightens their attractiveness to candidates and political parties. For these reasons, the Latino electorate has been considered *the* critical swing group and the "sleeping giant" of American politics.

But as Bill Knapp's chapter-opening quote suggests, the Latino population, when considered as a pool of potential voters, is substantially different from the national population as a whole. Primarily because forty percent of the Latino population is born outside the U.S. (U.S. Census Bureau 2007), their familiarity with American politics is not the same as it is for the native-born population. How these immigrants conceptualize basic political terms, such as *liberal* and *conservative* or *Democrats* and *Republicans*, is likely to vary from native-born Americans, given that these terms are unique to the U.S. political system. This unfamiliarity is reflected in survey responses from the 2006 Latino National Survey (Fraga et al. 2006), in which nearly one-third (31.6 percent) of Latinos did not consider themselves liberal, moderate, or conservative. In addition, the concept of multiparty politics is relatively new to some Latinos (Kasinitz et al. 2008). Take, for example, the case of Latinos of Mexican heritage: a one-party system led by the Institutional Revolutionary Party (PRI) ruled the country from 1929 to 2000 (Cothran 1994). The children of immigrants are also affected by this lack of familiarity because children learn about politics and acquire partisanship mainly through their parents (Vaillancourt 1973). The Latino population also differs from the rest of the U.S. population on indicators pertaining to socioeconomic well being. According to U.S. Census estimates, Latinos' median household income is lower than that of Anglos, Asians, and African Americans, and only about 60 percent of Latinos graduate from high school—the lowest graduation rate of any racial or ethnic group in the country (U.S. Census Bureau 2007). Approximately one out of five Latinos lives in poverty, and almost one out of three (32.7 percent) lack health insurance (U.S. Census Bureau 2007).

In light of the fact that socioeconomics and familiarity with politics are strong predictors of political participation (Verba et al. 1995), Latinos have yet to reach their full political potential. While their total share of the U.S.

population stands at 15 percent (U.S. Census Bureau 2007), Latinos make up 6 percent of the total American electorate. In 2004, about 9.3 million Latinos—less than a quarter of the total U.S. Latino population—registered to vote, with 7.6 million having reported voting. As a point of comparison, almost 16 million African Americans were registered in 2004, and 14 million reported voting (Abrajano and Alvarez, forthcoming). Thus, although Latinos constitute a larger share of the total U.S. population than do African Americans, they make up a smaller percentage of voters. This difference is partly because a significant number of Latinos face another hurdle before registering to vote—that of obtaining citizenship. The Current Population Survey estimates that only 63 percent of Latinos of voting age are citizens (U.S. Census Bureau 2009).[8]

Still, the growing size and influence of the Latino electorate presents a compelling opportunity for politicians to win over new voters and, ideally, lock in the allegiance of this group in the hope of future returns. Yet the particular demographic and political characteristics of the Latino electorate offer challenges to politicians as well, because it is not yet clear which strategies of campaigning are likely to win these voters over, and it is unclear whether Latino voters will behave like other, well-understood segments of the electorate. Conventional wisdom holds that candidates will advertise differently to ethnic and racial groups than they will to Anglos, because candidates are targeting a specific group of voters who presumably share something in common (Erie 1990; Popkin 1994; DeFrancesco Soto and Merolla 2008; Shea and Burton 2006). Among Latinos, that commonality is based on a shared language and, in some cases, a common cultural heritage. One can conceive of a group in much the same way that Bishin's work on subconstituency politics does, as "a constellation of people, either organized or not, who share a social identity owing to a common experience that leads to shared concerns and preferences" (2009, 5). Appealing to individuals based on culture is a powerful and relatively easy way to show voters that candidates understand and can relate to them (Popkin 1994). Indeed, politicians used ethnic campaigns on European immigrants who arrived in the U.S. in the late 1800s (Erie 1990; McNickle 1993). Presumably, then, these campaigns work, because politicians have been using them for decades. So we should expect nothing less of aspiring politicians today; when campaigning to our nation's largest immigrant group, they too should adopt a distinct ethnic political campaign.

The aim of this book is twofold. My first goal is to determine whether ethnic political campaigns are successful at winning ethnic minority votes. I challenge the conventional wisdom that all minorities will react to these campaign appeals in a positive way. The responsiveness of a given ethnic minority group to these political messages will vary based on the extent to which they have incorporated into American political life. My second goal is to examine the consequences, if any, that ethnic political campaigns have on the political health and well being of a segment of the ethnic group being targeted.

In addressing these issues, this book focuses specifically on the Spanish- and English-language televised political ads created for the 2000–2004 election cycles and examines the effects of the ads on Latino political behavior. Does exposure to these political ads influence who they vote for, whether or not they vote, and their knowledge of the candidates? Indeed, variations are likely to exist in the content of Spanish- and English-language ads, so that ads produced in Spanish may emphasize personal and non-policy-based appeals to a greater extent than do English-language ads. The reason for these distinctions, which serves as the basis for the theory of information based–advertising, is due to candidates' perceptions of Latinos' orientation to politics and to candidates' beliefs about the importance of ethnic identity as a factor in Latinos' political decision making. In general, because a large portion of the Latino population is relatively new to American political life, the campaign messages used to target this group of voters is fairly simple and symbolic in nature, focusing more on cultural cues and references than on candidates' policies and issue positions. The effectiveness of these campaign messages varies based on a Latino's familiarity with and knowledge of American politics and on the salience of ethnic identity in one's political behavior.

The research endeavor undertaken for this book is important for the well being of our nation's latest newcomers. First, if candidates are indeed advertising in the manner just described, it raises the possibility that the parties and candidates are acting in ways that systematically disadvantage some segments of the population in becoming informed participants in the political process. Because televised political ads aid in citizen learning by increasing one's knowledge of politics (Jackman and Vavreck 2009; Geer 2006; Patterson and McClure 1976; Brians and Wattenberg 1996), ads that mostly emphasize personal or cultural appeals make it difficult for individuals to learn anything about the candidates' policy positions. Adopting this type of advertising strategy also weakens the ability of certain communities to participate in politics the same way that others do, and, in turn, to have their voices heard. Finally, a bias in advertising could serve to undermine a basic principle of democracy—that all people are treated equally under the government. Several of these consequences are investigated in this book.

## The Power of Televised Political Advertising

In attempting to communicate with and win over voters, politicians have innumerable tools at their disposal, including campaign appearances, direct mailings, websites, televised debates and speeches, and door-to-door canvassing, to name just a few. But in the era of "new style" campaigning (Agranoff 1972), televised political advertisements have become the primary means by which candidates communicate with voters. This is clearly reflected in the way candidates allocate campaign funds. In the 2000 election cycle, approximately 85 percent of candidates' advertising budgets went to broadcast "spot" television advertisements (Segal 2002). The amount of money spent on advertising is staggering: in 2000, presidential candidate George W. Bush spent $75.3 million on televised campaign ads, while his opponent, Al Gore, allocated $77.1 million.

It is also by means of televised advertisements that candidates have most notably adjusted their behavior to take advantage of the growing influence of Latino voters. In the 2000 election cycle, both George W. Bush and Al Gore devoted approximately $4 million to Spanish-language television commercials. This spending marked the largest amount ever allocated by presidential candidates to Spanish-language advertising, and the millions of dollars devoted to appeals in Spanish has steadily increased since (Segal 2002).

That candidates spend such vast sums on television commercials is an acknowledgment of these advertisements' power to influence voters. The advent of televised political advertising in the presidential election of 1948 initially raised great concern about this power among scholars, the media, and the general public. This fear led to popular claims that political ads were deceitful and overly personalistic and lacked substantive material (West 2001, 44, 46). Scholars and the general public believed that, in advertisements, "the candidate's personality, image, and symbolic appeals [take] precedence over specific issue positions" (Atkin et al. 1973, 210). Berelson and colleagues (1954) alleviated some of these concerns; their research concluded that short-term effects, such as campaigns, had a minimal influence on voter decision making. Berelson and his colleagues argued that political campaigns did not provide new information to voters but instead triggered voters' previous beliefs and opinions. These findings led many scholars to support the "minimal effects hypothesis," which contends that campaigns have little or no impact on a voter's decision-making process.

Decades of research following Berelson's seminal work, along with technological advancements in measuring advertising exposure, leave little doubt that television ads influence voters' opinions and attitudes in presidential elections and nonpresidential elections alike (Brader 2006; Geer 2006; West 2001; Mendelberg 2001; Just et al. 1996; Herrnson and Patterson 2000; Kahn and Kenney 1999). As one might expect, more frequent advertising positively affects a candidate's vote share (Clinton and Lapinski 2004; Freedman and Goldstein 1999; Nagler and Leighley 1992; Shaw 1999). Using aggregate state-level data on voting from the 1988–1996 presidential elections, Shaw (1999) found a positive correlation between the amount of advertising candidates purchased and the share of the vote they won. Nagler and Leighley (1992) uncovered a similar relationship, finding that an increase in campaign advertising spending positively correlated with a candidate's share of the vote.

A televised political ad contains several distinct elements, all of which can affect the way voters assess candidates. One element of an ad is the tone, which refers to the way the message is crafted and is generally categorized as positive, negative, or comparative (Jamieson 1992; Shea and Burton 2006). The tone of political ads has received considerable attention from political scientists (Brader 2006; Geer 2006; Clinton and Lapinski 2004; Freedman and Goldstein 1999; Lau and Sigelman 2000; Kahn and Kenney 1999; Ansolabehere et al. 1994; Ansolabehere and Iyengar 1995). For example, whereas the extensive studies conducted by Ansolabahere and Iyengar find that attack advertising depresses turnout, Geer (2006) argues that negative ads tend to be more informative and substantive in their content than do positive ads.

In addition to the overall tone of an advertisement, how its message is presented—what political scientists call "framing"—can influence individuals' opinions and attitudes toward the particular issue under discussion (Nir and Druckman 2008; Winter 2008; Druckman 2004; Jacoby 2000; Iyengar 1991; Iyengar and Kinder 1987; Nelson et al. 1997; Entman 1993). A frame can be thought of as the point of view that a message takes (Popkin 1994; Tversky and Kahneman 1981). Framing is important because point of view determines which types of information and which considerations the message brings to mind for voters. As such, the standards by which an individual evaluates a campaign message may change depending on the frame being used in the advertisement. One way that issues can be framed is from a "group-centric" perspective. This approach is advantageous when an issue, such as crime, immigration, or welfare, specifically deals with or is identified with a particular group. Nelson and Kinder (1996) found that frames that focus on the groups associated with an issue (for example, African Americans and affirmative action), lead individuals to think about their attitudes toward the particular group rather than about the actual policy being addressed. Candidates may therefore be motivated to frame certain issues in a group-centric manner, either positively or negatively, to appeal to particular voters; a candidate might frame a commercial about immigration reform in a way that evokes Latino voters' positive feelings about economic opportunity in the United States or, alternatively, in a way that amplifies Anglo voters' negative feelings about Latino immigrants. In a related work, Winter (2008) offers evidence demonstrating how the discourse on welfare reform and Social Security over the past twenty years has been framed largely along racial lines. Thus, Anglo Americans' opinions on these issues have been shaped, to some degree, by racial bias.

Advertisements also attempt to prime voters to respond in particular ways. Priming is a concept drawn from the psychology literature on decision making (Kahneman et al. 1979). It refers to the idea that individuals will use the information that is most readily available and accessible to them when making decisions. Thus, a person's decision-making process is influenced to some extent by circumstance: the topics and themes of political ads viewed in the days leading up to the election are likely to affect how that person votes. Although priming does not overtly alter individuals' opinions and beliefs, it has the potential to influence the issues voters consider to be most important (Iyengar and Kinder 1987). Priming has also been found to be effective at activating voters' racial biases. When political advertisements contain subtle racial cues or negative stereotypes about racial and ethnic minorities, they can cause an individual's racial attitudes to also become more negative (Mendelberg 2001; Valentino et al. 2002).

The experimental work conducted by Mendelberg (2001) and Valentino and his colleagues (2002) found, however, that activating an individual's racial attitudes is effective only when the racial message is both visually and verbally implicit. Take, for example, the infamous Willie Horton ad, which criticized Democratic nominee Michael Dukakis for supporting weekend furlough programs in Massachusetts. Horton, an African American convict serving a life sentence for murder, committed armed robbery and rape while on furlough from prison. The effectiveness of this ad was attributed to the fact that, although it contained visual images of Horton, no mention was made of "racial nouns or adjectives to endorse white prerogatives, express anti-black sentiment, represent racial stereotypes, or portray a threat from African-Americans" (Mendelberg 2001, 8). The Willie Horton ad was framed in a way that encouraged voters to associate negative feelings about race with Dukakis's presidential bid or with the weekend furlough program, and it did so without explicitly mentioning race. The frames used in such political ads can prime voters' evaluations of the candidates featured in the ads and the policies that they discuss (Iyengar and Kinder 1987; Iyengar 1991), just as the Horton ad primed voters to carry prejudicial feelings with them to their polling places.

Finally, agenda-setting refers to the order in which political messages are discussed in an advertisement. If, for example, a candidate consistently emphasized education as his most important campaign issue, voters might perceive education as the issue most salient in their decision about which candidate to vote for. Extensive work by Iyengar and Kinder (1987) in this area finds that "those problems that receive prominent attention on the national news become the problems the viewing public regards as the nation's most important" (16). Both experimental work and survey data provide strong support for the argument that the issues a political ad emphasizes can influence which issues and policies individuals consider important (Herrnson and Patterson 2000).

All of these means of influencing voters help to make televised political advertising more effective than other tools at the candidates' disposal. Moreover, the content of political advertising is valuable in voter education. Political advertising can serve to reduce voters' misperceptions and uncertainty (Lupia and McCubbins 1998; Popkin 1994; Lupia 1994; Bartels 1993; Conover and Feldman 1989) as well as to provide cues that assist voters in their decision making (Lau and Redlawsk 2006; Popkin 1994; Lupia 1994). Information is costly to attain and thus provides voters with little incentive to gather it, but information shortcuts, or heuristics, can help reduce these costs (Kahneman et al. 1982). Such heuristics can take the form of reliance on campaign messages, on experiences from individuals' daily lives, or on using information experts, such as political commentators, as sources of knowledge (Lupia 1994; Popkin 1994). Some of the most readily available cues for voters are provided by the messages in the increasing number of televised political ads. But the type of information shortcut voters use depends on their stored levels of political knowledge; those who are less politically informed are more likely to evaluate a candidate based on the candidate's personal characteristics as opposed to his or her policy positions (Popkin and Dimock 1999). Thus, information shortcuts can be incredibly helpful to voters, but how they use them and the extent to which they help voters make decisions that are consistent with their own beliefs is also contingent on their familiarity with and knowledge of politics.

The authors of numerous studies have performed content analysis to determine what sorts of messages are being advertised in presidential and congressional campaigns (Spilliotes and Vavreck 2002; West 2001; Jamieson 1996; Joslyn 1980; Hofstetter and Zukin 1979; Patterson and McClure 1976). For instance, Jamieson (1996) finds that, with the exception of 1960 and 1976, domestic-related issues (for example, the economy, social issues, and taxes) are more prevalent in political ads than are messages relating to a candidate's personal qualities (for example, leadership, trustworthiness, and compassion).[9] And during the 2000 election, Jamieson notes that 60 percent of all commercials contained messages pertaining to policy matters, while only 31 percent mentioned a candidate's personal qualities. Moreover, regarding the 1998 election cycle, Spilliotes and Vavreck (2002) examined 1,000 advertisements by 290 candidates; they found that 92 percent of the ads contained some issue content. Although these studies reveal that many of the political ads produced over the past forty years include policy-related appeals, and, to a lesser extent, personality and trait appeals, it is unclear whether voters are persuaded more by policy or nonpolicy messages in their vote choice as well as in their likelihood of voting.

## Targeted Advertising Efforts

With the help of political consultants who draw on telephone surveys, focus groups, and myriad other resources, candidates make strategic decisions about what messages to advertise and to which voters. Scholars have offered a number of important insights into how these decisions are made. Candidates may be motivated to advertise more simple policy and character statements to Latinos than to Anglos depending on the candidates' ideological distance from the median voter of their district. The more ideologically distant a candidate is from the median voter in his or her district, the less likely that candidate will be to reveal his or her policy positions and, therefore, to advertise policy. Or it may be that candidates advertise policy messages only when they are in a highly competitive election (Kahn and Kenney 1999).[10] Although the existing research considers how the electoral context shapes candidates' advertising strategies, scholars have generally failed to account for one critical aspect of these strategies: the target audience. When deciding what campaign messages to use, today's candidates are more prone than ever before to consider who constitutes their potential group of supporters (Bradshaw 2004; Jamieson 1992) and how likely these voters are to respond to their campaign appeals.

In designing political ads with particular racial groups in mind, strategists assume that membership in a racial demographic carries with it shared concerns, interests, and experiences (Shea and Burton 2006). With advances in communication and technology, especially database technology, demographic targeting "has become a routine part of campaign operations" (56). Political consultants encourage candidates to develop an ethnic targeting program that "identifies what ethnic group an individual or family belongs to primarily by looking at and analyzing the last name." Once this has been done, "ethnic-based mailings can be sent on the basis of each ethnic group's presumed interests" (55).[11] But using an individual's last name to develop an ethnic marketing campaign is not a foolproof strategy. Given the increasing rates of intermarriage in the U.S., the surname Garcia or Rodriguez could refer to someone who is not of Latino descent.[12] Moreover, individuals with these surnames can have vastly different backgrounds—some may have immigrated to the U.S. within the past year, whereas others may have great-grandparents who were born in the U.S. Thus, assuming that all Latinos have similar concerns is problematic, as generational status and ethnic group background are just two categories in which we see differences among Latinos' political attitudes and behaviors (Abrajano and Alvarez, forthcoming; Branton 2007; Hood et al. 1997; de la Garza and DeSipio 1992).

Candidates can move away from a reliance on Spanish surname lists by targeting a significant number of Latinos in a medium that caters specifically to them and one that other individuals are not privy to. That is, politicians can communicate to a large segment of the Latino population *in* Spanish and *on* Spanish-language television. By doing so, candidates are guaranteed that most of their intended audience is being exposed to their campaign messages. Although not all Latinos rely on Spanish-language television, there are 28.1 million Spanish speakers in the U.S., 28.5 percent of whom do not speak English well or at all (Shin and Bruno 2003).[13] This means that candidates who advertise in Spanish are directly reaching out to a sizeable number of Spanish-dominant Latinos and potentially reaching out to an even larger number of bilingual Latinos. The estimates just cited from Shin and Bruno also offer insight about the Latino population. Because language acquisition has long been used as a proxy to measure a newcomer's rate of assimilation and level of incorporation of the values, beliefs, and behaviors of the host society (Portes and Rumbaut 1992; Bloemraad 2006; de la Garza et al. 1995), we can infer that Spanish-dominant Latinos are likely to be less incorporated into American society than are English-speaking Latinos. As such, Latinos who rely on Spanish are probably less politically active in, less interested in, and less knowledgeable about American politics than are English-dominant and bilingual Latinos. Overall, although advertising in Spanish does not ensure that candidates are reaching out to the entire Latino population, it is certainly more precise than relying on ethnic surname lists alone. Especially for those competing in national elections, broadcasting televised political ads in Spanish offers the most efficient way to reach out to the greatest number of individuals, because candidates can potentially communicate to millions of Latinos through the creation of just a handful of advertisements.

I now turn to some of the ads created in the 2000 presidential race. Gore's most frequently aired Spanish-language advertisement was titled "National Anthem." This ad begins with a visual image of a Latina stating, "They have arrived from far [away] but are looking to do things in which they are trained."[14] Next, another Latina states, "I have needs, I want more opportunities." In the final image of the political spot, an elderly Latina states, "For these and other reasons, this is why I am voting for Gore."

As a point of comparison, the political spot Gore used with the greatest frequency to target his English-speaking audience is called "Veteran." The commercial begins with images of students graduating from high school, with the narrator discussing Gore's plans for "$500 billion in targeted tax cuts," a "$10,000-a-year tax deduction for college tuition," and "welfare reform with time limits and work requirements."[15] The image then shifts to one of police officers, with the corresponding voice-over referencing a proposal for a "crime victims' bill of rights" as well as efforts to "fight violence and pornography on the Internet."

It seems clear that Gore targeted his Spanish-speaking and English-speaking populations with distinct campaign messages. Gore's Spanish-language ad makes absolutely no explicit references to his policy positions, proposals, or ideological beliefs. Instead, it focuses on Latinos' immigrant backgrounds, apparently with the goal of priming voters to think that voting for Gore will make them more likely to succeed in the United States. In stark contrast, Gore's English-language commercial is filled with more-detailed information about his proposed tax initiatives, welfare reforms, and crime legislation.

## The Argument

The variation in the content of these two Gore ads can be explained with the theory of information-based advertising: candidates will tailor their advertising messages on the basis of their perceptions of the ability of their target audience to respond to these messages. Candidates may wish to avoid broadcasting ads that contain overly complicated and detailed messages regarding their issue positions or policies to a group of voters that is fairly new to the political process. As this targeted group also shares a common cultural heritage, candidates may also find it advantageous to incorporate ethnic specific appeals in their ads. Research by political communication scholars (see Connaughton 2005; Connaughton and Jarvis 2004; Benoit 2000) explains this phenomenon through identification theory—candidates attempt to connect to voters by associating themselves, either through symbols, individuals, or personal experiences, with the particular group of voters being targeted.

As the findings from this book will demonstrate, the decision to target Latinos in this manner produces different effects among this group of voters. Spanish-language ads and other ads that specifically target Latinos who have yet to fully incorporate into U.S. political life (using, for example, an ad that features a Latino) influence their political behavior positively. Such ads make them more likely to vote and more likely to support the candidate who uses these ads. Yet politically incorporated Latinos will be less influenced by these ethnic-based appeals; instead, policy-based ads have a larger impact on their voting behavior. As these Latinos have become integrated and incorporated into American politics, their political behavior has mirrored that of the American electorate, so that a candidate's policies and positions affects who they vote for. (Alvarez and Nagler 1995; Page 1978; Downs 1957).

The normative implications from these different campaign strategies are twofold. First, I offer evidence demonstrating that the knowledge levels of the candidates' policies among Spanish-dominant Latinos were lower than for English-dominant Latinos, African Americans, and Anglos. I will also show

how Spanish-dominant Latinos are less likely to behave as issue voters when compared with English-dominant Latinos. Again, these differences arise because the content of Spanish-language ads is less informative than is the content of English-language ads.

## Organization of the Book

In Chapter 2, the specific framework of the central arguments is presented. I first provide an in-depth discussion of one primary aspect of the political acculturation process—the factors that contribute to an individual's knowledge of politics. This discussion is critical given that my theory of information-based advertising is grounded in the assumption that candidates use this indicator in deciding which messages to include in their Spanish- and English-language advertisements. The testable predictions from this theory are also presented in Chapter 2.

Chapter 3 discusses the historical and current-day campaign efforts used by candidates to appeal to Latinos in the U.S. Although advertising to such groups is not a recent phenomenon, the emergence of Spanish-language commercials makes it possible to systematically analyze how candidates target ethnic minorities, given that these efforts are clearly intended for a specific audience. Chapter 3 also provides readers with the campaign context and Spanish-language advertising efforts for the presidential, Senate, House, and gubernatorial elections that occurred from 2000 to 2004.

Chapter 4 begins with empirical tests of the theory of information-based advertising. I first examine the content of campaign advertisements used in the 2000, 2002, and 2004 election cycles. I take advantage of a unique data source that contains television ads reaching out to more than 80 percent of the U.S. population for these election periods. This data allows for an important advancement in our understanding of the campaign process, because it has been a challenge to gather data of such depth and magnitude in the past.[16] For each Spanish- and English-language advertisement, I compare the amount and types of policy and nonpolicy messages. Next, I examine which television shows these commercials aired on. Support for the theory of information-based advertising predicts that ads containing complex policy statements will be aired on shows with viewers most likely to understand them (for example, on local or network news), whereas the less-demanding policy messages will be aired on entertainment programs. Finally, I conduct an in-depth analysis of the congressional candidates' use of advertising to determine whether their district's level of education (used as a proxy for political knowledge), level of competition, or political ideology, or some combination of all three, best explains their decision to include policy in their commercials.

Chapter 5 turns to the impact of Spanish-language ads on Latino turnout and vote choice in the 2000 and 2004 presidential elections. In particular, the analysis examines whether Spanish-dominant, and thus less politically incorporated, Latinos were affected by Spanish-language ads in their voting behavior. I conducted this analysis using the National Annenberg Election Surveys (NAES) from 2000 and 2004, both of which contain a sizeable number of Latino respondents. The effect of both Spanish- and English-language political ads on the voting behavior of Latinos is also analyzed, based on their level of political incorporation.

Chapter 6 focuses on the implications of adapting an information-based advertising strategy for the civic and political health of the Latino electorate. Using the 2000 and 2004 NAES allows for an analysis of the campaign messages that most contributed to Latinos' knowledge of the two major presidential candidates. Which political ads did Latinos learn from, and did their learning depend on their level of political incorporation? Latinos' rates of political knowledge are then compared with the rates of political knowledge of non-Latinos. If the Spanish-language ads contained less policy content than the English-language ads, then we may see lower rates of learning for less politically incorporated Latinos than for more-incorporated Latinos, Anglos, and African Americans. Another implication of this campaign strategy pertains to the ability of all Latinos to behave as issue voters. Given the importance that issues play in one's vote decision, the lack of substantive policy messages that less politically incorporated Latinos are targeted with may make it more difficult for them than for acculturated Latinos to use their policy preferences in guiding their vote choice.

Chapter 7 summarizes the major findings from this research and discusses its theoretical contributions to the larger work on campaigns, political advertising, and political behavior. The implications of an information-based advertising strategy on the overall well being of the Latino electorate and for democracy in general are also discussed. Finally, Chapter 8 is a brief discussion of the 2008 presidential campaign efforts targeted to Latinos. Given the strategies used in the 2000–2004 campaigns, it is important to know whether candidates conducting subsequent campaigns have learned from previous experiences and the extent to which they have altered their strategies toward one of the most coveted voting blocs in American politics.

# 2  A Theory of Information-Based Advertising

PEOPLE'S FAMILIARITY WITH POLITICS is crucial during an electoral campaign because such awareness determines how receptive they will be to the countless campaign messages they are exposed to (Lau and Redlawsk 2006; Alvarez 1997; Zaller 1992). Without such awareness, it would be very difficult for voters to discern whether attack advertisements contain some truth to them, how candidates differ on their economic plans and foreign policy positions, and how this information squares with their own predispositions and values. This is especially true for any nation's newcomers, as their country of origin may have very different political structures, practices, and customs from those of their host, or receiving, country. Thus an immigrant's incoming conceptualization of politics may be distinct from the conceptualization of political knowledge in the receiving country, because the political circumstances are no longer the same.

For no population is this more true than for America's largest immigrant group, Latinos. This group comprises individuals hailing from more than twenty countries, whose political histories range from democracies and autocracies to military and single-party rule. A recently arrived immigrant from Latin America may therefore be unfamiliar with the two-party system that characterizes American politics, what the basic differences are between the two parties, and the ways that individuals can participate in politics.

Familiarity with politics plays an important role in deciphering the vast amount of campaign information in a given election, but those vying for elected office should also take into account when developing their campaign strategies the various levels of political familiarity among the electorate. As I briefly discussed in Chapter 1, the relationship between political familiarity, or political knowledge, and campaign advertising strategy serves as one foundation for the theory of information-based advertising.

In this chapter, I provide an in-depth explanation of my theory on advertising as well as the predictions that emerge from it. Moreover, because I test the predictions from the theory of information-based advertising by examining the ads candidates use to target the Spanish-speaking and English-speaking electorates, I also explore the levels of and factors that contribute to political knowledge for these two groups. The crux of my argument rests on the contention that differences exist in the levels of political familiarity between the Spanish-speaking and English-speaking electorates.

## Defining Political Familiarity

The extent to which an individual is aware of current political events and acquainted with the basic ins and outs of the political system is how I define political familiarity. How to measure a person's familiarity with politics has been the subject of much debate in the scholarly literature, with no consensus on a single measure. Some of the most frequently used measures of political familiarity or political knowledge include levels of political interest and participation, educational attainment, media use, and neutral factual knowledge pertaining to politics. Zaller's extensive work on this subject matter led him to conclude the following: "Neutral factual knowledge about politics, to a greater extent than any of the [other measures], captures political learning that has actually occurred—political ideas that the individual has encountered, understood and stored in his head" (1992, 335). Zaller also finds this measure to be theoretically satisfying because answers are not tainted by a respondent's social desire to appear politically knowledgeable, as is the case with self-reported levels of political interest. Moreover, questions about neutral factual knowledge require no subjective estimations of the respondents' levels of political familiarity.

But what factors contribute to one's knowledge of politics? Surely one's life experiences and personal interest in current events have to play some role. To gain a better understanding of this concept, I turn to Delli Carpini and Keeter's (1996) "path of political knowledge" to examine the factors that contribute to my conceptualization of political familiarity. In this path, Delli Carpini and Keeter differentiate between structural factors, which include demographics, years of formal education, income, and occupational opportunities, and behavioral factors, which include one's interest in politics and rate of political participation. I explore each of these factors in the following section, paying special attention to any variations that may arise between Latinos and Anglos.

The demographic characteristic of race plays a particularly important role in the types of structural opportunities (for example, employment opportunities and access to quality public education) available to individuals, thus affecting the distribution of political knowledge among the U.S. population. For the overall Latino population, nativity, or place of birth, is also an especially important factor affecting their level of political knowledge. As of 2000, an estimated 45.5 percent of the Latino population was foreign born (U.S. Census Bureau 2000a).[1] The result of having such a significant portion of the population born outside of the United States is that many Latinos' acculturation and socialization into American society and politics is markedly different from the socialization experiences of those born in this country (Portes and Rumbaut 1992; García Bedolla 2005).[2] Political socialization occurs primarily through formal education and family influences (Hyman 1959; Campbell et al. 1964; Easton and Dennis 1969; Greenstein 1965; Valentino and Sears 1998). Thus, one of the strongest forms of political socialization, the acquisition of partisanship through one's parents (Campbell et al. 1964), may be unavailable to these foreign-born immigrants. Although scholars have questioned the long-term effects of pre-adult socialization (Vaillancourt 1973), especially for partisanship, its long-term stability cannot be overlooked (Petrocik 1996).

Because a majority of foreign-born Latinos (70 percent) arrive in the United States as adults (Campbell and Lennon 1999), they are not exposed to any of the civic learning that takes place in high school or college. The remaining one-third of the foreign-born Latino population is under the age of eighteen. Unfortunately, these young immigrants are more likely than native-born Latinos to drop out of high school (Fry 2007). Thus, almost half of all Latinos in the United States either lack formal U.S. education or fail to complete that education. This makes it a challenge for many Latinos to learn the concepts and ideas that are foundational to knowledge about and interest in the American political system. Moreover, having parents who were born outside the United States virtually eliminates the possibility that foreign-born Latinos can become politically socialized at home. Most foreign-born Latinos eventually do become eligible voters as they naturalize and undergo the citizenship process (DeSipio 1996). But the absence of political socialization in school and at home means that many Latinos are learning about politics through a different process. This suggests that the path of political knowledge outlined by Delli Carpini and Keeter may need to be revised to explain it for immigrants.[3]

There is also strong evidence that the types of schools that racial minorities and Anglo students attend dramatically differ (Orfield and Lee 2006; Fry 2007). Schools with high minority enrollment receive approximately $1,000 less per student each year than schools with the lowest minority enrollments (Fry 2007). Schools with high Latino enrollment receive greater amounts of Title I funding (which is federal funding for schools with large percentages of poor children), suffer from higher teacher-student ratios, and receive more free lunches (one measure used to gauge the poverty rate in schools) than do schools with low Latino enrollment (Fry 2007). Orfield and Lee (2004) estimate that in public schools in which 80 to 90 percent of the population is Latino and African American, 85 percent of the students are living in poverty. Thus, Latino and African American students often have the structural disadvantage of attending schools that are underfunded and under-resourced (Orfield and Lee 2004). This is a significant disadvantage in the political education of these students, because "formal education is a key determinant of how knowledgeable citizens are about politics," and "schooling promotes the acquisition of political knowledge" (Delli Carpini and Keeter 1996, 278).

One of the major consequences of these inequalities is that the rates of civic knowledge of Latino and African American high school students are considerably lower than those of Anglo students. A 1988 survey of more than 4,000 high-school students conducted by the National Assessment of Education Progress found that Anglo students' average rate of civic knowledge (measured as the number of correct answers to civics questions) was 69 percent, compared with 58 percent for Latinos and 56 percent for African Americans. The survey, which included 150 questions related to civic engagement and knowledge of U.S. politics, also revealed that Latino and African American students systematically knew less about the structures and function of the U.S. government, state and local governments, political parties, lobbying, and the basic rights of citizens than did Anglo students.[4] These differences in civic knowledge cannot be attributed to any lack of political interest on the part of Latino and African American high-school students. In fact, a higher percentage of Latino students (51.2 percent) find government interesting to study than do Anglos (40.2 percent); African American students also report slightly higher rates of interest in government (44.1 percent) than do Anglo students (Niemi and Junn 1998).

The most important determinant of political learning for high-school students, Niemi and Junn find, is a school's civics curriculum. The extent to which current events and political issues are discussed as part of the school's curriculum predicts the level of Latino students' political knowledge.[5] Although Niemi and Junn do not directly account for the institutional discrepancies in the types of schools that Anglos and Latinos attend, variation in course offerings can be considered a suitable proxy, because schools with more funding can typically provide a wider array of classes than can schools with less funding. The underfunding of schools with a high minority student population helps to explain why Latinos are learning less about politics than are Anglos, because Latinos' exposure to current-events courses is probably limited due either to the shortage of adequately trained teachers or to an emphasis on other courses, such as vocational classes. In fact, according to Kozol (2005), in many schools with large minority populations, most of the courses offered are geared toward vocational skills, such as sewing and hairdressing. Offering civics- or current events–related courses is likely to be a low priority in schools in which the majority of its students are ethnic or racial minorities.

Although nearly 60 percent of Latinos age 25 or older graduate from high school, approximately 89 percent of non-Hispanic Anglos age 25 or older completed high school (U.S. Census Bureau 2007).[6] A comparison of the household income levels of Latinos, African Americans, and Anglos reveals a similar pattern. Information from the Pew Hispanic Center and the Kaiser Family Foundation reveals that 50 percent of Latinos surveyed in 2002 made less than $30,000 per year, compared with only 29 percent of Anglos and 44 percent of African Americans. Anglos were concentrated in the highest income category (42 percent), whereas only 17 percent of Latinos and 22 percent of African Americans earned enough to fall in that category. More Latinos also live in poverty (29 percent) relative to the three other racial groups (23.7 percent for African Americans, 10.7 percent for Asians, and 8 percent for Anglos).[7] And although the percentage of Latinos who own a home is just slightly lower than it is for African Americans, it is considerably lower than for Asians and Anglos.

These various structural indicators all point to the conclusion that because of hardships Latinos face in the educational system and the size of the foreign-born Latino population, their educational attainment levels are lower than those of non-Latinos, and their educational disadvantage spills over into differences in income and home ownership. The status of Latinos in America's racial paradigm makes it difficult to ignore how instrumental race is in determining their structural opportunities, and therefore their levels of political knowledge.[8] The direct impact of structural variables on political knowledge is evident in the strong correlation between years of formal education and levels of political knowledge (Delli Carpini and Keeter 1996; Niemi and Junn 1998; Nie et al. 1996).

Indirectly, one's schooling and occupation influences the likelihood of one's becoming involved and interested in politics, and political interest and attitudes constitute the behavioral, as opposed to structural, variables that affect political knowledge. How interested one is in politics, how often one pays attention to politics, the extent to which one discusses politics with family and friends, and one's feelings of political efficacy and civic duty are all influenced by structural variables. Those with higher levels of education and income are more likely to be involved in and attentive to politics and to be part of social networks than those with lower levels of education (Verba et al. 1995; Delli Carpini and Keeter 1996). The Citizen Participation Study, conducted by Verba and colleagues (1995), surveyed thousands of individuals regarding their civic and political participation rates, their knowledge of politics, and their political interest, efficacy, and information scores. They measured political interest as a summary score based on a respondent's reported interest in local and national politics.[9] They gauged political efficacy using several questions on whether respondents felt they could influence local and national government decisions and whether they believed that the government would respond to their needs. Across these measures of political attitudes, the study found Latinos to be among the least politically inclined of all the groups surveyed, with a score of 4.9. African American respondents scored an average of 4.9, whereas Anglos scored 5.8. Likewise, Latinos' levels of political efficacy were lower than those of African Americans and Anglos.

The Citizen Participation Study also provides insight on the different forms of political activity that groups engaged in. Latinos' reported rates of participation are lower across eight different types of political activity than those of African Americans and Anglos. Voting is the primary way that individuals participate in politics, and Latinos engage in this activity at much lower rates (40 percent) than do African Americans (65 percent) and Anglos

(72 percent).[10] Similarly, a smaller percentage of Latinos than of Anglos make campaign contributions, contact officials, get involved in informal community activities, and affiliate with organizations. The fact that Latinos, with little variation in citizenship status, contact elected officials at significantly lower rates than do Anglos is particularly troublesome, because contacting officials acquaints immigrants with the institutional aspects of the American political system.

On average, Latinos also participate in fewer political activities than do African Americans and Anglos. The Citizen Participation Study ranked political participation on an eight-point scale pegged to eight different political activities. The study found that rates of political involvement in the United States are fairly low across the board, but Latinos, who participate in an average of 1.2 activities, clearly lag behind African Americans, at 1.9 activities, and Anglos, at 2.2 (Verba et al. 1995, 232). Latino citizens participate in slightly more activities than the Latino population overall (1.4 versus 1.2), but their volume of political activity is still lower than that of Anglos and African Americans (232).[11] The one activity in which Latino citizens are more involved than African Americans and Anglos is protesting. This observation is consistent with the work of García Bedolla (2005) and Pardo (1997), who demonstrate Latinos' adeptness at using marches and protests as ways to speak out against public policies that detrimentally affect the Latino community (for example, Proposition 209 in California).

The indicators examined thus far suggest that Latinos' levels of political activity are lower than those of Anglos and African Americans. The evidence presented by Verba and associates (1995), who tabulated an average "political information score" for various racial and ethnic groups, confirms this hypothesis. Verba and colleagues measured the political information score using nine questions about "hard" political facts. Respondents were asked to name their members of Congress (both House and Senate), for example, and to explain the significance of the Fifth Amendment. Out of a possible score of 9, Anglos' political information scores were highest at 4.4, followed by African Americans with a score of 3.1, and then Latinos, who had an average political information score of 2.7. And as my analysis in Chapter 6 demonstrates, my own measure of political information reveals a similar pattern.

## The Theory of Information-Based Advertising

Given the differences in the levels of political familiarity and knowledge between Latinos and the rest of the U.S. electorate, candidates sometimes find it attractive to advertise distinct campaign messages to the Spanish-speaking electorate. In determining what messages to broadcast, they can select from two basic types—those that discuss their personal background, experiences, and characteristics, or those that focus on their policy beliefs and positions. The first type is straightforward; candidates' character-based messages often focus on their previous political experiences, family background, and military service as a way to relate and become more human to voters. These messages also tend to discuss those specific personal traits (for example, honest and hard-working) that make them suitable for elected office. The second type of message, however, is not as easy to produce. The way policy is conveyed in such advertisements can vary dramatically. Thus, not all of these issue appeals can be viewed in the same manner. Some may be quite simple and discuss policy as a goal that is shared by the majority of individuals (for example, "Candidate X is fighting for better schools"). Yet, policy statements can be complex, requiring the viewer to possess some existing knowledge of the issue. Finding that "more than 50 percent" of ads in a particular election or electoral year mention policy is not enough information to determine (1) what kind of policy information voters receive from these advertisements, (2) whether they are influenced by and can learn from these messages, and (3) whether some voters are more receptive to one type of policy statement than to others.

As such, the content of political ads needs to be examined in a way that distinguishes just how informative these messages are. To that end, I developed the policy complexity scale, which measures how difficult the policy messages are that are expressed in the advertisement. The following list presents the scale, which goes from the most to the least complex:

- *Complex policy statement.* The policy is phrased so that the viewer of the ad is required to know what the status quo (the current legislation or current status of an issue) is in order to have an opinion on the issue. Sample messages might be "Candidate X wants to privatize social security" or "Candidate X supports school vouchers."
- *Explained policy statement.* The policy is explained in the commercial, so the viewer knows what the issue is about from the text in the advertisement. For example, the candidate might say that "natural gas is safe, effective, and more cost efficient than electricity."
- *Simple policy statement.* The policy is stated in a way that would benefit everyone, and is expressed in a positive and universally acceptable

manner. For instance, "Candidate X is fighting for smaller class sizes, better education, and less crime." The policy is stated as a shared goal that everyone agrees with, and is not the candidate's actual position on an issue. Thus, it would be considered a "simple" policy message. All individuals, regardless of their knowledge of politics, can understand this type of message.

- *Character/Latino ad.* Commercials such as these would mention at least one personal quality or characteristic (for example, honest, trustworthy, or hard-working) of the favored or opposing candidate. There is no mention of policy in this ad. A targeted Latino ad is defined as one that features a Latino in the ad. Or, it could be an ad that references Latino ethnic identity. In both cases, there is no mention of policy.

The three types of policy statements are not mutually exclusive. A commercial could contain all three types of policy statements or it could contain none. It could include all of the policy statements and also mention the candidate's personal qualities.[12]

My theory of information-based advertising expects candidates to broadcast campaign messages that their targeted group would most likely respond to. Thus, people having little familiarity with politics should be targeted with the least complex campaign messages—simple policy and character statements—whereas more politically familiar voters should be targeted with the explained and complex policy ads.

## Why Use Ethnic Group Appeals?

We have seen that candidates sometimes choose to advertise issue appeals or to air commercials with no policy content at all. These nonpolicy ads may emphasize candidates' personal qualities and background. But another type of nonpolicy appeal is one that references or taps into an individual's ethnic group identity. As mentioned in Chapter 1, demographic targeting by candidates has made appeals based on ethnic identity increasingly popular in recent years. And as Chapter 3 demonstrates, historical accounts, the popular press, and the news media have all revealed the ways in which politicians have employed such strategies for centuries. The primary reason why political contenders have been drawn to ethnic campaigns is because a candidate showing that he or she is familiar with a group's culture sends a powerful signal to that group that the candidate understands and can relate to them. Such a strategy is a very personal way to connect with individuals, and one that does not require a lot of sacrifice or risk on the part of the candidate, as does, for example, taking a position on a controversial issue. Take, for instance, the attempt by sombrero-wearing Gerald Ford to connect with Mexican-American voters by eating a tamale—an attempt that backfired when the president, apparently having never encountered a tamale before, tried to eat it corn husk and all, thereby revealing his unfamiliarity with Mexican-American cultural practices (Popkin 1994). According to Popkin (1994), to Latino voters in Texas, this error "betrayed an unfamiliarity with their food which suggested a lack of familiarity with their whole culture. Further, tamales were a way of projecting from the personal to the political, of assuming that personal familiarity with a culture and the acceptability of a candidate's policies to a group were linked" (111).

Candidates have also turned to Spanish-language media for practical purposes. Political advertising through this media outlet not only enables candidates to directly communicate to Spanish-dominant Latinos but also can further demonstrate to Latinos that candidates are making a special effort to reach out to them—particularly when candidates themselves speak Spanish in the ads, a feat that both the 2000 presidential candidates attempted. The messages in many Spanish-language ads also make clear references to Latino culture and heritage. Several of Bush's 2000 campaign ads discussed his pride in the Latino blood line that exists in his family (his sister-in-law is Mexican), a discussion of the American Dream, and all of the available opportunities in the United States. Such references not only tap into group identity or cultural backgrounds, but also have been found to be emotionally satisfying (Steinhorn 2004).

Of course, part of the logic behind the creation of ethnic political ads is that they are effective, that Latinos will positively respond to them. Again, candidates can signal familiarity with and knowledge of a group's culture by communicating to them in this manner; that familiarity, in turn, can convey an understanding of their political concerns (Koslow et al. 1994; Popkin 1994). They may also see these campaign appeals as the safest ones to make to an ethnically and politically diverse group. Although candidates could target subgroups of Latinos even more specifically (for example, Cubans and Puerto Ricans), financial constraints and the costs associated with television advertising make it more cost efficient to target Latinos as a homogenous group. An additional explanation, then, for why the content of the two Gore ads discussed in Chapter 1 differed lies in perceptions of the types of messages that

Latinos want to hear: candidates' ads to Latinos strongly emphasize cultural and group cues because they believe that Latino ethnic identity is relevant to Latinos and that Latinos draw on this identity in deciding who to support politically.

Uncertainty about Latinos' policy preferences and concerns may also explain why candidates do not make many Latino-specific policy appeals. Latino- or group-specific policies include those related to immigration (particularly undocumented immigration), bilingual education, and affirmative action. Such policies affect a large share of the Latino population and are often associated with them. But less than 1 percent of all ads, whether in Spanish or in English, created in the 2000–2004 election cycles mentioned any Latino-specific policies.[13] It seems to be the case that although candidates may consider Latino group identity when advertising nonpolicy messages, they do not seem to include policy-related messages that speak directly to Latinos, perhaps for fear that doing so might alienate voters who do not hold the same views.

## How Political Incorporation Mediates the Effects of Political Advertising

It is not unreasonable for candidates to develop advertising strategies to exploit Latino group identity, as using such strategies can certainly prime an individual's previous dispositions (Bishin 2009; Clinton and Lapinksi 2004; Dimofte et al. 2003/2004; Koslow et al. 2004). But I do not expect all Latinos to be influenced by these ethnic group appeals. I argue that receptivity to these messages is conditional on the extent to which Latinos have incorporated into American society and politics. The classic view on immigrant incorporation is known as assimilation (Park 1928), which posits that immigrants will abandon their cultural ties and backgrounds as they advance at the socioeconomic, residential, and occupational levels. This process typically takes place over several generations; over time, a group's attachment to their cultural attachments should begin to decline. An alternative theory of immigrant assimilation known as acculturation (Gordon 1964) suggests that immigrants are able to retain their own culture while adopting the ways of the dominant society. In this view, immigrants do not need to completely relinquish all ties with their racial or ethnic culture to become part of the host society. Bloemraad (2006) defines political incorporation as "the process of becoming a part of mainstream [of the receiving country's] political debates, practices, and decision-making" (6). Thus, we can see how political incorporation is closely linked to political knowledge. If Latinos are new to the political process, then they are likely to possess less information about political matters than are those who are more fully incorporated into America's political system.

There is some evidence that campaign practitioners also take into account an immigrant's level of acculturation. Lionel Sosa, a veteran political consultant who worked on the Spanish-language campaigns for Ronald Reagan, George H. W. Bush, George W. Bush, and John McCain, classified and targeted "Hispanic [voters] based on their level of acculturation. This implied assessing the language and culture in which the Latinos felt most comfortable, and using this knowledge, along with other demographic data, to carefully craft the distinctive messages" (Subervi-Velez and Connaughton 2008, 279).

I define targeted Latino ads as those featuring a Latino in the ad or making some reference to Latino ethnic identity, with no mention of any type of policy. DeFrancesco Soto and Merolla (2008) define targeted Latino ads in a similar manner, although my definition also accounts for advertising messages that specifically reference Latinos. In light of the research on political incorporation, I theorized that targeted Latino ads would have a greater impact on the voting behavior of the less incorporated segment of the Latino electorate than on more-incorporated Latinos. The strongest evidence linking ethnic or racial group identity to political behavior comes from the research on African American voters. Dawson (1994) provides an in-depth explanation of this relationship, and the cornerstone of his argument rests on the "black utility heuristic," which he defines in the following way: "African Americans' evaluations of candidates, parties and public policies will be influenced by the extent to which they believe that it will impact the interests of the Black community, as a whole" (61). Dawson's reasoning is based on the historical experiences of African Americans with racism in the U.S. Until the late 1960s, the life chances and opportunities of African Americans were largely determined by their race. The structural barriers and discrimination faced by African Americans forced them to turn to their own leaders and organizations for cues about what would be best for them both socially and politically. Racial or ethnic identity therefore functions as a useful and meaningful heuristic, as long as group members truly identify with it when making political decisions.

García Bedolla (2005) develops an insightful explanation of Latino political identity that is comprised of three factors: power, place, and collective identity. The first factor, power, is closely related to stigma, which is "imposed on individuals who possess or are believed to possess some attribute, or characteristic, that conveys a social identity that is devalued in a particular social context" (5). Whether Latinos draw on stigma as a mobilizing or demobilizing tool is correlated with their political behavior and involvement. As García Bedolla demonstrates, the stigma surrounding Latinos in the wake of Proposition 187, a 1994 California ballot initiative intended to deny undocumented immigrants access to public education, social services, and health care, led hundreds of Latino high-school students in Los Angeles to organize and participate in marches, protests, and rallies against the initiative.

Where a Latino lives also plays a significant role in shaping his or her political identity. Contextual capital is especially important for immigrants because it determines which social networks they develop and which institutions they can access. If a recent Mexican immigrant settles in a neighborhood in which many Mexican-American-based organizations and groups already exist, he will have a ready-built social network, but also his ethnic identity may become more politicized as a result of his exposure to the shared histories and experiences in this neighborhood. Such was the case in the response to California's anti-Latino ballot initiatives of the 1990s, as it was mostly first-generation Latinos, those born outside of the U.S., that became politically active and vocal (García Bedolla 2005). Structural features such as where an individual resides may contribute to a positive conception of racial or ethnic identity, but the absence of such institutions is likely to result in the opposite. Living in a neighborhood with strong social networks could lead one to develop a strong collective identity with other coethnics, whereas living in a neighborhood with few or no social networks could lead one to develop a weak collective identity.

Thus, García Bedolla's construction of Latino political identity is primarily dependent on these three factors, many of which are not controlled by Latinos themselves but are largely determined by where they live, the institutions that exist in their neighborhoods, and how society responds to and interacts with them. Moreover, the importance of language retention and ethnic group identity is greater among first-generation Latinos than it is for later-generation Latinos (Abrajano et al. 2008). This existing work suggests that group-identity appeals should affect the political behavior of the less-incorporated segment of the Latino population.

For more–politically incorporated Latinos, however, the impact of targeted ethnic ads should be more moderate. Ethnic identity may have less of an effect on the political decisions of these Latinos; that is, in deciding whether to support a proposed policy or candidate, their ethnic or racial identity may not be so strongly tied to their political well being. Given that these Latinos have acculturated and adopted into American society, perhaps their political preferences are guided more by policy and issue concerns rather than by ethnic group identity. As more-integrated Latinos go through the process of political incorporation their ethnic and cultural ties may remain, as acculturation theory would predict, but this process leads them to increasingly make political decisions in the same manner as mainstream society. Thus, their political decisions are guided primarily by partisanship, ideological affiliation, and issue opinions.

## Summary

This chapter presented an explanation of and motivations behind the theory of information-based advertising. Because this theory is grounded in the concept of political familiarity, I first outlined the factors that contribute to one's overall familiarity with politics. I then focused on the reasons for the differences in the rates of political knowledge for Latinos and non-Latinos in the U.S. I also discussed my expectations for the effects of these political ads on Latino political behavior, which, I argue, is conditioned by level of political incorporation. The empirical tests of these predictions are presented in Chapters 4–6. Before turning to this discussion, I provide in Chapter 3 important background information on the elections on which the empirical analysis is based. The chapter also offers some insight on the previous strategies used to target racial and ethnic minorities in the United States.

# 3 Campaigning to Ethnic and Racial Minorities in the U.S.

THE GOAL OF THIS CHAPTER is to examine the historical circumstances that have led to the conventional wisdom regarding ethnic political advertising. The end of the nineteenth century brought a massive wave of immigrants from southern and eastern Europe, and the political machines employed numerous strategies to gain the support of these groups. It is useful to examine the appeals that were made to them in order to assess how these efforts compare with those aimed at Latinos, our nation's largest immigrant group today. These past efforts also help to place the theory of information-based advertising into a broader context.

Candidates, particularly at the local level, have competed for the votes of immigrants since the 1800s (Erie 1990; Dahl 1961; Katznelson 1981). Perhaps the most infamous political machine of all, Tammany Hall, led by William Marcy "Boss" Tweed, pioneered numerous efforts aimed at persuading immigrants to join the powerful Irish machine. These newcomers arrived in droves to the port city of New York, and by 1930, Jews and Italians made up 36 percent of the population of New York City. Party bosses appealed to these groups by offering them party posts and providing "coal, food and rent money to needy Jews and Italians on the Lower East Side" (Erie 1990, 102). Other actions were less substantive in nature; for example, Tammany's "Big Tim" Sullivan "shamelessly 'recognized' the new immigrants with symbolic gestures and donned a yarmulke to solicit Jewish votes" (103). Tammany bosses were also known to eat "corned beef and kosher meat with equal nonchalance" (McNickle 1993, 17) and to advertise in the Yiddish press to reach out to these new immigrants. To gain the support of Italian immigrants, the Irish sponsored legislation to honor Columbus Day as a holiday. Substantively, Congressman James Michael Curley of Boston advocated against literacy tests as one of the requirements for U.S. citizenship and also fought for less-restrictive immigration laws.

Not all immigrants were bowled over by these efforts. Instead of joining the Irish-led political machines, many offered their support to Tammany challengers. Jews became increasingly involved with the Socialist Party, particularly because of their concerns over labor and reform politics. Italian immigrants, though, lent their support to the Republicans.

As the earliest accounts on minority campaigning demonstrate, candidates have long believed that appealing to voters based on ethnic group membership is an effective and powerful strategy in gaining their support. The rationale for this behavior could be attributed to the perception that group membership is salient to the political decisions that individuals make. But as the responses from immigrant Jews and Italians indicate, such campaign appeals did not necessarily lead to unconditional support. Some immigrant groups were concerned about substantive matters, especially those that affected their community. Thus, although efforts to target ethnic minorities date back to the late nineteenth century, it is unclear what consequences these efforts may have had on the political well being of the immigrant or minority group in question.

## Historical Efforts at Latino Outreach

Latinos have been a presence on the American landscape for hundreds of years. In 1848, following the Mexican-American War, the northern portion of Mexico was annexed to the U.S and, thus, many individuals of Mexican descent became part of the American fabric. The first documented effort aimed at the Latino electorate can be traced back to the 1960 presidential election. John F. Kennedy, the Democratic contender, established Latino outreach efforts by way of his Viva Kennedy clubs. Concentrated primarily in the Southwest and Midwest, these grassroots associations focused on organizing Mexican Americans to support Kennedy. The clubs also indirectly served to incorporate and familiarize them with the electoral process. According to community leader Rodolfo Ramos, "The best thing we did with Viva Kennedy Clubs was that we organized independent local Democratic institutions" (Pycior 1997, 117). And although these clubs were officially part of the Kennedy presidential campaign, they operated independently from the state party Democratic committees (Garcia 2000). Moreover, much like presidential candidates do today, Kennedy sought endorsements from Latino elected officials, such as State Senator Henry Gonzalez of Texas and Los Angeles City Councilman Edward Roybal.

The fact that Kennedy was a Roman Catholic gave him a considerable advantage with this ethnic group, as most Mexican Americans are also of the Catholic faith (Pew Hispanic Center 2007). According to Garcia (2000), Kennedy's religious affiliation "represented a cultural bridge to the Mexican American community . . . it meant that he valued family and tradition" (59). Without a doubt, this shared faith was something that Kennedy and the Democrats intended to capitalize on. Moreover, because "[Kennedy's] wife Jacqueline understood and spoke Spanish, [it] meant that Kennedy could communicate with Mexican Americans and understand their needs" (Garcia 2000, 59).

The Kennedy campaign took advantage of Jacqueline Kennedy's Spanish-language proficiency to create the first-ever televised Spanish-language ad.[1] In a commercial that lasted slightly longer than a minute, she expressed the following sentiments:

> Dear friends, the wife of senator John Kennedy, candidate for the U.S. presidency, is talking to you. In these very dangerous times, when the world peace is threatened by communism, it is necessary to have in the White House a leader able to guide our destinies with a firm hand. My husband has always cared for the interests of all the portions of our society who need the protection of a humanitarian government. For the future of our children and to reach a world where true peace shall exist, vote for the Democratic Party on the eighth of November. Long live Kennedy![2]

The primary emphasis in this landmark political ad is on the personal qualities and traits of the candidate; there is also a subtle reference to Kennedy's commitment to underrepresented groups such as Latinos. Aside from the issue of communism, no mention is made about the policies that concerned Latinos during this time (for example, civil rights). His decision to target the Latino electorate turned out to be a prudent one; Kennedy captured 85 percent of the Latino vote, and some political analysts attributed Kennedy's victory in the close election to the support he received from Latinos (Schmal 2004).

Kennedy's outreach efforts are noteworthy for one main reason. The Viva Kennedy campaign brought Latinos, primarily Mexican Americans at that time, to the national spotlight. Latinos were thus recognized as a constituency that presidential candidates needed to court. In the 1968 Democratic presidential primaries, Eugene McCarthy and Robert F. Kennedy battled for the support of Latinos in the key states of Texas and California. Kennedy's campaign enlisted the aid of the Mexican American Political Association (MAPA) and its president, Bert Corona, to target thousands of potential supporters in East Los Angeles. Kennedy also made a series of campaign appearances in San Antonio, Chicago, and Los Angeles. Another key endorsement came from César Chávez, civil rights advocate and founder of the United Farm Workers, who used his extensive network to mobilize Latino voters. The concerted outreach efforts resulted in Kennedy's victory in California; according to media reports, "Mexican Americans contributed most of the slender margin by which Kennedy beat McCarthy in California" (Pycior 1997, 225). The organizational and political skills exhibited by Latinos through the Viva Kennedy clubs secured their position as an important part of the Democratic base; these clubs also enabled many Latinos to familiarize themselves with the electoral process.

By 1980, Democrats were not the only ones who had established Latino outreach efforts. Along with incumbent Democratic president Jimmy Carter, Republican challenger Ronald Reagan developed a specific campaign for the Latino electorate (Subervi-Velez and Connaughton 2008; Segal 2003). Because Reagan was then the governor of California, he likely recognized the importance of the Latino electorate. Latino rates of electoral participation, however, were quite low, with only 29.9 percent of Latinos turning out to vote in the 1980 presidential election. It is estimated that 60.1 percent of Latinos nationwide supported Carter, but among Hispanic voters in Florida, who are mostly Cuban American, 80 percent voted for Reagan (Schmal 2004). Thus, although both candidates made efforts to reach out to Latinos, Reagan's decisive victory over Carter (50.9 versus 41.1 percent) meant that the Latino vote was not as pivotal as it was in the 1960 presidential race.

Four years later, Reagan stepped up his Latino outreach efforts even more and, with the help of the Republican National Committee (RNC), crafted the "Hispanic Victory Initiative '84: A Proposed Strategy for the Reagan-Bush '84 Hispanic Campaign" (Subervi-Velez and Connaughton 2008). One of the highlights from this sixty-six-page document is a statement indicating that although campaigns may be able "to reach [Latinos] in English . . . you have to convince them in Spanish." Lionel Sosa, the political consultant that spearheaded Reagan's Latino outreach efforts, was confident that Latinos would be willing to support the Republican party—it was just a matter of reaching out to them and convincing them to do so. The two Spanish-language ads developed by Reagan and the RNC, "Democrat All the Way" and "New Tradition," reflected these sentiments. The theme of these ads focused on the notion that although Latinos traditionally have been aligned with the Democrats, they should consider supporting Reagan because of his leadership skills. No specific mention is made, however, about the types of policies enacted or supported by Reagan that would benefit Latinos. Given his success with Cuban Americans in the previous election, Reagan also paid special attention to this community by emphasizing his tough anticommunist position toward Cuba. Moreover, Vice President George H. W. Bush assisted in these campaign efforts by speaking Spanish at various events to attack Mondale.[3]

The Democratic candidate in this election, Walter Mondale, also targeted Latino voters. Adopting Kennedy's campaign slogan, Mondale courted Latinos in both the primary and general elections through his Viva Mondale campaign. He made great efforts in the primary season to reach out to Latinos in California, because they were considered to be a critical swing group in the state. During the general election campaign, Mondale continued these efforts by promising Latinos in Texas that he would appoint coethnics to his cabinet.[4] A surge in the number of national network television news stories covering Latino voters was also evident in this election season, up from seven stories in 1980 to twelve in 1984.[5] As in the previous presidential race, Reagan defeated his opponent by a considerable margin (18.3 percent); he also continued to win the support of the Cuban population in Florida, capturing 82 percent of their votes. But the Latino electorate as a whole continued to cast their ballots in favor of the Democratic candidate, 66 percent versus 32.6 percent.

In the 1988 presidential election, both candidates, George H. W. Bush and Michael Dukakis, made even greater efforts to gain the support and allegiance of Latino voters. The Bush campaign developed a grassroots organization, Hispanics for Bush, in order to target specific campaign messages to Latinos. Altogether, the campaign created four Spanish-language ads that were broadcast on Spanish-language media; some were also dubbed into English and aired on shows with large Latino audiences. The Dukakis campaign created five Spanish-language ads for the general election, a strategy many considered advantageous because the candidate was fluent in Spanish (Suberví-Velez and Connaughton 2008). But, somewhat surprisingly, the campaign spent less than $1 million broadcasting these ads (Segal 2003, 7). The explanation for this low figure was attributed to the well-accepted belief at the time that Latinos were already strong Democratic voters who were unlikely to defect and vote for Bush. Despite these efforts, however, Bush soundly defeated Dukakis by a margin of 7.8 percentage points. Latinos remained supportive of the Democratic candidate, with 70.2 percent of the Latino vote going to Dukakis.

Part of Bush's re-election campaign in 1992 involved targeting the Latino electorate. His challenger in the general election, Bill Clinton, also recognized the importance of the Latino vote. Clinton mostly relied on English-language media to communicate to Latinos and created only one Spanish-language ad, which was aired in the New York media market as a response to a negative ad broadcast by Bush. In contrast, Bush allocated millions to Spanish-language media, mostly in the markets of Illinois, Colorado, New Mexico, and Texas. Both candidates relied on endorsements from either Latino relatives or prominent Latino elected officials; Bush received endorsements from his Latino family members (his daughter-in-law and grandson), whereas Clinton turned to Henry Cisneros, then mayor of San Antonio. It was Clinton who received the lion's share of the Latino vote (71 percent). And although he was similar to his Republican predecessors, Bush captured just 70 percent of the Latino vote in Florida.

The 1996 presidential race also witnessed both the incumbent and the challenger, Republican Bob Dole, developing outreach efforts toward the Latino electorate. Clinton's campaign allocated more than $1 million to Spanish-language ad buys in New Mexico, Nevada, and Arizona. Clinton's political ads focused on jobs and national unity; he also created several attack ads focusing on Dole's positions on immigration and bilingual education. Although Dole targeted Latino voters in Florida, his record on immigration and bilingual education hampered these efforts. As a result, Dole's share of the Latino vote (21 percent) was the smallest of any Republican presidential candidate in the past twenty-five years. Approximately 10 percent of Latino voters supported the third-party candidate, Ross Perot.

Media coverage on Latinos was low in the 1996 election—only one television news story focused on the Latino electorate during that campaign season.[6] Perhaps the decrease was due to the dynamics of this presidential election, because Clinton had a good relationship with the Latino electorate. In fact, this was a landmark election for the Democrats, as it marked the first time since 1976 that a Democrat captured Florida. One reason for this shift has been attributed to the inroads that Clinton made with Cuban Americans. He received 35 percent of their votes, a 15 percent increase from his 1992 share of the Cuban vote. Latinos also proved to be pivotal in Clinton's historic victory in Arizona. He captured 90 percent of the Latino vote there, and the last time Democrats had won that state was 1948.

## Latino Appeals in the 2000 and 2004 Presidential Campaigns

As the quote that opens Chapter 1, from Gore campaign strategist Bill Knapp, reveals, even the most senior and well-seasoned campaign consultants openly admit the complexities in communicating to Latino voters. Given the constantly changing and extremely diverse demographic, ethnic, and racial composition of the Latino electorate, there is no single way to target them, much less a sure-fire way to win their support. As discussed in Chapter 2, the pan-ethnic label "Latino" captures a wide range of individuals who are of Hispanic origin (Espiritu 1992). Although candidates have historically used civil rights and social justice issues to appeal to African Americans, no overarching issue or policy exists that can unite a majority of Latinos living in the United States. Some believe immigration to be this issue, but Latinos who have lived in the United States for longer periods of time tend to favor tougher immigration policies than do recent Latino immigrants (Jimenez 2007; Hood et al. 1997).[7] Thus, candidates, especially those targeting Latinos on a large scale, are left with little choice but to seek the help of advertising agencies specializing in Latino consumers. These advertising agencies use focus groups and nationally representative telephone surveys to determine what messages will resonate best with Latinos. Such messages may focus on family values, opportunity, and inclusiveness (Segal 2003). Jamieson, who has conducted extensive research on political advertisements spanning the period 1952–2000, asserts that appealing to voters in a personal manner enables ads to "assert their relevance to [the voter's] lives" (1996, 517). One example of such an ad is a George W. Bush commercial in which the candidate's Latino nephew, George P. Bush, appears. He begins by saying, "I'm a young Latino in the U.S. and very proud of my bloodline. In many ways, I am like any other American."[8] He goes on to say that his uncle, like him, believes in "opportunity, a level playing field for everyone, and the achievement of the American dream for every Latino." Responses from Latino viewers indicate that this was Bush's most successful advertisement during the 2000 campaign; it also received the most publicity of any of his Spanish-language ads. Although it aired no more than one hundred times in the Miami, Albuquerque–Santa Fe, and Los Angeles media markets, the media attention that it drew greatly helped the Bush campaign.

Another Bush advertisement opens with the phrase "Es un Nuevo Día" (It's a New Day). Next, there are images of Bush being surrounded by Latino children. A narrator then states that "the George W. Bush plan believes in you, the people. The Democrats only believe in a big government. For the plan of George W. Bush, no one is forgotten." Then, toward the end of the ad, Bush expresses the following sentiment in Spanish: "The American Dream is for everyone in this nation. For everyone."[9] Like Bush's other ad, this commercial echoes the themes of the immigrant experience and of opportunities available in the United States; no mention is made of how Bush's policies and issue positions are actually going to help Latinos succeed in this country.

Likewise, Janet Murguia, director of constituent affairs for Democratic Party candidate Al Gore, states that the goal of his ads was to have a "broader marketing appeal versus hardcore political [appeal]" (Segal 2003, 21). Gore's campaign strategists felt that the Democratic Party needed to create several commercials that were not fact-laden but instead were more emotional in their approach to voters. Many of the campaign messages of Latino advertisements in 2000 alluded to Latinos' immigrant background and suggested that a vote for Bush or Gore would allow Latinos to succeed in the United States.

Both campaigns decided to target undecided Latino voters in battleground states by relying primarily on Spanish-language television media (Segal 2003). Most of the ads were therefore aired in the media markets of the major battleground states with considerable Latino populations: Miami–Fort Lauderdale, Orlando, Tampa, Albuquerque–Santa Fe, and Las Vegas.[10] Altogether, Republicans devoted $2 million to Spanish ads, and Democrats spent just slightly less at $1.75 million. The Gore campaign allocated the bulk of its spending to the Albuquerque–Santa Fe media market, outspending the Bush campaign there by a margin of 3 to 1. Gore supplemented these ads by making several appearances throughout New Mexico, many of which targeted Latinos, and he agreed to a number of interviews on Spanish-language radio stations. Gore also spent more than Bush in the Las Vegas media market, by a ratio of 4 to 1. Although Gore's strategy in New Mexico succeeded, he lost Nevada to Bush by a slim margin—approximately 4 percentage points. Overall, the 2000 presidential election demonstrates one reason why Latinos are so important to the success of any presidential hopeful: because a significant portion of the population is geographically concentrated in battleground states, Latinos can be pivotal in determining the vote outcome. As mentioned before, many political analysts firmly believe that a stronger Latino outreach effort in Florida would have handed that state to Gore.

As in the 2000 presidential campaign, efforts by the major party candidates in 2004 to reach out to Latinos were once again concentrated in the major battleground states. In fact, John Kerry, the Democratic candidate, and his campaign proudly announced on July 12, 2004, that they had made "the largest comprehensive Spanish-language ad buy in presidential campaign history" (Segal 2004, 10). Altogether, Spanish-language advertising costs were estimated at $8,729,000 for this election cycle; Bush and Kerry combined created 46 Spanish-language ads, which is almost double the number created by Bush and Gore in 2000. Kerry and the Democratic National Committee (DNC) spent approximately $2.6 million on Spanish-language ad buys, whereas Bush spent $3.2 million (Segal 2004). The New Democratic Network (NDN), an independent 527 group, also joined in the effort and allocated $2.3 million to Spanish-language advertising on behalf of Kerry. Both candidates aired these ads in the Florida media markets of Miami, Orlando, and Tampa. As in the previous presidential race, Florida was once again considered a key battleground state in the 2004 election, particularly with respect to the Latino electorate.[11]

The first Spanish-language ad aired by Bush, "Safer, Stronger," was a direct translation of the controversial English-language ad that contained images of 9/11 and discussed the need for leadership in these difficult times. Kerry's first Spanish-language ad aired during Memorial Day weekend, and, appropriately enough, emphasized his military service in Vietnam and recognized the military contributions of Latino soldiers. Another Kerry Spanish-language ad, titled "Husband and Father," focused on his personal background and traits. The accompanying script to this ad is as follows: "We introduce to you a man of faith; a man of family; a man of honor; a man for our community. His name is John Kerry. And for more than twenty years, he has defended working people. And has fought to make our dreams come true. John Kerry: as president, he will be our hope for a better future."[12] Kerry's Spanish-language ad "Culture" continued to discuss the importance of values and faith in the selection of a leader. More importantly, this was the first Kerry ad to mention immigration reform—the commercial promised that in "his first 100 days as president, John Kerry will present a plan to reform immigration and help reunify families."[13] These examples echo the same themes used in the Spanish-language ads from the 2000 presidential election—with the exception of immigration reform, no mention was made of Kerry's policy positions. Even though Kerry mentions immigration reform in the "Culture" ad, there is no detailed explanation of exactly how Kerry would change the current system or of how he plans to reunite immigrant families. Consistent with the Spanish-language ads discussed thus far, Kerry's Spanish-language ads reached out to Latinos based on shared cultural or ethnic traits between himself and this community—a similar faith (Kerry is Catholic), military service, and the belief that all Latinos care about the immigration issue. Appealing to Latinos based on a shared religious faith is reminiscent of the strategy used by Kennedy's campaign in the 1960 presidential election.

The messages used in Bush's Spanish-language ads focused on some Latino-specific appeals, but also tried to differentiate his issue positions from those of his opponent. For instance, in the "Accountability" ad, the focus was on education and highlighted how "President Bush signed the most sweeping education reforms in thirty-five years." The ad then states that although Kerry initially supported Bush's education reforms (the No Child Left Behind Act), Kerry changed his position due to pressure from the school unions, so that Kerry's proposed education plan would offer "less responsibility and accountability to parents."[14] One example of a Latino-targeted ad was titled "Our Country, Our President." The ad begins by saying that "it doesn't matter where we came from or why we came . . . we live in a country that has opened its heart, and has given us real opportunity. The United States. Our country. George W. Bush. Our president."[15] The corresponding visual images were of the flags from a variety of Latin American countries, as well as of the elderly, children, and Bush. This Latino-targeted ad clearly recognizes the diversity and heterogeneity of the Latino community and recognizes the immigrant experience that many Latinos share in. But no mention is made of Bush's policy record or plans. And although Bush's "Accountability" ad does touch on an issue that concerns many Latinos, the ad does not provide much information on how Bush's education reforms helped students, Latino or otherwise. These examples offer some insight into the advertising strategies used to communicate to the Latino electorate. Once again, targeted Latino messages, along with relatively simple policy appeals, describe some of the content in the Spanish-language ads used by the 2004 presidential campaigns. How the content of candidates' Spanish-language ads compares with that of their English-language ads is the focus of Chapter 4.

How well do these past advertising efforts support the theory of information-based advertising? These descriptive accounts show that there is some reason to believe that candidates use culturally based appeals when communicating to the Latino electorate. Moreover, Connaughton and Jarvis's (2004) content analysis of the Spanish-language ads produced by the presidential nominees from 1984 to 2000 finds that the ads primarily focused on the La-tino community as opposed to the candidate's policy positions or personal qualities. In particular, they observed Latinos being portrayed as a group that "happily stood side by side with other Americans . . . depicted as a fully as-similated pan-Latino community" (51). The Spanish-language ads also were largely positive in tone and contained messages that were verbally empower-ing, as Latinos were told that they are a growing force in politics, and visu-ally empowering, because Latinos, rather than the candidate, were the main focus of the ads (Connaughton and Jarvis, 48). They also found that the use of American symbols (for example, the U.S. flag) was a recurring theme in these ads. Of the thirty-six Spanish-language ads produced from 1984 to 2000, 39 percent contained American symbols. It is not clear, however, how this percentage compares with that of American symbols used in English-language ads, because the analysis focused only on Spanish-language ads. Moreover, whether the Spanish-language ads contained more or fewer policy messages than did English-language ads, and the degree of policy complexity in the ads, was beyond the scope of their research. Overall, it is likely that the content of presidential Spanish-language ads is skewed in the direction of cul-tural and symbolic appeals. Such a possibility is an indication that the theory of information-based advertising could explain the campaign strategies for targeting Latinos and non-Latinos during these presidential races. Whether or not this is true for other election settings remains to be seen.

## Campaigning to Latinos in Statewide Races, 2000–2004

Numerous U.S. gubernatorial and Senate races took advantage of Spanish-language media in the 2000–2004 election cycles. Table 3.1 summarizes those elections in which at least one candidate advertised in Spanish; it also provides information on the content of these Spanish-language ads, along with some contextual information about the competitiveness of the election and the per-centage of Latinos in a given district. Previous research has demonstrated the importance of electoral competitiveness in candidates' advertising strategies (Kahn and Kenney 2001); demographic targeting is another strategy that can-didates have grown to rely on (Shea and Burton 2006). As such, both of these

**Table 3.1** Gubernatorial and Senate campaigns using Spanish-language advertising (2000–2004)

| Race and State | Year | Candidate | Types of ads broadcast | Competitive election? | Percent Latino in district |
|---|---|---|---|---|---|
| *Governor* | | | | | |
| NM | 2002 | B. Richardson (D) | Simple, Explained, Character | Yes | 43.4 |
| TX | 2002 | R. Perry (R) | Simple, Character, Latino | No | 32.0 |
| | | T. Sanchez (D) | Simple, Explained, Latino, Character | | |
| IL | 2002 | R. Blagojevich (D) | Simple, Latino | Yes | 12.3 |
| MD | 2002 | B. Ehrlich (R) | n/a | No | 4.3 |
| | | K. Townsend (D) | | | |
| FL | 2002 | J. Bush (R) | Explained, Simple, Character, Latino | Yes | 16.8 |
| | | B. McBride (D) | Explained, Simple | | |
| CA | 2002 | G. Davis (D) | All types | No | 32.4 |
| | | B. Simon (R) | Character, Simple, Latino | Yes | |
| | 2004 | G. Davis (D) | Simple, Character, Latino | | |
| | | C. Bustamante (D) | Latino | | |
| NY | 2002 | G. Pataki (R) | Character, Simple, Explained, Latino | Yes | 15.1 |
| | | C. McCall (D) | Latino, Complex, Simple, Character | | |
| | | T. Golisano (I) | All types | | |

*Senate*

| State | Year | Candidate | Ad types | Latino | |
|---|---|---|---|---|---|
| NM | 2000 | J. Bingaman (D) | Latino | Yes | 43.4 |
| | 2002 | B. Richardson (D) | Character, Simple, Explained | Yes | |
| NV | 2000 | J. Ensign (R) | Explained, Simple | Yes | 19.7 |
| | 2004 | H. Reid (D) | Character, Latino, Complex, Simple | Yes | |
| NY | 2000 | H. Clinton (D) | Explained, Simple, Latino | Yes | 15.1 |
| | | R. Lazio (R) | Explained | | |
| | 2004 | C. Schumer (D) | Simple, Character, Latino | No | |
| FL | 2000 | B. McCollum (R) | Character | Yes | 16.8 |
| | 2004 | B. Castor (D) | Complex, Simple, Latino, Explained | Yes | |
| | | D. Gallagher (R) | Complex, Simple, Character | | |
| | | M. Martinez (R) | Character, Latino | | |
| TX | 2000 | K. Hutchison (R) | Latino | No | 32.0 |
| IL | 2004 | B. Obama (D) | Policy, Latino | No | 12.3 |
| | | B. Hull (D) | Character, Latino, Simple | | |
| | | G. Chico (D) | Character, Latino, Simple | | |
| CO | 2004 | K. Salazar (D) | Character, Latino, Simple | Yes | 17.1 |
| CA | 2000 | D. Feinstein (D) | Simple | No | 32.4 |

SOURCE: The American Almanac of American Politics (2000–2004) for competitive election information; U.S. Census for the percentage of Latinos in a district; Ad content was discerned using data from the Wisconsin Advertising Project, 2000–2004.

NOTE: *Complex, Explained, Simple, Latino* and *Character* ads constitute the policy complexity scale, explained in Chapter 2. *All types* means that the candidate advertised at least one type of ad from the policy complexity scale.

factors should be taken into account when examining candidates that choose to advertise in Spanish. Altogether, a total of fifteen candidates in eight gubernatorial races and a total of seventeen candidates in twelve Senate races campaigned to Latinos using this media outlet.

I turn first to the gubernatorial elections. It should come as no surprise that candidates from states with sizeable Latino populations chose to advertise in Spanish. The Latino population exceeded 10 percent of the state population in seven of the eight states in question (the exception was Maryland).[16] It is also noteworthy that in five of the eight gubernatorial races, the election was considered to be competitive. Perhaps one reason why these candidates advertised in Spanish was that Latinos are often considered the all-important "swing vote." In most of these races, both the Republican and Democratic gubernatorial candidate in each state targeted Latinos through televised Spanish-language ads. Regarding the content of these ads, some variation exists. Only two of the fifteen candidates—Tom Golisano in 2002 (New York) and Gray Davis in 2002—used all types of ads outlined in Chapter 2. The majority of the gubernatorial ads used simple policy messages (86 percent), character messages (71 percent), and targeted Latino appeals (71 percent). Only 21 percent of the ads included a complex policy message, and 50 percent featured an explained policy message. These Spanish-language gubernatorial ads show that candidates chose to emphasize nonpolicy and easily understood policy messages rather than complex policy statements.

The amount of money spent to broadcast these ads was considerable. For example, in the 2002 California election, Gray Davis spent more than $1.7 million during the general election and $200,000 in the primary on Spanish-language commercials. To date, this is the largest amount spent by a gubernatorial candidate in California on Spanish-language media. The Davis campaign developed a number of unique Spanish-language television and radio ads that aired in the state's largest media markets: Los Angeles, San Francisco, San Diego, Fresno, and Sacramento. Also, recall that Davis was one of the only candidates to use all types of ad messages. His "Un Mejor Amigo" (A Good Friend) ad specifically references the fact that he worked "side by side" with then–lieutenant governor Cruz Bustamante, who is Mexican American, and that he improved education in California by expanding "the Healthy Families program to cover more than 300,000 Latino children. And he signed legislation making it easier for immigrant children to attend college" (Kinnard 2002).[17] His Republican challenger, Bill Simon, spent a much smaller amount, approximately $250,000, on Spanish-language ads. One of Simon's radio ads focused on the issue of education. In the 2002 New York election, challengers Tom Golisano and Carl McCall spent more than $3 million combined to communicate to Latinos in Spanish, while incumbent governor George Pataki allocated approximately $820,000 to Spanish-language ads. In the same year, Tony Sanchez, the Democratic challenger in Texas, devoted a vast sum to Spanish-language advertising, more than $1.8 million. Meanwhile, the incumbent governor, Rick Perry, spent less than half that amount on Spanish-language television ads. Despite these efforts, Perry defeated Sanchez by a considerable margin—58 percent to 40 percent.

Compared to these amounts, the Spanish-language advertising budgets of Bill Richardson, for governor of New Mexico, and Rod Blagojevich, for Illinois governor, appear rather modest. Richardson spent approximately $155,000 on Spanish-language ads and, as the incumbent, came out victorious, easily winning the election with 57 percent of the vote. Democratic nominee Rod Blagojevich advertised $180,000 worth of Spanish-language commercials. This proved to be a wise move on his part, as Blagojevich won the election by only 7 percentage points.

Like their gubernatorial counterparts, contenders for the U.S. Senate in New York, New Mexico, Texas, Florida, Illinois, Colorado, Nevada, and California took advantage of this media outlet. A considerable amount of overlap exists between the gubernatorial races that used Spanish-language ads and the Senate races that used such ads. Although both Democrats and Republicans created Spanish-language ads for the 2000 New York and the 2004 Florida Senate races, Democratic contenders in the Colorado, Nevada, California, Illinois, New Mexico, and New York Senate races advertised in Spanish, whereas their Republican opponents chose not to do so. In only three instances did the opposite scenario occur (the Republicans advertised in Spanish, whereas the Democrats did not), and this was in the 2000 Florida, Texas, and Nevada Senate elections. Thus, in the 2000–2004 election cycles, it appears as if Democratic candidates made a greater effort to attract the Latino electorate through Spanish-language campaigns than did the Republican candidates.

Consistent with the demographic patterns that emerged from the gubernatorial elections that featured Spanish-language ads, the Latino population in each state in these Senate races made up more than 10 percent of the population, ranging from a low of 12.3 percent in Illinois to a high of 43.4 percent in New Mexico. Eight out of the twelve elections (75 percent) were considered to be competitive, which is consistent with the assertion that candidates competing in close races will turn to Spanish-language advertising as a means to attract swing voters such as Latinos. The content of these ads tended to focus on targeted Latino messages, character appeals, and simple policy statements. A majority of the Spanish-language ads produced for Senate elections from 2000 to 2004 contained these types of messages, whereas a quarter or fewer featured complex or explained policy messages. Once again, as with Spanish-language gubernatorial ads, these Spanish-language ads targeted Latinos with cultural and character-based appeals to a greater extent than they did with informative policy appeals.

I turn now to a brief discussion of each these campaigns. Florida's 2000 U.S. Senate race was between the Republican candidate Bill McCollum and Democrat Bill Nelson. Only McCollum broadcast Spanish-language ads, the content of which emphasized his personal qualities, such as his integrity and principles, but gave no policy-related information. Because the majority of the Latino population in Florida consists of Cubans, who are decidedly pro-Republican, it is easy to understand why McCollum advertised in Spanish. In the 2004 election to replace Florida's retiring U.S. Senator Bob Graham, several candidates appealed to the Latino electorate through Spanish-language commercials in both the primary and general elections. Ultimately, in this close election, the Republican candidate Mel Martinez came out victorious.

The other Senate races in which candidates used Spanish-language ads took place in states that contained a moderately sized Latino population and an open seat race. The open seats generally made for competitive races. For instance, the Illinois Senate election in 2004 led all three Democratic candidates in the primaries to advertise in Spanish. Interestingly, all the candidates adopted a similar advertising strategy by featuring Latinos in their ads. Two out of the three candidates also mentioned their personal qualities and characteristics, as well as simple policy statements, in the ads. In the 2000 open seat election in Nevada, the Republican contender, John Ensign, broadcast Spanish-language ads containing explained and simple policy messages. In yet another open seat race, great efforts were made to target Latino voters by the Democratic candidate, Hillary Clinton, and by the Republican challenger, Rick Lazio, in the 2000 New York U.S. Senate race. To mobilize Clinton's base, her campaign implemented a major get-out-the-vote effort in both African American and Latino areas. Clinton also created several Spanish-language ads and broadcast them a total of 195 times. One of Clinton's ads included an endorsement from prominent Latino leader Fernando Ferrer, in which he praises Clinton but attacks her opponent for his support of the Puerto Rican island of Vieques as a U.S. Navy bombing range and weapons-testing site. The Vieques issue was an important one to Ferrer, who is of Puerto Rican descent, and to the Latino population in New York, which is predominantly Puerto Rican. Clinton's other television ads featured policy messages that were immigrant-specific: health care for immigrant children, laws targeting the children of immigrants, and amnesty for immigrants. Although Lazio also targeted Latino voters through one Spanish-language ad, this ad aired only eleven times during the entire campaign.[18]

In Texas's U.S. Senate election, only the incumbent, Kay Bailey Hutchison (R), used Spanish-language advertising; her ad focused on policy achievements while in office. The 2000 race for one of California's U.S. Senate seats featured only the Democratic incumbent, Dianne Feinstein, investing in Spanish-language advertising. Her ads included simple policy messages and featured her with prominent Latino politicians, such as then–Lieutenant Governor Cruz Bustamante. In Colorado's 2004 Senate race, it was also the Democratic contender who advertised in Spanish. Ken Salazar targeted Latinos with simple and character-driven appeals and also highlighted Latino culture in his ads. This concerted effort to target Colorado's burgeoning Latino community may have contributed to Salazar's victory, as he edged out his opponent by only 3.9 percentage points.

Overall, candidates' spending on Spanish-language ads appeared to have paid off. Of the twenty statewide races in which candidates used Spanish-language commercials, a majority of the candidates emerged victorious. Although other factors clearly contributed to these election outcomes, including incumbency, name recognition, and campaign resources, targeted Latino campaigns may have also played some role in the victories.

## Spanish-Language Campaigns in House Races, 2000–2004

During the 2000–2004 election cycles, twenty-one House races saw at least one candidate using Spanish-language ads. In total, twenty-six candidates advertised in Spanish, with only one candidate advertising in all three election cycles that I examine (see the next section, on New Mexico's 1st congressional district, for a more detailed discussion). Table 3.2 lists those House races with candidates that advertised in Spanish, along with the same information

**Table 3.2** House races using Spanish-language advertising (2000–2004)

| State and district | Year | Candidate | Types of ads advertised | Competitive election? | Percent Latino in district |
|---|---|---|---|---|---|
| AZ-2 | 2000 | E. Pastor (D) | Simple, Character | No | 62.5 |
| CA-9 | 2004 | C. Bermudez (R) | Simple, Latino | No | 17.3 |
| CA-20 | 2000 | C. Dooley (D) | Simple, Latino | Yes | 63.7 |
| | | R. Rodriguez (R) | Latino | | |
| | 2004 | J. Costa (D) | Simple, Latino, Character | No | |
| | | L. Quigley (D) | Complex | | |
| CA-30 | 2000 | X. Becerra (D) | Simple, Character | No | 64.3 |
| CA-39 | 2002 | L. Sanchez (D) | Latino | No | 61.2 |
| | | T. Escobar (R) | Simple, Latino | | |
| FL-8 | 2002 | M. Diaz-Balart (R) | Latino, Explained, Simple, Character | Yes | 17.6 |
| | | E. Diaz (D) | Explained, Latino | | |
| FL-18 | 2004 | I. Ros-Lehtinen (R) | Simple | No | 70.5 |
| IL-4 | 2000 | L. Gutierrez (D) | n/a | No | 74.5 |
| NM-1 | 2000 | H. Wilson (R) | Explained, Simple, Character | Yes | 42.6 |
| | | J. Kelly (D) | n/a | | |
| | 2002 | H. Wilson (R) | Character, Latino | Yes | |
| | 2004 | H. Wilson (R) | Explained, Simple, Latino, Character | Yes | |

| District | Year | Candidate | Ad content | Competitive | % Latino |
|---|---|---|---|---|---|
| NM-2 | 2000 | M. Montoya (D) | Latino | Yes | 47.3 |
|  | 2002 | S. Pearce (R) | Latino, Complex, Explained, Simple, Character | No |  |
|  | 2004 | J. Smith (D) | Character, Explained, Latino | No |  |
|  |  | G. King (D) | Character, Latino |  |  |
| NM-3 | 2000 | T. Udall (D) | Latino | Yes | 36.3 |
| TX-16 | 2004 | S. Reyes (D) | Character, Latino | No | 78 |
| TX-23 | 2000 | W. Garza (D) | Character, Simple, Latino | No | 65.1 |
| TX-28 | 2004 | H. Cuellar (D) | Explained, Latino | Yes | 77.5 |
|  |  | C. Rodriguez (D) | Latino |  |  |
| TX-32 | 2004 | M. Frost (D) | Complex, Latino | No | 36.2 |
|  |  | P. Sessions (R) | Character, Latino |  |  |

SOURCE: *The American Almanac of American Politics* (2000–2004) for competitive election information; U.S. Census for the percentage of Latinos in a district; ad content was discerned using data from the Wisconsin Advertising Project dataset, 2000–2004

NOTE: *Complex, Explained, Simple, Latino,* and *Character* ads are based on the policy complexity scale, explained in Chapter 2. *All types* means that the candidate advertised at least one type of ad from the policy complexity scale.

presented in Table 3.1. As in the statewide races, House candidates that used Spanish-language ads competed in a district with a considerable number of Latino voters; in fact, many of these districts were majority and even super-majority Latino districts. At the low end of the population scale were California's 9th and Florida's 8th congressional districts—in each district Latinos constituted approximately 17 percent of the population. At the high end, 77.5 percent of the 28th congressional district in Texas are Latino, and in the 4th district of Illinois, Latinos make up 74.5 percent of the population. The content of the ads targeting the House districts reflects the same general pattern as those used in the statewide races—the majority of the ads featured images of Latinos, as well as simple policy and character statements.

Forty percent of the elections were considered to be competitive, whereas the number of statewide races deemed competitive was considerably higher (75 percent). This difference could perhaps be attributed to the nature of House elections, because House members have smaller constituencies than do senators, and many representatives are long-time incumbents. As such, they may advertise in Spanish as a gesture of goodwill to their Latino constituents more than as a bid for votes. Of the twelve noncompetitive elections in which at least one candidate advertised in Spanish, five were incumbents. They were Luis Gutierrez (IL-4), Ed Pastor (AZ-2), Ileana Ros-Lehtinen (FL-18), Silvestre Reyes (TX-16), and Xavier Becerra (CA-30). Also note that in these five elections, the challengers did not create a Spanish-language advertising campaign. And with the exception of Ileana Ros-Lehtinen, all the incumbents are Democrats. Yet, Republican incumbents, such as Henry Bonilla (TX-23), Steve Pearce (NM-2), and Joe Skeen (NM-1), did not advertise in Spanish, even when their Democratic challengers chose to do so. Thus, there appears to be some partisan bias, because Democrats, at least in these three election cycles, were more apt to use this media outlet than were Republicans. This difference can perhaps be attributed to the long-standing relationship that Democrats have had with the Latino electorate. It is also interesting to note that of the sixteen Latino candidates competing in these elections, only one—former congressman Henry Bonilla (TX-23)—did not target his Latino electorate through Spanish-language ads.

## Case Study: New Mexico's 1st Congressional District

During the 2000–2004 election cycles, Heather Wilson of New Mexico's 1st congressional district was the lone candidate who consistently developed a Spanish-language advertising campaign. Some characteristics of her district offer insight on why Wilson used such a campaign in each of these election cycles. Her district is 42.6 percent Latino, 25.5 percent of whom are Spanish speaking (U.S. Census Bureau 2000a). Moreover, only 1.2 percent of the population consists of foreign-born individuals (U.S. Census Bureau 2000a). Thus, more than half of the Latinos in her district could be exposed to her Spanish-language ads, and, more importantly, they are likely to be eligible voters (given that virtually all Latinos in this district are U.S born). Finally, that Wilson faced a formidable competitor in all of her reelection bids, as evidenced by a margin of victory of 10 percent or less in each election, can also help explain why she regularly employed a targeted Latino campaign.[19] The one recurring theme in her Spanish-language ads was a mention of the personal qualities of either Wilson or her opponent, and although Latinos were not featured in her 2000 commercials, she did include them in her subsequent campaign ads. Wilson also discussed policy in her Spanish-language ads, with a preference for simple and explained policy messages over complex policy statements.

This case study offers a number of insights about candidates' Latino-specific campaigns, and it helps support the theory of information-based advertising. Wilson's concerted efforts to campaign to Latinos, despite the fact that she is a Republican, reinforces the conventional wisdom that Latinos are considered a valuable swing group. And although Latinos have traditionally been aligned with the Democratic party, Wilson exemplifies the efforts made by the Republican party to appeal to this group of voters. She made her appeal by communicating messages that primarily focused on her or her opponent's personal characteristics and on easily understood policy statements. Specifically recognizing Latinos in her Spanish-language ads, either by featuring them or by having them speak in the ad, is another regular component of her campaign strategy. That the content of these Spanish-language ads focused more on character and cultural appeals, with less of an emphasis on substantively motivated policy messages, lends some initial support for the theory of information-based advertising. Of course, this case study is not conclusive evidence, because the focus is only on the content of Wilson's Spanish-language ads. Nonetheless, it offers a glimpse into the campaign strategies used by the same candidate in three different races.

## Summary

Clearly, politicians competing for both national and statewide races realize the importance of developing a specific campaign strategy directed toward

Latinos. In a growing number of states across our nation, a successful bid for most elected offices requires that some effort be made to win the support of the Latino electorate. Particularly in states in which Latinos make up more than a third of the population, and therefore a sizeable part of the electorate, it is almost a given that candidates competing in statewide offices need to secure their allegiance. Just as California's Latinos were pivotal to Robert Kennedy's bid for the Democratic presidential nomination, Latinos play an equally, if not more, prominent role in today's elections. How much the theory of information-based advertising can explain candidates' advertising strategies remains to be seen, as the analysis in this chapter focused solely on their Spanish-language campaigns. But this analysis shows that gubernatorial, Senate, and House candidates prefer to advertise character, Latino, and simple policy messages to a greater extent than they do complex policy statements. Chapter 4 turns to an empirical analysis of both English- and Spanish-language ads to determine whether the theory of information-based advertising explains candidate behavior in the 2000–2004 election cycles.

Those seeking elected office have long understood the importance of targeting specific groups within the electorate who they believe may behave in a politically homogeneous manner. Although appeals to our nation's newest arrivals have resulted in candidates swapping corned beef for tamales, the motivations for such behavior appear to remain the same—candidates believe that campaigning to immigrants based on their ethnicity or culture is effective. That is, politicians believe that such efforts signal to these ethnic groups that politicians understand them and care about them. Candidates hope that, in turn, these groups will respond positively to the campaigns and will cast their ballots in favor of the candidate who appeals to them in this way.

This conventional wisdom appears to have carried over to the campaigns developed for the country's largest immigrant and minority group today. Given the technological advances in communication and the access that Latinos have to myriad Spanish-language media outlets, aspiring politicians can use these media sources to target ethnic messages to Latinos. Just as candidates have allocated the bulk of their campaign resources to televised political advertising for the general public, candidates have also turned to this medium in reaching out to Latino voters.

# 4 Candidates' Advertising Strategies

THE RISE OF TELEVISED SPANISH-LANGUAGE ADS makes it possible to determine whether candidates indeed use different advertising strategies to target Latinos and non-Latinos in the U.S. This chapter is devoted to making this determination. To test the empirical predictions from the theory of information-based advertising, I examine the types of policy messages and targeted Latino appeals used by the candidates and compare them with the messages used to target non-Latinos.

## Testing the Theory of Information-Based Advertising

The first step in testing this theory is to examine the content of the ads using the policy complexity scale discussed in Chapter 2. Before beginning my analysis, I give a brief review of this scale, which consists of complex, explained, simple, and character/targeted Latino statements. Complex policy statements are those in which the policy is discussed such that the viewer of the ad is required to know what the status quo is in order to understand and process the candidate's position on the issue. Although I refer to these policy appeals as "complex," it should be understood that they are complex relative only to the other types of policy messages used in commercials, not to policy discussions generally. Second on the complexity scale are explained policy statements, in which a policy is described so that the viewer knows what the issue is about from the text of the commercial. Simple policy messages are expressed as shared policy goals in a way that does not actually reveal the issue positions of the candidates, as in a statement that a candidate is in favor of "better education" or a "strong economy." Or a political advertisement may contain no policy statements whatsoever. The most popular type of nonpolicy message focuses on the personal background or characteristics of either the favored candidate or the candidate's opponent. The other type of nonpolicy message focuses specifically on the Latino community. To understand the factors that influence whether candidates advertise in Spanish or English, I examine only those elections in which at least one candidate used a Spanish-language commercial.

Different types of elections may also lead candidates to employ distinct advertising strategies. Because presidential candidates have to appeal to a much larger audience than do congressional candidates, presidential candidates may be more likely to rely on character appeals, targeted Latino appeals, and simple policy messages when pursuing Spanish speakers than will candidates advertising to non-Spanish speakers. But congressional or gubernatorial candidates should be less inclined than presidential candidates to include simple policy messages, because, as West (2001) points out, these candidates have less name recognition and may need to convey their issue positions to a greater extent than do presidential hopefuls. Also, because gubernatorial and congressional candidates can tailor their campaign messages to their constituents better than presidential candidates can, they may have the ability to discuss issues in greater depth and to include more specific information. Given that candidates may appeal to Latinos based on their ethnic group identity, however, we may find that the proportion of nonpolicy messages is greater in their Spanish- than in their English-language ads.

After candidates decide what messages to include in their commercials, they then have to decide on what television programs to broadcast them. This choice is limited to a certain extent by candidates' financial resources, because it is more costly to advertise during prime time (from 8 to 10 p.m.) than in the morning or the afternoon. Nonetheless, within these time slots, candidates have some idea of the types of shows that their commercials will be broadcast on—the early evening time slot makes it likely that ads will air during the local news programs, whereas advertising in the mid-afternoon time slot raises the possibility that the ad will be broadcast on a talk show such as *Oprah*. As such, we may expect candidates to account for the potential audience of a television program in their decision making. Given that those who watch the news tend to possess higher levels of income and education than those who do not (Delli Carpini and Keeter 1996), news watchers are more likely to be able to comprehend complex policy statements. Therefore, a greater number of complex policy ads should be aired on news programs than on entertainment programs. But because simple and nonpolicy messages are straightforward, candidates may advertise such commercials more on entertainment shows (for example, soap operas and talk shows) than on news programs. I conducted my analysis of these hypotheses using the same data as for the content analysis, because information is available regarding the show during which each commercial aired.

Although comparing the content of the commercials themselves could provide some basis for determining the validity of the theory of information-based advertising, variations in the candidates' partisanship and characteristics specific to their constituents could also influence their advertising decisions. To determine which of these factors best explains candidates' advertising decisions, I employed multivariate regression analysis.

All three analyses use political ads developed by candidates competing in the presidential, congressional, and gubernatorial races spanning from 2000 to 2004. The data is available from the Wisconsin Advertising Project (Goldstein et al. 2002; Goldstein and Rivlin 2005, 2007a, 2007b). The advertising data was gathered by the Campaign Media Analysis Group (and uses information from Competitive Media Reporting [CMR]). CMR monitored the satellite transmissions of the national networks (ABC, CBS, NBC, and FOX) and twenty-five national cable networks, such as CNN, TBS, and ESPN. Each advertisement was compiled as a storyboard, which is the complete text of the commercial as well as images taken at intervals of three to four seconds. In addition to the text and images of the commercials, the database contains information about the commercials' length and estimated cost of broadcast, as well as the times each commercial aired and on which shows and stations. The 2000 political commercials are from the top seventy-five media markets in the United States, which cover more than 80 percent of the U.S. population. By 2002, the number of media markets had expanded to one hundred. In the 2000 election season, over 970,000 advertisements were broadcast; in 2002, the number was more than 1 million. In the 2004 election cycle, more than 1.5 million political commercials were broadcast. Because the Wisconsin Advertising Project did not code advertisements according to the parameters outlined in the policy complexity scale, I conducted my own content analysis. The coding scheme and a detailed explanation of the coding process can be found in Appendix A.

Table 4.1 presents several descriptive statistics regarding the ads used

**Table 4.1**  Basic descriptive statistics of political ads, 2000–2004

| | Spanish-language ads | | | English-language ads | | |
|---|---|---|---|---|---|---|
| | 2000 | 2002 | 2004 | 2000 | 2002 | 2004 |
| *Ads created* | | | | | | |
| Number of unique ads created | 72 | 130 | 99 | 3,089 | 4,365 | 3,366 |
| Average length of ad (in seconds) | 29.9 | 32.9 | 30.6 | 30.4 | 30.2 | 31.5 |
| *Ads broadcast* | | | | | | |
| Number of times ads were broadcast | 5,046 | 20,073 | 15,607 | 330,312 | 340,420 | 796,562 |
| Average cost to broadcast an ad[a] | $539,905 | $733,920 | $601,574 | $743,342 | $824,890 | $699,923 |
| Percentage of ads broadcast on the news | 30.7 | 35.0 | 50.9 | 48.6 | 41.9 | 41.6 |
| Percentage of ads broadcast a month prior to election | 31.3 | 57.7 | 60.7 | 57.6 | 51.4 | 76.5 |
| State where the largest percentage of ads were broadcast | California | Texas | Florida | Michigan | Texas | Ohio |

[a] This figure is the average cost to broadcast an ad based on the number of times it was broadcast.

for these elections. Altogether, fifteen elections in 2000 featured Spanish-language advertisements: the presidential election, six Senate races, and eight House elections. In these fifteen elections, seventy-two unique ads were created in Spanish and broadcast a total of 5,046 times. In 2002, a greater number of candidates advertised in Spanish. Twenty-two races in 2002 included at least one televised Spanish-language ad; eight of them were gubernatorial elections, three of them U.S. Senate races, and eleven of them House elections. This increase coincides with a jump to 130 in the number of unique Spanish-language advertisements created. In the 2004 election cycle, fourteen contests featured Spanish-language ads: the presidential race, one gubernatorial race, eight House elections, and four Senate races. The number of Spanish-language ads developed for this election cycle dropped from that of 2002, from 130 to 99, as did the frequency with which these ads were broadcast. Nonetheless, there is a significant increase from 2000 to 2004 in the number of ads created for the Spanish-speaking electorate.

As one would expect, when compared with the number of English-language ads produced and broadcast, these numbers are small. The number of times English-language ads aired more than doubled from 2000 to 2004, indicating just how important this mode of political communication has become. The cost of broadcasting Spanish-language ads varied over these three election cycles, and appears to have been more expensive in nonpresidential election years. A similar pattern is also evident in the costs associated with broadcasting English-language ads. Of course, these comparisons are all relative, as the price of broadcasting these paid political ads is staggering, exceeding more than half a million dollars for a mere 30-second spot. The length of these ads remained fairly constant across the three election cycles as well as across language type.

These comparative statistics indicate a notable shift in which programs candidates decided to broadcast their Spanish-language ads on; whereas approximately a third were broadcast on news programs in 2000 and 2002, half of all Spanish-language ads were broadcast on such programs in 2004. This jump can perhaps be attributed to candidates adopting an advertising approach more similar to the one used in their English-language campaigns, in which the tendency was to broadcast ads on news programs. It is also worthwhile to note that, over time, candidates have begun to spread out their Spanish-language ads across the campaign seasons. In 2000, 68.7 percent of the Spanish-language ads were broadcast less than a month before the general election, yet in 2002, 42.3 percent of Spanish-language ads were aired less than a month before, and in 2004, this figure dropped even further to 39.3 percent. Candidates in 2000 may have perceived Latinos to be largely undecided a month before the general election and thus decided to broadcast their Spanish-language ads closer to the general election in hopes of influencing Latinos' votes. And candidates seemed to prefer broadcasting their Spanish-language ads much closer to the general election than they did their English-language ads. Only in the 2002 midterm elections did candidates broadcast their Spanish- and English-language ads at somewhat comparable rates.

Across these three election cycles, there was not much overlap in where candidates directed their advertising efforts. For example, in the 2000 election cycle, the greatest number of Spanish-language ads was broadcast in California, but in the next presidential election year, the majority of Spanish-language ads was broadcast in Florida. This shift in advertising strategy could be a result of the pivotal role that Florida played in the 2000 presidential election, particularly with respect to the Latino electorate. Recall that Gore's Latino outreach campaign spent a minimal amount of resources on Spanish-language ad buys in Florida, and as discussed in Chapter 1, such a decision may have cost him the presidency. In the midterm election year, and the only case with overlap, the largest number of Spanish- and English-language commercials was aired in Texas; this can most likely be attributed to the highly competitive gubernatorial race that occurred in that state.[1] The fact that Michigan in 2000 and Ohio in 2004 are where the greatest number of English-language ads was broadcast can be attributed to their status as battleground states.

Although these basic indicators do not reveal the entire picture of the variations in the English- and Spanish-language campaigns used in the 2000–2004 elections, they do offer an initial look at the advertising efforts put forth by presidential, congressional, and gubernatorial candidates. The next section specifically compares the types of political ads created by the candidates, and thereby leads to the initial test of the information-based theory of advertising.

## Content Analysis

Table 4.2 presents the distribution of Spanish- and English-language spots, based on their content and the type of election in which they were used. In the most basic of comparisons, aggregating across all ads produced for these three election cycles, a larger percentage of policy messages appeared in English-language ads (86.7 percent) than in Spanish-language ads (78.6 percent). Moreover, and consistent with expectations from the theory of information-based advertising, complex and explained policy messages were more prevalent in English than in Spanish. A gap of 10 percentage points exists in the number of complex messages advertised in English as opposed to Spanish; this difference also exists for explained policy messages, but the gap declines to approximately 6 percent.

Messages that are relatively straightforward (simple policy), however, appeared with greater frequency in Spanish-language ads than in English-language ones. Fifty-eight percent of Spanish-language ads contained a simple policy message, compared to only about half of English-language ads. Moreover, the difference in the percentage of Spanish- and English-language ads containing character messages is considerable. Whereas 41 percent of Spanish-language ads mentioned a candidate's personal qualities, only 28 percent of English-language ads did so. Not surprisingly, a much larger percentage of Spanish-language ads contained visual images of Latinos (47.6 percent, compared with 7.1 percent for English-language ads).

These comparisons at the aggregate level suggest that candidates do indeed

**Table 4.2** Content of Spanish- and English-language advertisements (2000–2004), by election type

| Percentage of Ads with | Total | | Presidential | | Senate | | House | | Gubernatorial | |
|---|---|---|---|---|---|---|---|---|---|---|
| | English | Spanish | English | Spanish | English | Spanish | English | Spanish | English | Spanish |
| Policy (overall) | 86.7 | 78.6 | 99.1 | 90.7 | 86.6 | 63.3 | 85.1 | 79.9 | 72.5 | 70.1 |
| Complex policy | 25.4 | 14.8 | 43.2 | 20.4 | 12.7 | 9.0 | 20.7 | 4.0 | 14.8 | 7.7 |
| Explained policy | 42.9 | 37.4 | 55.2 | 50.4 | 35.7 | 23.5 | 35.2 | 36.3 | 32.9 | 21.0 |
| Simple policy | 49.5 | 58.2 | 49.0 | 65.4 | 38.2 | 46.2 | 49.5 | 53.4 | 50.1 | 63.0 |
| Character ad | 28.1 | 40.9 | 19.9 | 21.4 | 28.5 | 49.3 | 25.9 | 37.1 | 37.7 | 61.0 |
| Targeted Latino ad | 7.1 | 47.6 | 11.7 | 43.6 | 5.7 | 53.3 | 2.6 | 17.9 | 3.6 | 64.6 |
| N (broadcast) | 670,732 | 25,119 | 807,008 | 14,423 | 123,984 | 2,873 | 26,878 | 2,624 | 267,486 | 15,793 |

SOURCE: 2000–2004 Wisconsin Advertising Project data.
NOTE: These are only the advertisements for races in which at least one candidate ran a Spanish-language ad. The columns do not sum to 100 percent because an ad could have mentioned more than one issue. A difference of means test was performed for all the bivariate distributions, and each test statistic was significant at $p < .01$ level.

target Spanish speakers in a manner distinct from the rest of the population. But such differences may be less pronounced depending on the type of election that candidates compete in. That is, presidential candidates may behave differently from gubernatorial and Senate candidates, given the variations in their targeted audiences. To determine whether this is so, I also present in Table 4.2 the distribution of ad content based on election type. Looking at the ads created in the presidential campaigns of 2000 and 2004, one sees the same general patterns emerge in the content variation between Spanish- and English-language ads. For example, twice as many complex policy messages are featured in English-language ads than in Spanish-language ones. Moreover, a greater percentage of explained policy messages was used in English-language ads, although the gap is not as large as it was in the aggregate. More-straightforward policy appeals, however, continue to occur with greater frequency in presidential candidates' Spanish-language ads than in their English ones. Whereas 65 percent of Spanish-language ads contained a simply policy message, just 49 percent of English-language ads did. These distributions once again highlight a preference among presidential contenders to advertise more simple policy statements in their Spanish-language ads than in their English-language ones. I turn now to the final category of interest, nonpolicy campaign messages. Presidential candidates advertised character messages at nearly the same rate in Spanish as in English, 21.4 percent versus 19.9 percent. Clearly, the difference here is much smaller than it was for the distribution on the aggregate level. A substantial difference, however, was seen in the use of targeted Latino ads. In the presidential ads created during these two election cycles, targeted Latinos ads were four times more likely to appear in Spanish than in English.

Moving on to the ad content distribution from Senate and House races employing Spanish-language campaigns, one generally finds continued support for the theory of information-based advertising. In the most basic of comparisons, these congressional races featured a larger percentage of policy messages in English-language ads than in Spanish-language ones. A 23-percentage-point difference exists between the number of Senate policy ads in English and those in Spanish, whereas for House ads the gap is significantly smaller, at 5 percent. Moreover, for both of these election types, the most substantive policy messages are more frequently advertised in English as opposed to Spanish. The discrepancy is especially pronounced in the political ads produced for House elections, in which only 4 percent of Spanish-language ads contained complex policy messages, compared with 21 percent of English-language ads.[2] Recall that such patterns are consistent with the distribution from the presidential ads as well as with the aggregate-level data.

The use of explained policy messages in candidates' televised political ads also varied depending on the congressional election they were competing in. Senate ads featured a greater percentage of these policy statements in English than in Spanish, whereas House competitors advertised at almost equal rates in both languages. Once again, when House and Senate candidates are compared, greater parity seems to exist in the way House candidates advertised this type of policy message as well as those messages referencing legislation. In advertising simple policy and character messages, both Senate and House contenders adhered to the same strategy employed by presidential candidates. As a result, a larger percentage of Senate and House candidates advertised simple policy statements, character messages, and Latino-specific appeals in their Spanish-language ads as opposed to their English-language ones. In the three election types (presidential, Senate, House) examined thus far, the average difference in the proportion of simple policy messages advertised in Spanish versus English is approximately 9 percent, whereas the average difference in the proportion for character statements is 11 percent. And as with presidential ads, targeted Latino ads developed for Senate and House races appear with much greater frequency in Spanish than in English.

Gubernatorial elections constitute the final type of race in which candidates advertised in Spanish. The final two columns in Table 4.2 present the distribution of gubernatorial candidates' ads based on content and language. The content variation between these English- and Spanish-language ads is consistent with expectations from the theory of information-based advertising.

Had candidates accounted for ethnic group identity in their decision to broadcast Spanish-language policy ads, Latino-specific policies (for example, bilingual education) should have prevailed in their ads. This does not seem to have been the case, however. Looking at the aggregate-level data, one can see that only 0.4 percent of candidates' Spanish-language commercials mentioned bilingual education, and 3 percent referenced the issue of immigration.[3] The bulk of the candidates' Spanish-language ads containing policy messages focused on education (56.3 percent) and health care (22.4 percent)—the same two issues that they mentioned most frequently in their English-language ads. Thus, not much evidence exists to support the idea that candidates' advertising efforts toward Latinos entailed the inclusion of policies that directly affect Latinos.

Comparing the policy and nonpolicy content of ads in English and Spanish offers some initial insight into the belief that candidates competing for various elected offices appealed to Spanish- and non-Spanish-speakers differently. Overall, candidates competing in presidential, Senate, House, and gubernatorial elections consistently advertised more complex policy messages in their English-language ads than in their Spanish-language ones. Candidates also consistently advertised simple policy, character, and Latino-specific appeals in their political ads. Regardless of the elected office for which candidates competed, Spanish-language ads contained these particular appeals to a larger extent than did English-language ads. Finally, in only one case did the distribution of explained policy ads somewhat deviate from the theory of information-based advertising. Although this type of policy message appeared with slightly greater frequency in House candidates' Spanish-language ads than in their English-language ones, the difference is quite small (1.1 percent). When compared with the differences in the percentages of complex policy, simple policy, and character messages advertised in Spanish versus English, this gap is small.

The advertising patterns from the 2000–2004 election cycles suggest that candidates' decisions about broadcasting commercials are not made haphazardly. Instead, it appears that candidates have a tendency to tailor their policy, character, and ethnic-specific messages to the voters who are likely to respond to and be persuaded by them.

## Broadcasting the Advertisements

The next step in testing the theory of information-based advertising is to examine which television shows different types of commercials aired on. If the theory holds, then ads with complex policy statements should have been broadcast with greater frequency on news programs, whereas those containing simple policy and character statements should have appeared more frequently on entertainment shows. Table 4.3 presents the distributions of which type of commercials aired on one of six types of television shows: local or network news, news programs or talk shows, entertainment shows, soap operas, sports programs, and game shows.[4] I defined news programs and talk shows as shows such as the *Today Show*, *Good Morning America*, and *Oprah*. As Baum (2003) notes, such programs can be informative, particularly for those

**Table 4.3**  Broadcast of policy and character advertisements, by type and language of television show

| Content of advertisement | Policy (total) | Complex policy | Explained policy | Simple policy | Character ad | Targeted Latino ad |
|---|---|---|---|---|---|---|
| *English: Type of show* | | | | | | |
| Local or network news | 45.7 | 45.6 | 44.8 | 46.5 | 45.4 | 45.4 |
| News program or talk show | 18.5 | 19.2 | 19.1 | 19.9 | 20.6 | 19.4 |
| Entertainment | 28.4 | 27.9 | 28.1 | 26.4 | 26.3 | 27.5 |
| Soap operas | 1.6 | 1.5 | 1.6 | 1.5 | 1.3 | 1.6 |
| Sports | 1.3 | 1.5 | 1.3 | 1.3 | 1.3 | 1.3 |
| Game shows | 4.3 | 4.1 | 4.2 | 4.4 | 4.2 | 4.2 |
| *Spanish: Type of show* | | | | | | |
| Local or network news | 41.0 | 49.6 | 41.9 | 39.8 | 36.0 | 41.9 |
| News programs or talk shows | 14.1 | 11.6 | 13.5 | 12.3 | 17.8 | 17.6 |
| Entertainment | 36.1 | 31.4 | 30.1 | 39.3 | 40.1 | 32.4 |
| Soap operas | 2.2 | 3.8 | 3.6 | 3.8 | 1.9 | 1.4 |
| Sports | 1.4 | 1.5 | 1.2 | 1.0 | 1.8 | 1.5 |
| Game shows | 0.1 | 0.1 | 0.1 | 0.0 | 0.2 | 0.3 |

SOURCE: 2000–2004 Wisconsin Advertising Project data.

NOTE: Cell entries denote the percentage of ads aired for the given type of show. A difference-of-means test was conducted for each relationship, and each test statistic was significant at the $p < .01$ level.

who are inattentive to politics. Programs such as *Entertainment Tonight,* sitcoms, and dramas were categorized as entertainment shows.

Looking first at Spanish-language policy ads, one can see that 41 percent were aired on the local news, 14.1 percent on news programs and talk shows, and 36.1 percent were broadcast on entertainment programs. The remaining ads were broadcast on soap operas, sports programs, and to a much lesser degree, game shows. Thus, while it is indeed the case that a larger percentage of policy ads were advertised on the news than on entertainment programs, the difference is fairly moderate, at approximately 5 percent. In examining broadcast rates based on type of ad, the same general trend emerges, with some exceptions. Half of the Spanish-language complex policy ads (49.6 percent) were broadcast on the news, whereas fewer than one-third (31.4 percent) were broadcast on entertainment programs. A similar distribution is seen with explained policy ads—42 percent were broadcast on the local or network news and 30 percent on entertainment shows. Of the three different types of policy ads, complex policy ads were broadcast with the greatest frequency on local or network news. This seems to offer some support for the expectation that candidates target their campaign messages to specific audiences, at least with respect to their Spanish-language ads. Yet, although the theory predicts that the bulk of simple policy and character ads in Spanish will be aired on non-news programs, the evidence is mixed. Candidates' simple policy ads were broadcast almost evenly between the local or network news and entertainment shows. And while it is the case that a larger number of character ads were broadcast on entertainment programs as opposed to the news (40 percent versus 36 percent), the difference is fairly moderate. Thus, the evidence is not conclusive in either direction.

Do candidates make the same decisions about their English-language commercials? Put simply, the answer is no. Regardless of their content, 45 percent or more of all English-language spots used in the 2000–2004 elections were broadcast on the local or network news, while less than 30 percent aired on entertainment programs. It is clear that English-language ads, no matter what their content, were predominantly broadcast on the news. Perhaps this is to be expected, because those who watch the news are also those most likely to vote (Delli Carpini and Keeter 1996; Freedman and Goldstein 1999).

One possible reason why candidates do not broadcast as many Spanish-language ads on the news as English-language ads may be due to financial constraints. Although candidates devote the majority of their campaign funds to paid political spots, the portion of these funds allocated to advertising in Spanish-language media is quite small. As a result, if candidates can spare some money for Spanish-language advertising, they may choose to cast a wider net by appealing to as many Latinos as possible, not just to likely voters. By placing their ads on shows with the largest audiences, such as soap operas, they can get more "bang for their buck." But many of the Latinos who watch these entertainment shows may be noncitizens, and thus the effectiveness of candidates' commercials would be lost on viewers who are ineligible to vote. In contrast, because candidates possess a significantly larger advertising budget for their commercials in English, they can target the audience that is most likely to turn out and vote.

This second test of the theory of information-based advertising suggests that candidates are only marginally influenced by the Spanish-speaking electorate's prior levels of political knowledge in deciding which shows to broadcast their Spanish-language commercials on. In comparison, their strategy of broadcasting English-language ads is motivated more by their assessment of which viewers are most likely to vote, as opposed to viewers' familiarity with politics.

## Comparing Theories of Political Advertising

Although the main contention of this book is that content variations in Spanish- and English-language ads arise due to candidates' perceptions of voters' familiarity with politics and proclivity to group appeals, other explanations certainly exist. Petrocik (1996) finds that candidates often choose to discuss only issues or policies that they or their party "own." For instance, Republicans are traditionally considered to be better at foreign policy and tougher on crime than are Democrats, whereas Democrats are thought to perform better on social issues than are Republicans. But candidates also have the option of developing their own unique platform, especially one that is built around widespread consensus (Page 1978). One example is the policy platform of building a stronger economy—a policy goal with which no one would disagree. Brasher (2003) finds these advertising decisions to be motivated primarily by the degree to which a candidate's party owns a particular issue, issues that he or she can claim credit for, and issues that are currently on the congressional agenda.

Other scholars have argued that candidates advertise policy messages that are closest to the ideological position of the median voter in their district (Downs 1957), with the hope of maximizing their vote share. This strategy can be difficult for candidates running for higher offices, which have broader constituencies that are more divided in their opinions (Page and Shapiro 1992). Also, voters' issue positions have the potential to change over time (Zaller 1992). Instead of taking an exact position on an issue, candidates may be better off adopting ambiguous positions, so as to avoid alienating voters (Shepsle 1972; Conover and Feldman 1989). Another option for candidates is to create televised ads featuring affective messages, such as emotional appeals or those discussing candidates' personal characteristics, as voters do rely on these messages to evaluate candidates (Brader 2006; Markus 1982).[5]

The competitiveness of an election also affects candidates' advertising strategies. Research by both Simon (2002) and Kahn and Kenney (1999) finds that the amount of electoral competition between Senate candidates determines whether or not they discuss issues in their advertisements. Closer races make candidates more likely to include policy content in their commercials than do less competitive elections. The logic is rather straightforward: close elections require candidates to differentiate themselves from their opponents, and advertising their issue positions is one way to do this. But policy ads are risky, because candidates' policy stances may not be favorable to all voters; thus, candidates may advertise their policy positions only when they are left with few other options. Simon's (2002) research confirms this assumption: he finds that the reason why little or no dialogue exists in campaigns is that honest discussion about policy is the least attractive option for rationally motivated candidates. These findings suggest that the context of an election influences what types of messages candidates will use in their political spots.

### Case Selection and Research Design

In determining which of these theories best explains candidates' advertising decisions, I used multivariate statistical analysis. The first set of analyses focuses on House races from 2000 to 2004, because the ideological preferences of the median voter in a congressional district can be estimated with great accuracy.[6] This makes it possible to examine the relationship between candidates' advertising decisions and how well their ideologies correspond to those of the average voters in their district. The second set of analyses concentrates on the political ads developed by gubernatorial and Senate candidates from 2000 to 2004. These additional cases help shed light on which factors influence the advertising decisions of statewide candidates and how these factors compare with those influencing the advertising decisions of House candidates. At the statewide level, a Senate or gubernatorial candidate's ideological distance from the preferences of the median voter is not accounted for, given that the estimation procedures are less precise than they are at the House level. Nonetheless, examining the Spanish- and English-language commercials produced by statewide candidates along with those created by House contenders offers a systematic and in-depth look at the factors that influence their decisions to advertise specific types of policy messages in certain election types and in one language or the other.

The advertising decisions of House, Senate, and gubernatorial candidates are therefore analyzed based on the language of the ad and type of message used. As such, two sets of analyses were conducted—one looks at the factors explaining a candidate's decision to advertise policy and character messages in Spanish, and the other focuses on the factors influencing a candidate's decision to advertise policy and character statements in English.

The content of the ad (based on the categories from the policy complexity scale) serves as the dependent variable in the multivariate analysis. I estimate four different models, in which the dependent variable in each model is the decision to advertise a simple policy ad, explained policy ad, complex policy ad, or character ad.[7] Each of these variables is coded in one of two ways, with 1 indicating that the message in question is mentioned, and 0 indicating otherwise.[8] These models are estimated separately for English-language ads and Spanish-language ads.

In addition to broadcasting policy and character messages, candidates, as previously discussed, can advertise specific messages targeting ethnic and racial minorities. What influences a candidate to advertise in Spanish or feature an ethnic or racial minority ad? To answer these questions, I once again use multivariate analysis to estimate several models of political advertising. The dependent variables in these models are (1) whether or not the ad is in Spanish, (2) whether a Latino is the ad, (3) whether an African American is in the ad, and (4) whether an Asian American is in the ad. The last three types of ads can be considered as targeted Latino, African American, and Asian American appeals, given that the inclusion of these visual images is intended for a particular audience. The presumption is that ethnic and racial minorities who see their respective coethnics in these ads will respond to them positively, as the ads would serve to activate one's ethnic group identity and group consciousness (Clinton and Lapinksi 2004). Moreover, the inclusion of coethnics in these ads could also act as a signal or "information shortcut" to these voters that candidates care about them and their needs. But the findings by Garcia Bedolla (2005) and Dawson (1994) show that these targeted ethnic appeals are effective only if one's ethnic or racial identity is linked to one's political behavior. What motivates candidates to advertise these minority-specific appeals is particularly important given that little, if any, research in the campaign advertising literature has explored this topic.

The explanatory variables in these models of campaign advertising include a variety of indicators that account for my theory of advertising, as well as for those advanced in previous research.[9] To test the theory of information-based advertising, I accounted for familiarity with and knowledge of politics based on the percentage of individuals in the district with a high-school degree.[10] In this analysis, the average percentage of individuals in a district with a high-school degree is 81.5 percent, with a low of 29.1 percent and a high of 94.1 percent. Although this definition of political knowledge does not fully capture my definition outlined in Chapter 3, as education is just one component of political knowledge, this is the best available measure at the aggregate level. Thus, although this measure may underestimate the impact of political knowledge on advertising decisions, we would still expect that the greater the percentage of individuals in a district with a high-school degree, the more likely candidates are to mention policy in their advertisements.[11]

To account for Kahn and Kenney's (1999) contention that the level of electoral competitiveness determines whether candidates advertise policy in their commercials, I also control for district competitiveness in a given election. The level of competitiveness in the district is measured as the Democratic share of the two-party vote in the 1996 presidential election for those candidates advertising in 2000 and the two-party Democratic vote share in the 2000 presidential race for candidates' commercials in 2002 and 2004. This variable can be interpreted in the following manner: in districts in which the difference in two-party vote share is large, the degree of competitiveness will be low. By the same logic, in a district in which the difference in the two-party vote share is small, the election is deemed to be a competitive one. There is ample variation in the amount of electoral competition for the 2000–2004 House races, ranging from 28 to 94 percent, with the average Democratic share of the two-party vote for a district being 22.9 percent. Based on Kahn and Kenney's research, the expectation is that in electorally competitive districts, candidates will advertise more policy than nonpolicy messages because they have to distinguish themselves from their opponents.

I also created a measure to represent the ideological distance of the candidate from the median voter in his or her district.[12] A candidate who is ideologically distant from his or her district's median voter should be less likely to include policy messages in commercials, because the candidate has no incentive to reveal his or her support for policies that are not closely aligned with the median voter's ideology.

The models of campaign advertising also take into consideration the demographic context of a candidate's district by controlling for its percentage of Latinos, African Americans, and Asians. [13] It is certainly reasonable for candidates to consider the size of their minority population when deciding whether to advertise minority-specific commercials. As the size of a particular minority population increases, candidates should be more likely to feature members of this population in their televised campaign ads. Likewise, candidates may feel compelled to advertise in Spanish when they represent a sizable Latino population. As documented in Chapter 3, House candidates competing in districts with a majority or supermajority Latino population advertised in Spanish, even though many were long-time incumbents and faced very little competition. Thus, the decision to produce Spanish-language ads may be more of a symbolic gesture in cases in which candidates represent a large number of Latino voters and are in an uncompetitive race. For these House elections, the percentage of Latinos in a district ranged from a low of .01 percent to a high of 77.7 percent, with the average being 6.3 percent. The mean percentage of African Americans in a district is relatively comparable, at 5.8 percent, and ranged from .003 to 65.9 percent. Finally, the average number of Asians in a congressional district was significantly lower, at 1.1 percent, with a range from .01 to 28.8 percent.

Regional variations may also influence what types of policy or nonpolicy ads candidates broadcast. I include a geographic indicator that denotes whether the congressional district is located in the South.[14] Finally, I account for the partisanship of the candidate who created the political spot. Although previous research has no clear guidance on how partisanship affects policy advertising, it may be the case that Republicans are more inclined to advertise certain types of policy messages than are Democrats or vice versa. I estimate each of these models using probit analysis, which is appropriate given that the dependent variables are all dichotomous in nature.

### Findings from Congressional Campaigns

Table 4.4 presents the probit estimates from the campaign advertising model in which the dependent variable is the probability of broadcasting the different types of policy and character statements in Spanish, while in Table 4.5, the results from the analysis of English-language ads are shown. In the estimates presented in Table 4.4, the interaction term capturing the percentage of Latinos in a district and the percentage of that district with a high-school degree is statistically significant and signed in the expected direction in each of the advertising scenarios analyzed. Substantively, these interaction terms indicate that candidates from districts with an educated and sizeable Latino population are more likely to advertise explained policy and complex policy messages in Spanish. But districts with such characteristics have a lower probability of advertising Spanish-language ads containing simple policy and character messages. Based on the predictions from the theory of information-based advertising, one would expect candidates to account for the levels of political knowledge of their targeted audience, measured here by educational

**Table 4.4**  Probit estimates: Factors influencing House candidates' Spanish-language advertising decisions

| Independent variable | Simple policy | Explained policy | Complex policy | Character ads[a] |
|---|---|---|---|---|
| | Estimated coefficient (standard error) | Estimated coefficient (standard error) | Estimated coefficient (standard error) | Estimated coefficient (standard error) |
| Ideological distance | 1.36* (.11) | 1.41* (.27) | −2.31* (.54) | −.89 (.54) |
| Percent district with high-school degree | −.19 (.02) | −.01* (.002) | −.01* (.003) | −.01* (.003) |
| Percent Latino | 1.54* (.40) | −.04* (.00) | −.002 (.03) | .02* (.003) |
| Competitiveness | −.11 (.02) | .003 (.003) | −.01 (.01) | −.03* (.01) |
| Percent Latino × Percent district with high-school degree | −.02* (.004) | .02* (.001) | .04* (.01) | −.05* (.01) |
| *Candidate specific* | | | | |
| Democratic candidate | —[b] | −1.26* (.07) | —[b] | —[b] |
| Constant | 17.77* (2.43) | 1.18* (.20) | −.72* (.32) | −.01 (0.38) |
| N | 3,322 | 3,669 | 3,798 | 4,169 |
| Log-likelihood | −561.69 | −2037.31 | −605.71 | −567.20 |

NOTE: Estimates are for 2000–2004 House elections, and the sample is limited to House candidates who created Spanish-language ads. Entries not in parentheses are the probit coefficients; entries in parentheses denote the corresponding robust standard errors to the probit coefficients, and are clustered by congressional district. The dependent variable is coded as *1* for the type of message listed in the column, and *0* otherwise.

[a]The dependent variable is coded as *1* if the ad discusses either the favored candidate or the opposing candidate's personal qualities only, and *0* otherwise.

[b]Variable was dropped due to a lack of variation in the partisanship of the candidates who ran Spanish-language ads. Eighty percent of the candidates who ran Spanish-language ads were Democrats.

*$p < .01$

attainment, in their advertising decisions. This appears to have been the case for House candidates who created Spanish-language ads containing complex policy messages: they were more likely to do so when there was a large Latino population that exhibited high levels of political knowledge. Candidates faced with this demographic combination were also less likely to use simple policy and character messages. Thus, at least in the case of House candidates, the campaign strategies directed at their Spanish-speaking electorate were motivated by the political knowledge and magnitude of the intended audience. As the predicted probability estimates in Table 4.6 reveal, the impact of these factors is rather substantive in the decision to advertise Spanish-language explained and complex policy messages.[15] A one-standard-deviation increase in the percentage of Latinos and level of education in a district results in a 12 percent increase in the probability of advertising an explained policy message and an 8 percent increase in the probability of advertising a complex policy message. The substantive impact of these factors on advertising a character message, however, is more understated (−.02). Given that policy messages are more costly to advertise because candidates must publicly reveal

**Table 4.5** Probit estimates: Factors influencing House candidates' English-language advertising decisions

| Independent variable | Simple policy Estimated coefficient (standard error) | Explained policy Estimated coefficient (standard error) | Complex policy Estimated coefficient (standard error) | Character ad Estimated coefficient (standard error) |
|---|---|---|---|---|
| Ideological distance | .13* | .12* | −.10* | .49* |
| | (.01) | (.01) | (.02) | (.02) |
| Percent district with high-school degree | −.02* | .03* | −.02* | −.01* |
| | (.002) | (.002) | (.002) | (.003) |
| Percent Latino | −.01* | .03* | −.08* | .02* |
| | (.004) | (.002) | (.04) | (.004) |
| Percent Asian | .13* | −.04* | −.01* | −.18* |
| | (.004) | (.001) | (.002) | (.003) |
| Percent Black | −.05* | .02* | −.09* | .05* |
| | (.003) | (.003) | (.004) | (.004) |
| Competitiveness | .02* | −.03* | .04* | −.02* |
| | (.001) | (.001) | (.01) | (.004) |
| South | −.10* | −.15* | .07 | −.10* |
| | (.05) | (.005) | (.05) | (.01) |
| *Candidate specific* | | | | |
| Democratic candidate | −.09* | .16* | −.21* | −.03* |
| | (.004) | (.004) | (.05) | (.01) |
| Constant | 2.00* | −.34* | −.49* | −.77 |
| | (.03) | (.02) | (.03) | (.03) |
| N | 344,315 | 349,067 | 349,067 | 414,397 |
| Log-likelihood | −195,090.33 | −237,266.25 | −180,155.53 | −89,737.77 |

NOTE: Estimates are for 2000–2004 House elections; the sample is limited to House candidates who ran at least one Spanish-language ad. Entries not in parentheses are the probit coefficients; entries in parentheses denote the corresponding robust standard errors to the probit coefficients and are clustered by congressional district. The dependent variable is coded as *1* for the type of policy message listed in the column, and *0* otherwise.

*$p < .01$

**Table 4.6** Predicted probability estimates: Factors influencing a House candidate's advertising decisions

| | Type of advertisement (dependent variables) | | | |
| --- | --- | --- | --- | --- |
| | Simple policy message | Explained policy message | Complex policy message | Character message |
| *Spanish-language ads* | | | | |
| Candidate goes from being a Republican to a Democrat | —[a] | −.47 (.02) | —[a] | —[a] |
| Education level goes from the mean to the maximum | −.003 (.001) | −.10 (.02) | −.01 (.002) | −.01 (.002) |
| Competitiveness goes from the mean to the maximum | .02 (.01) | .04 (.04) | −.01 (.01) | −.06 (.02) |
| Percent Latino goes from the mean to 19 percent | −.01 (.004) | .06 (.004) | .0004 (.0001) | −.003 (.001) |
| Percent Latino × Percent education increases by one standard deviation | .01 (.007) | .12 (.06) | .08 (.03) | −.02 (.003) |
| Distance goes from the mean to one-standard-deviation increase | .22 (.08) | .08 (.02) | −.01 (.003) | −.004 (.002) |
| *English-language ads* | | | | |
| Candidate goes from being a Republican to a Democrat | .004 (.002) | .06 (.001) | −.06 (.001) | −.003 (.001) |
| Education level goes from the mean to the maximum | −.13 (.002) | .02 (.001) | −.01 (.001) | −.01 (.004) |
| Competitiveness goes from the mean to the maximum | −.03 (.001) | −.03 (.001) | .003 (.001) | −.04 (.004) |
| Percent Latino goes from the mean to 19 percent | −.06 (.002) | .02 (.002) | −.03 (.001) | .04 (.001) |
| Percent Black goes from the mean to 16 percent | −.02 (.001) | .01 (.001) | −.03 (.001) | .01 (.001) |
| Percent Asian goes from the mean to 3 percent | .09 (.001) | −.03 (.001) | −.01 (.001) | −.03 (.003) |
| Nonsouthern to southern district | −.01 (.002) | −.06 (.002) | .002 (.002) | −.01 (.001) |

NOTE: Entries not in parentheses are changes in predicted probabilities and indicate the likelihood of advertising the given statement when all the independent variables are held at their mean or mode. Entries in parentheses are the standard errors. Estimates were calculated using the CLARIFY package in STATA. Predicted probabilities were calculated based on the estimates from Tables 4.4 and 4.5.

[a] These entries could not be estimated in Tables 4.4 and 4.5, and as such, no predicted probabilities were calculated.

their issue positions, this may perhaps explain why a shift in the demographic and political characteristics of the congressional district has a bigger impact on policy-related advertising decisions than on candidate-quality-related advertising decisions.

Other factors also influenced the decision to broadcast particular messages in Spanish; most notable is that a candidate's ideological distance from the median voter of the district is significant in all of these advertising scenarios. As a candidate's political ideology strays from that of the average voter in his or her district, the likelihood of advertising simple and explained policy messages increases. This finding makes a great deal of intuitive sense because candidates who do not share the political perspectives of the average voter would have little reason to reveal this fact in their Spanish-language campaign ads. Instead, we would expect them to advertise exactly these types of policy appeals—simple and with a normative focus, so as to reveal little that might alienate the typical voter in their district. A candidate may wish to advertise an explained policy statement as a way to outline and describe her policy proposals, so that even if she does not share the same ideological preferences of the average voter in her district, voters may be persuaded by the merits of the policy itself. As the ideological distance increases by a standard deviation, the probability of broadcasting this type of policy message increases by 8 percent. Under this same scenario, in which the candidate is ideologically distant from the median voter, the chances that a candidate will advertise a complex policy message are low. A one-standard-deviation increase in ideological distance results in a 1 percent decrease in the likelihood of advertising a complex policy statement. This finding is consistent with the median voter theory, as such a policy message would be wasted among constituents who do not possess the same ideological preferences. A candidate exposing himself in this manner might not be the wisest of strategies, as it has the potential to alienate his base of support. Fear of alienating voters, however, is not as great a factor as the size of the target population (Latinos) and their level of political knowledge. The same is true for the decision to advertise an explained policy message; an increase in the percentage of Latinos and the political information levels for a given district makes a candidate 12 percent more likely to use such a statement, whereas greater ideological distance leads to an 8 percent increase.

The factors explaining House candidates' English-language advertising decisions are presented in Table 4.5. The results indicate that a district's political and demographic characteristics, along with the candidate's partisanship, influence which messages are used. The level of political knowledge in a district is important in determining which types of policy statements to advertise; it also influences the extent to which a candidate advertises a character message. As candidates did with Spanish-language ads, those representing districts with a politically aware electorate are more likely to advertise explained policy messages and less likely to include simple policy and character statements. A more politically knowledgeable district has the greatest influence on the decision to advertise a simple policy message. Based on the predicted probability estimates presented in Table 4.6, a one-unit increase in the district's level of political knowledge decreases the chances of advertising this type of message by 13 percent. In comparison, an increase in district political knowledge has a more subdued effect on the decision to advertise the other types of policy messages.

Along with the political knowledge of a district, its political ideology, ethnic and racial composition, regional location, and degree of electoral competitiveness all influence which types of messages candidates include in their English-language ads. I look first at district and candidate ideology. Candidates whose political ideology is distant from that of their median voter are more likely to advertise both simple and explained policy messages in their ads. The same is true for the decision to advertise a character ad. But ideological distance negatively influences the decision to feature a complex policy message in an English-language commercial. These results follow the same general pattern as those found in candidates' Spanish-language advertising decisions; they also reinforce the importance of the ideological congruence between candidates and their "average" voter in determining the types of campaign messages used.

The ethnic and racial makeup of a congressional district also influences which policy messages a candidate advertises, although it varies based on the ethnic or racial group in question. For instance, the percentage of Latinos in a district positively affects the likelihood of advertising an explained policy or character ad, but negatively affects the probability of including a simple or complex policy ad. A sizeable Asian and African American population is also associated with less advertising of complex policy messages. Possibly, the magnitude of these racial and ethnic minority populations serves as some sort of proxy for political awareness and familiarity, given that a large percentage of the Asian population is also foreign born. Thus, in districts containing a sizeable immigrant community, candidates may be less inclined to feature complicated policy messages in their political ads. If this were a broader phenomenon affecting all the advertising decisions that candidates make, districts with large Asian and Latino populations should lead candidates to advertise more-straightforward policy messages as well as character ads. Although this is true for the size of the Asian population and the decision to advertise simple policy ads, as denoted by its positive and statistically significant coefficient (.13), the coefficient capturing the percentage of Latinos in a district is signed in the opposite direction (−.01). And whereas a larger Latino population is associated with an increased probability of advertising character ads, a sizeable Asian population decreases the chances of advertising such ads. This analysis shows that the size of racial and ethnic minority populations apparently influences only candidates' decisions to advertise complex policy messages. Substantively, a change in the ethnic and racial composition of a House district has the largest impact on the decision to advertise simple policy messages. A one-standard-deviation increase in a district's Latino population decreases the chances of advertising simple policy statements by approximately 6 percent; a similar change in the Asian population makes a candidate 9 percent more likely to feature a simple policy message in an English-language ad.

Regional location also plays a role in advertising choices. Candidates competing in Southern House districts have a lower probability of advertising simple and explained policy messages and character ads than do those in non-Southern congressional districts. Why those competing in Southern districts are less likely to feature these types of messages may be due to other contextual features not accounted for in these models, or it may be a result of the electoral dynamics that are unique to the South.

Finally, the amount of competition that candidates face from their opponents is another factor in these advertising decisions. Candidates competing in very close elections have a higher probability of revealing their policy positions in their ads than do those competing in less competitive elections; this result is consistent with the argument put forth by Kahn and Kenney (1999). It appears, however, that this decision is conditional on the specific type of policy message advertised. A candidate including simple policy statements in his political ads would seem like the ideal strategy for a contender in a tight election, as it would differentiate him from the opponent but not reveal so much as to alienate undecided voters and his base of support. An extremely competitive election also induces a candidate to broadcast a complex policy ad, which is certainly one way that she can distinguish herself from the opponent. But such a strategy also carries potential risks because her electorate might respond negatively to the policy appeal, or her opponent might use the information to his advantage. It is important for the candidate to keep in mind that this policy message may resonate with only a select group in the electorate. A lot of electoral competition, however, decreases one's chances of advertising an explained policy or character message. Just like a simple or complex policy message, advertising an explained policy message can help a candidate distinguish herself from the opponent. Unlike a complex policy message, however, an explained policy statement runs the risk of alienating a larger group of individuals because it will likely be understood by the vast majority of the electorate. Electoral competitiveness also decreases the probability of advertising character-based commercials. This finding further confirms Kahn and Kenney's (1999) work regarding Senate elections and as these results demonstrate, a similar dynamic takes place in House races.

The candidate-specific trait of partisanship also carries some weight in politicians' advertising choices. Democratic candidates are less likely to advertise policy statements (with the exception of explained policy messages) than are Republican candidates. Democrats also have a lower likelihood than their Republican counterparts of featuring character-based messages in their political ads. Again, because the existing research has provided little theoretical motivation behind the relationship between partisanship and policy advertising, it is not immediately clear why Democrats are less likely to use policy messages. Perhaps if these particular policy messages are "owned" by the Democrats, which is a point raised by Petrocik (1996), then it would be reasonable to assume that more Democrats than Republicans would choose to advertise them. Unfortunately, these questions are beyond the scope of this study, and the estimates here are unable to test for such a relationship.

### Findings from Statewide Campaigns

Table 4.7 examines the factors influencing the Spanish-language advertising decisions made by Senate and gubernatorial candidates.[16] The findings shown here indicate once again that the levels of political knowledge within the Latino electorate affect candidates' advertising decisions. The interaction term (*Percent Latino × Percent district with high-school degree*) is signed in the expected direction for all four advertising models. Thus, as the percentage of

**Table 4.7**  Probit estimates: Factors influencing statewide candidates' Spanish-language advertising decisions

| Independent variable | Simple policy<br><br>Estimated coefficient (standard error) | Explained policy<br><br>Estimated coefficient (standard error) | Complex policy<br><br>Estimated coefficient (standard error) | Character ad<br><br>Estimated coefficient (standard error) |
|---|---|---|---|---|
| Percent district with high-school degree | .36*** (.04) | −.69*** (.04) | −1.31*** (.05) | .78*** (.05) |
| Percent Latino | .24*** (.04) | −.77*** (.04) | −1.41*** (.05) | .84*** (.07) |
| Competitiveness | −.03*** (.005) | .03*** (.01) | −.03*** (.004) | −.03*** (.01) |
| Percent Latino × Percent district with high-school degree | −.02*** (.004) | .03** (.002) | .06*** (.002) | −.04*** (.003) |
| *Candidate specific* | | | | |
| Democratic candidate | —ᵃ | −.64*** (.07) | —ᵃ | −.56*** (.09) |
| Constant | −5.62*** (1.21) | 13.83*** (1.05) | 31.49** (1.27) | −17.78 (1.48) |
| N | 10,536 | 13,298 | 13,854 | 13,740 |
| Log-likelihood | −6,769.25 | −7,127.77 | −5,858.19 | −2,104.89 |

NOTE: Estimates are for the 2000–2004 Senate and gubernatorial elections, and the sample is limited to candidates who created Spanish-language ads. Entries not in parentheses are the probit coefficients; entries in parentheses denote the corresponding robust standard errors to the probit coefficients and are clustered by congressional district. The dependent variable is coded as *1* for the type of policy message listed in the column, and *0* otherwise.

ᵃ Variable was dropped due to lack of variation in the partisanship of the candidates who ran Spanish-language ads. That is, 80 percent of the candidates who ran Spanish-language ads were Democrats.

*$p < .10$

**$p < .05$

***$p < .01$

politically knowledgeable Latinos in the electorate increases, the likelihood of candidates broadcasting explained and complex policy messages in Spanish also increases. In contrast, districts with a large percentage of politically knowledgeable Latinos result in candidates having a lower propensity to feature simple policy and character statements in their ads. The magnitude of these effects ranges from 3 percent for character ads to almost 30 percent for explained policy ads.[17]

The impact of district characteristics on Senate and gubernatorial candidates is consistent with their impact on the advertising decisions of congressional candidates. For instance, the competitiveness of the election influences

which policy and nonpolicy messages statewide candidates choose to advertise. A highly contested election reduces the probability that a candidate will
advertise simple, complex, and character messages. Explained policy messages are the only ones that candidates are likely to advertise when they face
tough competition from their opponents because such messages enable candidates to distinguish themselves from one another. This finding supports the
existing work on campaign strategies.

## Motivations for Advertising to Racial and Ethnic Minorities

Thus far, the discussion has focused on the factors motivating congressional
and statewide candidates to advertise policy and nonpolicy messages in their
Spanish- and English-language ads. In this section I turn attention to the
variables influencing House candidates' decisions to develop targeted ethnic
and racial campaigns. Table 4.8 presents the estimates from these models. In
Table 4.9, I present the predicted probabilities to determine the substantive
impact of these estimates.

Overall, these findings further highlight the relationship between district
characteristics and advertising decisions. As seen from the data in Tables 4.8
and 4.9, whether candidates make targeted campaign appeals to racial and
ethnic minorities can largely be explained by the racial and ethnic composition of the district. In fact, the percentage of Latinos in a district factors into
of all of these advertising decisions. The probability that a candidate advertises in Spanish and features a Latino, African American, or Asian American
in an ad are all positively correlated with the size of the Latino population in
a House district. Thus, as the Latino population increases, the likelihood that
candidates will advertise in these ways increases. A one-standard-deviation
increase in the Latino population of a typical House district results in a 5 percent jump in the probability that a candidate will advertise in Spanish, and a
9 percent higher probability that a candidate features a Latino in an ad. That
candidates would factor in the size of their Latino population when deciding whether to advertise these targeted Latino appeals should come as no
surprise. It is rather intriguing, however, that the size of the Latino population also influences a candidate's decision to feature African Americans
and Asian Americans in his or her ads. These findings could be attributed
to the relatively high residential overlap that exists between Latinos, African
Americans (Kaufman 2003; McClain and Karnig 1990) and, to somewhat a
lesser extent, Asian Americans (Horton 1995). As the percentage of Latinos

**Table 4.8**  Factors influencing a House candidate's targeted ethnic and racial ads

| | Type of advertisement | | | |
|---|---|---|---|---|
| | Spanish-language ad | Latino in ad | African American in ad | Asian American in ad |
| | Estimated coefficient (standard error) | Estimated coefficient (standard error) | Estimated coefficient (standard error) | Estimated coefficient (standard error) |
| *District characteristics* | | | | |
| Distance | −.11* (.04) | −.58* (.03) | −.26* (.02) | −1.20* (.05) |
| Percent with high-school degree | −.01* (.001) | −.03* (.004) | −.01* (.003) | −.02* (.001) |
| Percent Latino | .01* (.001) | .04* (.005) | .03* (.004) | .01* (.001) |
| Percent African American | .01 (.04) | .004* (.001) | .02* (.003) | .01* (.001) |
| Percent Asian American | .01* (.004) | .11* (.002) | .05* (.002) | .09* (.003) |
| Competitiveness | .01* (.004) | .01* (.002) | .01* (.0002) | .02* (.004) |
| South | .03 (.02) | −.51* (.01) | .14* (.01) | −.47* (.02) |
| *Candidate specific* | | | | |
| Democratic candidate | .52* (.02) | .21* (.01) | .09* (.01) | .63* (.02) |
| Constant | −2.70* (.07) | .20* (.05) | −.68* (.03) | −1.20* (.07) |
| N | 418,376 | 338,574 | 333,967 | 331,194 |
| Log-likelihood | −18,659.11 | −45,130.17 | −129,129.78 | −15,447.41 |

NOTE: Estimates are for the 2000–2004 House elections. Entries not in parentheses are the probit coefficients; entries in parentheses denote the corresponding robust standard errors to the probit coefficients. The dependent variable is coded as *1* for the content listed in the column, and *0* otherwise.
*$p < .01$

in a district goes from its average level to a one-standard-deviation increase (from 4.6 percent to 19 percent), candidates are 12 percent more likely to include African Americans in their ads. The same size increase in the Latino population, however, has a much smaller impact on the decision of political contenders to create ads featuring Asian Americans.

Candidates also take into consideration the size of their African American and Asian American electorates in their minority ad campaigns. Of course, the larger the size of the African American and Asian American populations

**Table 4.9**  Predicted probability estimates: Targeted ethnic and racial ads

| Scenario | Spanish-language ad | Latino in ad | African American in ad | Asian American in ad |
|---|---|---|---|---|
| *Candidate specific* | | | | |
| Candidate goes from being a Republican to a Democrat | .01 (.002) | .02 (.001) | .02 (.001) | .01 (.003) |
| *District characteristics* | | | | |
| Percent of Latinos in district goes from the mean to 19 percent | .05 (.01) | .09 (.002) | .12 (.002) | .01 (.004) |
| Percent of African Americans in district goes from the mean to 16 percent | .003 (.001) | .003 (.001) | .07 (.001) | .003 (.0003) |
| Percent of Asian Americans in district goes from the mean to 3 percent | .01 (.004) | .02 (.004) | .02 (.001) | .04 (.002) |
| District competitiveness goes from the mean to one-standard-deviation increase | .01 (.001) | .02 (.001) | .05 (.001) | .01 (.0003) |
| Percent with high-school degree goes from the mean to 94 percent | −.001 (.001) | −.02 (.002) | −.03 (.001) | −.003 (.0001) |
| Distance goes from the mean to one-standard-deviation increase | −.001 (.0003) | −.01 (.003) | −.01 (.001) | −.002 (.001) |

NOTE: Entries not in parentheses are changes in predicted probabilities and indicate the likelihood of advertising the given statement when all the independent variables are held at their mean or mode. Entries in parentheses are the standard errors. Estimates were calculated using CLARIFY package in STATA. For each of the calculations, the increase in the variable of interest was based on a one-standard-deviation increase. These estimates were calculated based on the probit estimates from Table 4.8.

in a district, the more likely candidates will be to include African Americans and Asian Americans in their ads. A one-standard-deviation increase in the size of the African American population in an average congressional district increases the chances of African Americans appearing in an ad by approximately 7 percent. The size of the African American population has the greatest impact on ads that feature African Americans. From a substantive perspective, the size of the Asian American population matters only in a candidate's decision to feature Asian Americans in their political commercials. Even so, an increase in the size of the Asian American population increases a candidate's likelihood of running an Asian American ad by only three percentage points. Given that the three largest ethnic and racial groups in the U.S. reside together in major urban centers across the country (for example, Los Angeles, New York, and Chicago), as well as in smaller cities (such as Monterey Park, California), candidates seem to be affected by the racial and ethnic diversity of their districts in developing outreach efforts targeted at racial and ethnic minorities.

The ideological composition of the district and the amount of electoral competition also affect candidates' targeted minority campaigns. A candidate having an ideology that is distant from that of the district's median voter makes him less likely to develop minority-specific ads, to include minorities in his televised ads, and to advertise in Spanish. The magnitude of these effects is quite minimal, however, with .01 being the largest value. Thus, it seems that the size of the targeted audience factors into these advertising decisions to a greater extent than does the candidate's ideological congruence with her constituents.

The extent to which candidates face a tough competitor once again helps to explain their advertising decisions. Electoral competition impacts all four of these advertising scenarios. More competitive elections results in an increase in the likelihood that a candidate will target minorities via these ethnic ads. Given that ethnic and racial minorities, and Latinos particularly, function as a crucial swing vote in many close races, politicians may indeed use targeted ad campaigns to win their support. Although electoral competitiveness has been found to play a key role in a candidate's decision to advertise policy messages (Kahn and Kenney 1999), it also influences the degree to which a candidate engages in campaign efforts that target racial and ethnic minorities.

Finally, a candidate's partisanship influences these advertising decisions, with a strong bias toward Democratic candidates. Democrats are more likely to use all four minority-specific advertising strategies than are Republicans. These findings further reaffirm the strong relationship between ethnic and racial minorities and the Democratic party; this relationship is in large part due to the historical efforts made by Democrats to advance the interests of ethnic and racial minorities in the United States (Abrajano and Alvarez, forthcoming). Moreover, congressional candidates representing minority constituents are overwhelmingly Democratic in their party affiliation (Alvarez and García Bedolla 2003; DeSipio 1996; Cain et al. 1991), although in recent years, Republicans have made attempts to portray themselves as a more ethnically diverse and inclusive political party, using, for example, the appearance by George W. Bush's half-Latino nephew at the 2000 Republican National Convention. But the predicted probability estimate for one's party identification, given in Table 4.9, shows that it has a much smaller impact on candidates' advertising decisions than do the demographic characteristics of their district.

Overall, these findings offer another lens with which the predictions of the theory of information-based advertising can be examined. Candidates do appear to be accounting for their intended audience when developing minority ad campaigns, and therefore they seem to be tailoring their messages in hopes that ethnic and racial minorities will respond positively to them.

## Summary

Analyzing the policy and nonpolicy content of the thousands of ads produced during the 2000–2004 election cycles indicates that candidates are, for the most part, motivated to tailor their Spanish- and English-language advertising messages according to the theory of information-based advertising. At the aggregate level and across the various elections, campaign messages in Spanish-language commercials differed from those in English-language commercials. As such, these results confirm the conventional wisdom on minority advertising. They also suggest that these differences are the deliberate result of candidate decision making—that the variations are carefully thought-out rather than accidental. It is no mere coincidence that the total number of Spanish-language advertisements used in the 2000–2004 election cycles contained more simple policy statements and character messages than did the English-language ads, and it is not an accident that the English-language commercials contained a larger number of complex policy messages than did the Spanish-language spots.

Such differences exist because candidates are targeting voters with messages based at least in part on the candidates' beliefs about how well their constituents will respond to such messages. Overall, Spanish speakers were exposed to more nonpolicy appeals than were English-speakers because candidates perceive that the Spanish-speaking community will be receptive to messages that refer to their immigrant background or to candidates' characters. In deciding which kinds of programs to broadcast commercials on, though, the results are mixed. Only with respect to one type of policy ad did the distributions support the theory of information-based advertising. When it came to advertising complex policy messages in Spanish, a greater percentage of ads were aired on the news than on entertainment programs. But regardless of content, the majority of English-language ads were broadcast on the news.

The level of political knowledge in a candidate's district and the demographic composition of the district exercise much influence over both statewide and House candidates' decisions to advertise policy and character messages in their commercials. Candidates competing in districts with a large percentage of politically informed Latinos are more likely to advertise policy messages in Spanish than are those representing a less politically informed Latino electorate. Additional contextual factors, such as the competitiveness of the election and the demographic makeup of the electorate, also played a role in these choices. In particular, the percentage of minorities in a candidate's district affected whether candidates developed ethnic-specific ads.

Thus, based on these analyses, one has reason to believe that politicians target Latino voters with campaign messages that the candidates expect them to respond favorably to. The question remains, how do these ads affect Latino political behavior? Chapter 5 explores this question by looking at Latino turnout and vote choice.

# 5 Advertising Effects on the Latino Vote

TELEVISION ADVERTISING HAS EMERGED as the primary means used by political campaigns today to communicate to voters. The campaigns from 2000 to 2004 demonstrated that candidates spent millions of dollars on this advertising medium, each with the hope that he would capture more votes than his opponent. Among those who have researched the effects of these political ads, the general consensus is that campaign messages *can* and *do* affect voters.[1] Of course, the primary goal of these ads is to influence the outcome of an election (Simon 2002; Shaw 1999; Nagler and Leighley 1992). They do so in a number of different ways, from striking a certain tone (Ansolabehere and Iyengar 1995; Geer 2006), to making emotional appeals (Brader 2006). But rather surprisingly, given the important role that policy plays in an individual's political behavior (Downs 1957; Carmines and Stimson 1980; Alvarez and Nagler 1995), very little research has focused on the effects of policy-focused campaign ads on how voters cast their ballots, develop their political attitudes, or add to their levels of political knowledge. With the exception of recent work by Vavreck (2009), this paucity in the campaign research literature has largely been due to data limitations because it has been difficult to systematically analyze the content of political ads in the past.

As Chapter 4 highlighted, policy ads come in all shapes and sizes. We also saw how Spanish-language ads, overall, contained a larger percentage of character-based appeals than did English-language ads. This chapter explores how these different policy ads affected Latino political behavior. Among Spanish-dominant Latinos, did exposure to the Democratic contender's

Spanish-language ads increase their likelihood of voting for him? Did exposure to Spanish-language targeted ethnic appeals make Spanish-dominant Latinos more likely to support them? This chapter also examines the impact of both Spanish- and English-language ads on the vote decisions made by bilingual Latinos.

In addition to directly influencing the election outcome, exposure to political ads can produce some spillover, or secondary, effects. In particular, being exposed to campaign ads can contribute to voter learning and decision making (Zhao and Chaffee 1995; Brians and Wattenberg 1996; Alvarez 1997; Freedman et al. 2004; Craig et al. 2005; Geer 2006; Brader 2006) and can influence citizen participation and interest (Freedman et al. 2004; Ansolabehere and Iyengar 1995; Lau and Pomper 2004). I explore one of these secondary effects, voter turnout, in this chapter. Understanding the factors in an ad, particularly its language and content, that can mobilize Latinos to the polls is important because Latinos' rates of turnout are still not commensurate with those of African Americans and Anglos (Abrajano and Alvarez, forthcoming).

The conventional wisdom expects Latinos to respond positively to these campaign appeals. But at the same time, Latinos, particularly those who are second- and third-generation Americans, care very much about matters that affect their daily lives—from jobs and the economy to education and health care (Abrajano 2005; Abrajano et al. 2008; Abrajano and Alvarez, forthcoming). Thus, as Latinos become acquainted with and incorporated into the American political system, they are likely to exhibit the same political attitudes as the average citizen. Socially and politically incorporated Latinos, then, should be more persuaded in their decision to vote and in their vote choice by political ads that contain policy messages than by ads with group identity appeals. But those Latinos who have yet to fully incorporate into American politics and society should be positively influenced in their political behavior by these ethnic group appeals.

## The Impact of Political Ads on Latino Vote Choice and Turnout
In testing these expectations, I drew on information about Latino voters and their political preferences from the National Annenberg Election Survey (NAES) of 2000 and 2004. Both of these surveys were designed as national, rolling cross-sectional studies and asked respondents a wide variety of questions pertaining to their political attitudes, demographics, and, most

importantly, whether they voted and who they would vote for in the presidential race. So in 2000, respondents were given the choice of Bush versus Gore,
whereas in 2004, respondents were asked to select Bush or Kerry.[2] Altogether,
for the 2000 survey, more than 70,000 interviews were conducted from December 1999 through January 2001. For the 2004 survey, 98,711 individuals
were interviewed from October 2003 through November 2004. Because I am
interested in the effects of political ad exposure on vote choice and turnout,
I focus on the interview waves conducted from September to November in
both election cycles, as this is when the majority of televised campaign commercials were broadcast. In the 2000 survey, a total of 1,553 respondents who
identified themselves as of Hispanic or Latino origin were interviewed; of
these respondents, 69.4 percent took the interview in English and 30.6 percent took it in Spanish. In the 2004 survey, 1,474 Latino respondents were part
of this interview wave, with 35.7 percent taking the survey in Spanish and
64.3 percent taking it in English. This breakdown is fairly representative of
census estimates of language use and English-language ability for the Latino
population in the U.S.; among those Latinos who speak Spanish, 71.8 percent
are bilingual and 28.2 percent are Spanish dominant (do not speak English
well or at all). The language in which the respondent took the survey serves as
my measure of political incorporation. Unfortunately, other measures of political incorporation, such as generational status or salience of ethnic group
identity, were not available in this survey. Nonetheless, language acquisition
is a suitable measure because it serves as a fundamental indicator of one's level
of incorporation and assimilation into mainstream society (Bloemraad 2006;
Portes and Rumbaut 1992). The ability to speak in the host country's primary
language has long been the main hallmark of assimilation (Dahl 1961; Portes
and Rumbaut 1992). It is therefore reasonable to infer that respondents who
opted to take the interview in Spanish are likely to be less politically incorporated than those who chose to be interviewed in English.

   Determining the types and number of ads that Latinos were exposed to
was the next step in assessing the impact of advertising on their political
behavior. Obtaining this kind of data has been a challenge for researchers,
with most relying on survey questions asking respondents if they recall seeing a television ad during the campaign. This measure of advertising exposure, however, does not capture the number of commercials that respondents
were exposed to, and it does not indicate the content of a commercial's campaign message. For these reasons, I depart from this measure of advertising

exposure and instead use one that relies on the cost per household of airing a political spot. My measure serves as a proxy for the likelihood that a given household watched the ad when it aired because television stations usually charge based on audience size. Moreover, the cost of broadcasting each commercial should be directly proportional to the number of people exposed to each ad.[3] Luckily, this information is available from the same data set used to analyze candidates' advertising decisions in Chapter 4; the advertising data includes both the cost of broadcasting an ad and its rate of broadcast.[4]

The construction of this measure does not permit me to actually observe the number of commercials that a respondent was exposed to; also, it assumes that voters in a given media market watched television ads at an equal rate. The measure is therefore just a rough estimate of actual advertising exposure. But any measurement error should, if anything, only reduce the estimated effects of exposure, and any campaign effects that are revealed are thus likely to underestimate, rather than overestimate, the actual impact of televised ads. Using this measure, I then categorized commercials based on their sponsor (Bush or Gore in 2000 and Bush or Kerry in 2004) and policy content (using the policy complexity scale), because my predictions examine the impact of specific campaign messages on voters. [5] The turnout model is consistent with previous efforts (see DeFrancesco Soto and Merolla 2008) in that it does not differentiate the political ads based on their sponsor. The primary interest in estimating a model of turnout is to understand which types of policy messages affected one's likelihood of voting, so knowing who sponsored the ad is not that relevant. But in the vote choice model, it is important to know the factors that make one either more or less likely to vote for a specific candidate.

Next, the measure of ad exposure was assigned to survey respondents who were potentially exposed to the commercials, and, because ad exposure is based on the cost of broadcast for a given media market, each individual was matched with the advertisements that were broadcast in his or her media market.[6] From this measure, I created several specific measures of exposure, based on language, content, and ad sponsor. For Spanish-dominant Latinos, the impact of Spanish-language political ads was the focus, as these were the only ads that they were exposed to.[7] But Latinos who took the survey in English could have been exposed to both the Spanish- and English-language political ads. Although this could also include some Latinos who speak no Spanish, given that 79.6 percent of the Latino population speaks Spanish at home (Shin and Bruno 2003), it is likely that they saw at least some of the Spanish-language ads produced by Bush and Gore in 2000 and Bush and Kerry in 2004. Thus, English-dominant Latinos were potentially exposed to the policy messages and to the targeted Latino ads in both English and Spanish. If the conventional wisdom holds, Spanish-dominant Latinos should be responsive to targeted Latino ads in both their vote choice and turnout. Exposure to cultural appeals, then, should be positively associated with a Spanish-dominant Latino's likelihood of supporting the presidential candidate who broadcast such ads. If targeted Latino ads indeed had a mobilizing effect on Spanish-dominant Latinos, as found by DeFrancesco Soto and Merolla (2008), a positive relationship between ad exposure and rates of turnout should also exist. But I expect exposure to policy-based messages to have a greater effect on the voting behavior of English-dominant Latinos than does exposure to ethnically based political ads. In this expectation, I depart from conventional wisdom.

By estimating a multivariate model of vote choice, one can determine whether or not these expectations are realized. The dependent variables for the vote-choice models are the probability of supporting Gore in 2000 and the probability of supporting Kerry in 2004, coded as $1$ if the respondent reported voting for Gore or Kerry, and $0$ if the respondent voted for Bush. [8] In the turnout model, the dependent variable is also treated dichotomously, with $1$ indicating that the respondent reported voting in the 2000 or 2004 presidential race, and $0$ indicating otherwise.

Along with the primary explanatory variable of interest—exposure to the various types of political ads—I also control for the standard predictors of vote choice and turnout. I account for a respondent's gender, household income, education, marital status, and age. Because political disposition plays a very important role in a person's vote decision, I also control for political ideology and partisanship, as these have been the strongest and most consistent predictors of vote choice in American politics (Campbell et al. 1964). Finally, in the vote-choice model, I control for a respondent's positions on two issues that were salient in the 2000 presidential campaign—abortion and Social Security. Along with partisanship and ideology, a person's own issue positions have long been recognized by the voting behavior literature as playing a critical role in vote decisions (Downs 1957; Petrocik 1996; Alvarez and Nagler 1995). It is therefore essential to account for the positions of a respondent on at least a handful of issues.

The existing research on political participation has also found one's personal orientation to politics, which includes factors such as interest in government and degree of political attentiveness, to affect the likelihood of voting (Wolfinger and Rosenstone 1980; Rosenstone and Hansen 1993; Verba et al. 1995). Thus, in the turnout model, I account for the frequency with which a respondent watches television news and reads the newspaper, as well as for his or her self-reported levels of interest in government and current affairs. Research on Latino political participation also notes differences between subgroups in their rates of political involvement (de le Garza and DeSipio 1992); Cubans tend to be more active participants in political matters than are Mexicans and Puerto Ricans. In light of these variations, I control for a Latino respondent's ethnicity in the turnout model.

Table 5.1 presents the multivariate estimates from the vote-choice model that examines the impact of Spanish-language ads on Latinos' vote intentions. Table 5.2 contains the predicted probability estimates. Overall, exposure to Spanish-language policy and nonpolicy ads produces different effects on the vote decisions of English- and Spanish-dominant Latinos. Exposure to Gore's Spanish-language policy ads increased the likelihood of English-dominant Latinos having voted for him; in substantive terms, if Spanish-dominant Latinos had been exposed to more of these ads, they would have been about 5 percent more likely to support Gore.[9] The same can be said of the 2004 presidential race, because English-dominant Latinos who were exposed to Kerry's Spanish-language policy ads were more likely to support him. Greater exposure to these policy-based Spanish ads had a strong impact on their vote intention, making them 64 percent more likely to cast their ballots in favor of Kerry. Kerry's targeted Latino ads also positively affected the vote direction of English-dominant Latinos, though the magnitude of the effect was not as great as that of Kerry's policy ads.

The impact of Spanish-language ads on the vote intentions of Spanish-dominant Latinos appears to be less consistent across these two election cycles. Only in 2000 did the exposure of this group to Gore's targeted Latino ads positively impact their decision to vote for him. Spanish-language policy ads carried no weight on the voting decisions of Spanish-dominant Latinos in either presidential election.

The political dispositions and issue concerns of Latinos also impact their vote choices. Not surprisingly, Democrats were more likely to vote for Gore and Kerry than were Independents. As expected, Republicans exhibited a lower probability of supporting Gore or Kerry than did Independents. Also,

**Table 5.1** The impact of Spanish-language ads on Latino vote choice in the 2000 and 2004 presidential elections

| | 2000 (probability of voting for Gore) | | 2004 (probability of voting for Kerry) | |
|---|---|---|---|---|
| | Estimated coefficient | Standard error | Estimated coefficient | Standard error |
| Constant | .23 | .39 | −.26 | .25 |
| *Political dispositions* | | | | |
| Liberal ideology | .14** | .07 | .19*** | .04 |
| Democrat | 1.08*** | .15 | .99*** | .10 |
| Republican | −.94*** | .17 | −.92*** | .11 |
| Restrict abortion | -.57** | .13 | −.10*** | .03 |
| Social Security | −.13 | .11 | .04 | .09 |
| *Demographics* | | | | |
| No high-school degree | −.18 | .19 | −.27** | .13 |
| High-school graduate | −.09 | .16 | −.25** | .08 |
| Income | −.01 | .04 | −.04* | .02 |
| Married | −.19 | .14 | −.03 | .09 |
| Women | −.04 | .13 | −.04 | .08 |
| Age | .00 | .01 | −.004 | .003 |
| Interview in Spanish | −.06 | .18 | .43*** | .12 |
| *Advertising exposure* | | | | |
| Gore/Kerry Spanish policy | 4.57** | 1.95 | 3.88** | 1.91 |
| Gore/Kerry targeted Latino | −.27* | .16 | 3.30** | 1.58 |
| *Advertising exposure ×<br>Interview language* | | | | |
| Gore/Kerry Spanish policy ×<br>Spanish | −2.12 | 3.57 | 3.12 | 4.89 |
| Gore/Kerry targeted Latino Ad ×<br>Spanish | .65* | .39 | −2.97 | 4.16 |
| *N* | 548 | | 1,254 | |
| Log-likelihood | −264.89 | | −602.76 | |
| Baseline | 50.23 | | 61.73 | |
| Percent correctly predicted | 62.26 | | 65.49 | |

NOTE: For the 2000 data, the dependent variable is coded as *1* if respondent voted for Gore, and *0* if respondent voted for Bush. For the 2004 data, the dependent variable is coded as *1* if respondent voted for Kerry, and *0* if respondent voted for Bush.

*$p < .10$
**$p < .05$
***$p < .01$

**Table 5.2** Predicted probability estimates: The impact of the amount of ad exposure on Latino vote choice and turnout

| Type of ad and voter | Likelihood of voting | Likelihood of voting for Gore | Likelihood of voting for Kerry |
|---|---|---|---|
| General political ads × Spanish-dominant respondent | .03 (.01) | — | — |
| Spanish-language ads × Spanish-dominant respondent | .28 (.16) | — | — |
| Targeted Latino ads × English-dominant respondent | .09 (.05) | — | — |
| Spanish-language ads × English-dominant respondent | −.05 (.02) | — | — |
| Gore/Kerry Spanish-language policy ad | — | .05 (.02) | .64 (.06) |
| Gore/Kerry Spanish-language targeted Latino ad | — | −.03 (.02) | .34 (.05) |
| Gore targeted Latino ad × Spanish-dominant respondent | — | .04 (.02) | — |
| *English-dominant Latinos* | | | |
| Gore/Kerry complex policy ad | — | .19 (.07) | — |
| Gore/Kerry explained policy ad | — | .30 (.14) | .28 (.10) |
| Gore/Kerry targeted Latino ad | — | .06 (.03) | .15 (.07) |
| Bush explained policy ad | — | −.20 (.11) | — |
| Bush targeted Latino ad | — | — | −.22 (.07) |

NOTE: Cell entries not in parentheses report the difference in the probability of voting for the Democratic presidential candidate in the 2000 and 2004 elections and of voting when a respondent goes from being exposed to the mean number of ads to a one-standard-deviation increase in advertising spending. Entries in parentheses denote the standard errors of the probability estimates. The estimates were calculated using the probit estimates in Table 5.1 and were computed using the CLARIFY package in STATA.

how people conceive of themselves ideologically affects their vote decision in the expected manner, so that Latinos who consider themselves liberals had a higher probability of supporting the Democratic presidential nominee. Only one issue mattered to Latinos in these presidential elections: those holding a restrictive view on abortion were less likely support the Democrat in both presidential elections. Finally, Latinos' education and income influenced their vote decisions, although only in the 2004 presidential election. Less-educated Latinos were not as likely to support Kerry as were more-educated Latinos. But, more-affluent Latinos displayed a lower likelihood of casting their ballots in favor of Kerry when compared with Latinos in the lower-income brackets.

Recall that the campaign environment of English-dominant Latinos varied considerably from that of Spanish-dominant Latinos. English-dominant Latinos had the potential to be exposed to the multitude of English-language ads produced by the presidential contenders. The estimates presented in Table 5.3 account for this possibility, and therefore focus on the impact of advertising exposure from both Spanish- and English-language ads on this group's vote decisions. As the estimates suggest, exposure to political ads played a role in the vote decisions of English-dominant Latinos in both the 2000 and 2004 presidential elections. In the 2000 election, exposure to Gore's more-sophisticated complex and explained policy ads positively influenced the likelihood of these Latinos voting for him. In the 2004 election, only Kerry's explained policy ads increased the probability that English-dominant Latinos would support him. The finding that more-incorporated Latinos are affected by political ads in their vote decision is in line with the arguments presented in this book as well as the existing research on Latino voting behavior. But not all policy messages had the same effect on voting behavior. Only ads containing the most informative types of policy messages influenced these voters; exposure to the simple policy ads produced by Bush, Gore, and Kerry appeared to have no significant impact on the vote decision.

Political ads containing targeted Latino appeals also increased the chances that English-dominant Latinos would lend their support to the Democratic candidate. Thus, even for the socially and politically incorporated segment of the Latino electorate, campaign ads that tap into their culture are salient in their political decisions. These estimates, however, do not indicate whether targeted Latino ads had a greater impact on their knowledge of the candidates' policy positions than did policy ads. This question is addressed later in the chapter.

Exposure to Bush's commercials also played a role in the vote decisions of English-dominant Latinos. In the 2000 presidential race, those exposed to his explained policy ads were less likely to vote for Gore. But in the 2004 election, it was Bush's targeted Latino ads that affected the vote choice of English-dominant Latinos. Those who were exposed to such messages were less likely to favor Kerry. In the parlance of Zaller (1992), the impact of countervailing messages does not appear to have been consistent across these two election cycles, particularly regarding the content of the ads. It is difficult to draw any conclusions from these results about the effects of an opponent's political appeals on voter decision making. Instead, the results lend support to Zaller

**Table 5.3** The impact of Spanish- and English-language ads on the vote choice of English-dominant Latinos

| | 2000 (probability of voting for Gore) | | 2004 (probability of voting for Kerry) | |
| --- | --- | --- | --- | --- |
| | Estimated coefficient | Standard error | Estimated coefficient | Standard error |
| Constant | −.09 | .48 | −.47 | .33 |
| *Political dispositions* | | | | |
| Liberal ideology | .27*** | .09 | .31*** | .06 |
| Democrat | 1.27*** | .19 | .71*** | .13 |
| Republican | −1.01*** | .22 | −1.20*** | .15 |
| Restrict abortion | −.48*** | .17 | −.13*** | .04 |
| Social Security | −.10 | .12 | — | — |
| *Demographics* | | | | |
| No high-school degree | −.26 | .26 | −.45** | .20 |
| High-school graduate | −.18 | .19 | −.12 | .14 |
| Income | −.04 | .05 | −.05 | .03 |
| Married | −.25 | .18 | −.22* | .12 |
| Women | −.05 | .16 | .10 | .11 |
| *Advertising exposure* | | | | |
| Gore/Kerry complex policy | 4.00** | 1.80 | −.16 | .14 |
| Gore/Kerry explained policy | 1.93** | .88 | .60* | .33 |
| Gore/Kerry simple policy | .56 | .40 | −.36 | .34 |
| Gore/Kerry targeted Latino | 1.64** | .81 | 3.23* | 1.71 |
| Bush complex policy | 3.04 | 1.98 | −.25 | .35 |
| Bush explained policy | −1.29* | .70 | .52 | .65 |
| Bush simple policy | −.54 | .37 | .23 | .54 |
| Bush targeted Latino | 3.52 | 2.93 | −2.94** | 1.42 |
| | | | | |
| N | 403 | | 826 | |
| Log-likelihood | −171.64 | | −337.21 | |
| Baseline | 57.66 | | 59.71 | |
| Percent correctly predicted | 65.84 | | 68.19 | |

NOTE: The dependent variable is coded as *1* if the respondent voted for Gore, and *0* if the respondent voted for Bush; the sample is restricted to Latinos who conducted the survey in English.

*$p < .10$

**$p < .05$

***$p < .01$

(1992) and Alvarez (1997), who find that campaign messages have the ability to reinforce existing political dispositions and attitudes. But campaign appeals do not seem to be able to actually change the attitudes of individuals. We also see from these results that the political dispositions of English-dominant Latinos influence their vote choice too. Partisanship, political ideology, and the issue of abortion all factor into English-dominant Latinos' decision-making process.

Although these multivariate analyses offer important insights on the factors that best explain Latino voting behavior, I could not determine, as I mentioned above, whether Gore's and Kerry's explained policy commercials or targeted Latinos ads had a larger impact on the vote choice of English-dominant Latinos. Predicted probability estimates need to be calculated to know the magnitude of these advertising effects. These estimates, which I present in Table 5.2, are similar to the ones calculated in Tables 4.6 and 4.9 on candidate advertising.[10] An English-dominant Latino who was exposed to a one-standard-deviation increase of Gore's complex policy messages had a 19 percent higher likelihood of voting for Gore. Gore's explained policy ads had a greater impact on one's vote choice; an increase in this type of advertising exposure resulted in a 30 percent higher likelihood of supporting Gore. Notice that the magnitude of the effect of targeted Latino ads is smaller than the effect of the two policy ads on one's vote choice. English-dominant Latinos who were exposed tothese nonpolicy messages had a 6 percent higher likelihood of supporting Gore and a 15 percent higher likelihood of supporting Kerry.

The impact of countervailing messages was also fairly substantial. An increase in exposure to Bush's explained policy ads in 2000 resulted in Latino voters becoming 20 percent less likely to support Gore. In 2004, English-dominant Latinos were 22 percent less likely to vote for Kerry as a result of increased exposure to Bush's targeted Latino ads. So although only one of Bush's four advertising appeals resonated with Latino voters, its impact was far from trivial. In fact, its magnitude was relatively similar to those of complex and explained policy ads.

Overall, the results from these models of vote choice support the conventional wisdom that Latinos will be responsive to advertising messages that directly target their community. The major caveat of this belief is that *not all* Latinos are equally affected by this type of campaign appeal in deciding which presidential candidate to support; the degree to which Latino voters have incorporated themselves into American society determines which political ads most influence their vote. These results also confirm the prediction that policy ads, particularly those that are informative in nature, have a greater impact on the voting decisions of the politically and socially incorporated segment of the Latino electorate than do ads that only emphasize Latino culture. Among their less politically incorporated counterparts, however, ethnic-specific appeals resonate the most on this group's vote intentions.

The other form of political behavior in which ad exposure can be influential is turnout. As mentioned earlier, one of the indirect or "spillover" effects of advertising exposure is that it can mobilize individuals to turn out and vote on election day. We have just seen how political ads directly affected the political behavior of Latinos; such ads may also make them feel that candidates are paying attention to them by advertising in Spanish or making ethnic-group appeals. Moreover, as recent newcomers to the political process, Latinos may feel that these appeals are a personal attempt to include them in the political process, thereby increasing their levels of political efficacy and personal agency. As a result, viewing such ads may encourage and energize them to vote. To determine whether this could be so, I calculated a model of turnout, with the estimates presented in Table 5.4. The predicted probability calculations can once again be found in Table 5.2.

The estimates indicate that exposure to political ads affects the turnout rates of both English- and Spanish-dominant Latinos. As expected, Spanish-dominant Latinos exposed to Spanish-language ads were more likely to vote. This result is consistent with the work by DeFrancesco Soto and Merolla (2008), as they too note a positive relationship between turnout and Spanish-language advertising. It seems also that exposure to general political ads among Spanish-dominant Latinos has a positive impact on their likelihood of voting. But seeing Spanish-language ads appears to have a larger impact on Spanish-dominant Latinos' probability of voting. More exposure to Spanish-language ads resulted in a 28 percent greater likelihood of voting, whereas a similar increase in general ad exposure caused only a 3 percent greater likelihood of voting.

The effect of Spanish-language ads appears to have a negative affect on the turnout rates of English-dominant Latinos, reducing their probability of voting by about 5 percentage points. Exposure to targeted Latino ads, however, positively influences their probability of voting by 9 percentage points. Whereas the first finding is rather counterintuitive, the second is consistent

**Table 5.4** The impact of Spanish- and English-language ads on Latino turnout

| | Estimated coefficient | Standard error |
|---|---|---|
| Constant | 1.41*** | .24 |
| *Political dispositions* | | |
| Partisan | .17** | .08 |
| No interest in government | −.09** | .04 |
| Watch news daily | .03** | .01 |
| Read newspaper daily | .03 | .02 |
| *Demographics* | | |
| No high-school degree | .12 | .12 |
| High-school graduate | .01 | .09 |
| Income | .004 | .02 |
| Married | .07 | .08 |
| Women | .12 | .08 |
| Age | .01*** | .003 |
| Mexican | .02 | .09 |
| Cuban | .19 | .19 |
| Puerto Rican | .02 | .12 |
| Interviewed in Spanish | −2.10*** | .11 |
| *Advertising exposure* | | |
| Spanish-language ads | −6.44* | 3.80 |
| General political ads | −.02 | .09 |
| Targeted Latino ads | 1.98* | 2.46 |
| *Advertising exposure × Interview language* | | |
| Spanish ads × Spanish | 6.41* | 3.80 |
| General political ads × Spanish | .04** | .02 |
| Targeted Latino ads × Spanish | −2.11 | 2.46 |
| | | |
| *N* | 1711 | |
| Log-likelihood | −756.24 | |
| Baseline | 61.47 | |
| Percent correctly predicted | 68.76 | |

NOTE: The dependent variable is coded as *1* if respondent voted in the 2000 or 2004 presidential election, and *0* otherwise.

*$p < .10$
**$p < .05$
***$p < .01$

with existing research and the conventional wisdom. Watching Spanish-language ads may have a negative impact on turnout rates because the ads lack substantive information when compared with English-language ads. And because these Latinos can access both types of political ads, they may feel demobilized to vote by the lack of informative content in Spanish-language commercials.

Yet, targeted Latino appeals serve as a positive signal to English-dominant Latinos that candidates are making special efforts to reach out to them. Thus, these targeted ads can also affect English-dominant Latinos indirectly by encouraging them to vote. Perhaps its null effect among Spanish-dominant Latinos can be attributed to the fact that they are less likely to participate in politics to begin with than are English-dominant Latinos; being exposed to political ads, then, is not enough to induce them to vote. In addition to political advertising exposure, certain political dispositions and demographic traits influence the likelihood that Latinos will vote. Those who report a high interest in government and current affairs are more likely to vote than are Latinos with little interest in government, and those who watch the news daily are more likely to vote than are occasional news watchers. Partisans are also more likely to vote than are Latinos who do not identify with a political party. Older Latinos have a higher probability of turning out than do their younger counterparts. One's own political dispositions and personal attributes have long been acknowledged to be important determinants of political participation (Wolfinger and Rosenstone 1980; Rosenstone and Hansen 1993; Verba et al. 1995), and other studies on Latino turnout have also shown this to be true (Shaw et al. 2000; Barreto 2007; DeFrancesco Soto and Merolla 2008).

## Summary

This chapter explored the impact of televised campaign ads on the political behavior of the Latino electorate. Even though considerable resources are devoted to Spanish-language ad buys, rather little is known about the effects of these televised commercials on the way Latinos cast their ballots and on their rates of turnout. My analysis reveals that political ads are affecting Latino voters both directly and indirectly. Exposure to political ads of the sponsoring candidate increases the chances that Latinos will support that particular candidate. Not all political ads influence Latino vote choice in the same manner, however. The degree to which Latinos are incorporated into American life determines which types of political ads affect their vote decisions and likelihood of voting. Only those political ads that tap into the ethnic identity of Spanish-dominant Latinos, who are still in the process of becoming politically and socially incorporated, play a role in deciding which presidential candidate they will support. And although politically incorporated Latinos also respond positively to ethnic appeals, the impact of these ads on their vote decisions is not as great as that of ads containing policy-related information. Exposure to the more-informative policy ads has a greater impact on the vote choice of English-dominant Latinos than does exposure to targeted Latino ads. Ethnic attachments tend to decline as immigrants become more incorporated into their host society (Portes and Rumbaut 1992). Thus, political ads that focus only on ethnic and cultural ties may become less salient to the voting decisions of the politically incorporated. As a result, over time, possibly even over generations, Latinos may gradually shift from evaluating candidates based on their cultural familiarity to evaluating them based on their policy positions and issue beliefs.

Exposure to political ads also produces an indirect effect by mobilizing or demobilizing the Latino electorate. Targeted Latino ad exposure increases the rates of turnout among English-dominant Latinos, whereas exposure to Spanish-language ads had the opposite effect. Thus, a Latino's ethnic identity influences his or her decision to engage in one of the most fundamental forms of political expression—voting. Spanish-dominant Latinos had an increased likelihood of voting after exposure to both Spanish-language ads and general ads.

Given the vast socioeconomic, ethnic, and cultural diversity within the Latino population, it would be simplistic to assume that campaign messages would influence their political behavior in the same way. This research is a first attempt to explore this relatively underexplored subject, and the possibilities for further work in this area are considerable. With substantial technological advances in the fields of political advertising, campaigns, and communications (see Jackman and Vavreck 2009), future researchers will be able to examine the effects of Spanish-language advertising in other election settings as well as on other types of political behavior. The decision to advertise differently to Spanish and non-Spanish speakers may have detrimental effects on the political well being of the Latino community and on the overall health of American democracy. Chapter 6 explores this possibility and focuses on two specific consequences of adopting an information-based strategy of advertising.

# 6 The Consequences of an Information-Based Advertising Strategy

POLITICAL ADVERTISING CAN INFLUENCE what citizens know about candidates and about public policy. In some instances, exposure to political ads can contribute to increased learning when compared with exposure to the information found in newspapers or television news (Ridout et al. 2004; Brians and Wattenberg 1996; Just et al. 1996; Patterson and McClure 1976). Patterson and McClure's (1976) classic work on this subject found that people learned more about the policies of Nixon and McGovern in the 1972 presidential campaign from political commercials than from television news. Brians and Wattenberg's (1996) research echoes this finding by demonstrating that political advertising was the only factor that contributed to one's ability to recall the issue positions of the presidential candidates in the 1992 election. Learning, as some scholars have argued (Hitchon and Chang 1995; Pfau et al. 2002; Faber and Storey 1984), depends also on the specific characteristics of an ad and on the viewer's personal attributes. For instance, experimental work by Hitchon and Chang (1995) found that the sex of the candidate running the ad matters; voters learned more from issue ads sponsored by women than by men. Tone matters too—neutral and positive ads contributed to more learning than did negative ads. Pfau and colleagues (2002) also uncovered a relationship between learning and ad sponsor. They discovered that ads sponsored by candidates promote a higher degree of learning than do ads sponsored by interest groups. Along the same lines, Faber and Storey (1984) showed how citizens have better issue recall when the political spot is sponsored by the favored candidate rather than by the opposing one. Jackman and Vavreck (2009) found that, in presidential elections, a reduction in voter uncertainty occurs as the election nears. They also noted that some variation in learning occurred between battleground and non-battleground states.

One reason why campaign messages, especially those found in televised political spots, are so valuable to voters is that they function as "information shortcuts." Also known as heuristics (Kahneman et al. 1982), information shortcuts enable voters to rely on the campaign messages delivered in televised commercials, on daily life experiences, or on the opinions of information experts, such as political pundits, as sources of political information (Lupia 1994; Popkin 1994). Generally, such information is difficult and costly to attain, but these shortcuts reduce the costs. And because candidates have become increasingly reliant on television advertising as a means of reaching out to voters, political commercials have become an accessible and low-cost heuristic tool (West 2001).

The goal of this chapter is to examine the consequences of adopting an information-based advertising strategy for the Spanish- and English-language ads produced in the 2000–2004 election cycles. It is likely, given the existing research, that the content of certain ads will contribute to political learning more than will others. For instance, exposure to simple policy or targeted Latino appeals should play a muted role in one's ability to recall the issue positions of the major presidential candidates because these ads are not providing any information about the policy positions of the candidates. But more substantive issue appeals, such as complex and explained policy ads, should provide more information from which to recall the candidates' issue positions.

Recall that the percentage of sophisticated policy messages in Spanish-language ads was lower, on average, than it was in English-language ads, and so the educational benefits associated with exposure to political ads may not be the same for Spanish- and English-dominant Latinos. Given that Spanish-dominant Latinos were generally exposed to more non-policy-based campaign appeals than were their English-dominant counterparts, exposure to political ads may have contributed very little to their knowledge of politics. But because English-dominant Latinos were exposed to both English- and Spanish-language ads, their issue recall ability should be better with advertising exposure.

Another repercussion from this advertising strategy is the manner in which individuals use their ideological and issue positions as a basis for their vote decisions. Again, given the variation in the number of policy-based ads produced in Spanish and in English, Spanish-dominant Latinos may be less able to behave as "issue voters" than can English-dominant Latinos. That is, a Spanish-dominant Latino's policy positions and political ideology should have a more moderate impact on their vote choice when this group is compared with English-dominant Latinos. This second consequence is highly correlated with the first; if Spanish-dominant Latinos do not learn much about the candidates' policy stances from Spanish-language ads, then they may also have difficulty assessing which of the candidates is closest to their own policy preferences.

## Latino Political Knowledge in the 2000 and 2004 Elections

In line with the existing academic research described earlier, and with the discussion on political knowledge in Chapter 2, I define voter knowledge as a citizen's ability to recall the issue positions of the two major presidential candidates in the 2000 and 2004 elections. Luckily, the NAES asked respondents to identify both presidential candidates' positions on a wide range of issues, including education, abortion, Social Security, Medicare, and so on.[1] To measure knowledge, I calculated the number of correct answers a respondent provided to twenty-four neutral political questions. Overall, voter knowledge in 2000 ranged from a minimum of 0, meaning that a respondent did not correctly identify any of the candidates' issue positions, to a maximum of 24, indicating that a respondent correctly identified the candidates' issue positions on all the questions. In 2004, the NAES did not ask as many questions pertaining to candidates' issue positions; thus, the variable for voter knowledge ranged from 0 to 8 for that election. As discussed throughout this book, one's familiarity with politics varies not only between immigrant and nonimmigrant groups, but also within an immigrant group. In particular, political knowledge should vary based on an immigrant's level of political incorporation. Table 6.1 presents Latinos' average levels of knowledge in the 2000 and 2004 presidential campaigns based on several indicators of political incorporation—language use, citizenship status, educational attainment, and income level.

The patterns across these distributions indicate that Latinos who were more politically incorporated and acculturated knew more about politics than did Latinos who have not fully incorporated into American politics and society. Spanish-dominant Latinos in 2000 had a mean level of knowledge of 2.92, compared with 5.28 for English-dominant Latinos. In 2004, Spanish-dominant Latinos also exhibited lower levels of knowledge when compared

**Table 6.1** Latinos' mean levels of political knowledge, by measures of incorporation

| 2000 | Mean level of knowledge | Standard deviation | Range | N |
|---|---|---|---|---|
| *Interview language* | | | | |
| Spanish | 2.92 | 3.11 | 0–19 | 499 |
| English | 5.28 | 4.43 | 0–18 | 993 |
| *Citizenship* | | | | |
| Non-U.S. citizen | 2.86 | 2.98 | 0–15 | 391 |
| U.S. citizen | 5.08 | 4.40 | 0–19 | 1,097 |
| *Education* | | | | |
| No high-school degree | 3.19 | 3.19 | 0–15 | 424 |
| High-school degree | 4.19 | 3.92 | 0–19 | 430 |
| Some college or beyond | 5.67 | 4.63 | 0–18 | 603 |
| *Income* | | | | |
| Less than $25,000 | 3.53 | 3.46 | 0–17 | 589 |
| $25,000–$49,999 | 5.20 | 4.30 | 0–19 | 408 |
| $50,000–$99,999 | 6.17 | 4.78 | 0–18 | 278 |
| $100,000 or more | 6.58 | 5.29 | 0–18 | 217 |
| **2004** | | | | |
| *Interview language* | | | | |
| Spanish | 2.29 | 1.37 | 0–8 | 649 |
| English | 3.14 | 1.88 | 0–8 | 1,396 |
| *Citizenship* | | | | |
| Non-U.S. citizen | 2.85 | 1.79 | 0–8 | 1,622 |
| U.S. citizen | 2.94 | 1.74 | 0–8 | 423 |
| *Education* | | | | |
| No high-school degree | 2.34 | 1.45 | 0–8 | 456 |
| High-school degree | 2.66 | 1.66 | 0–8 | 550 |
| Some college or beyond | 3.22 | 1.89 | 0–8 | 1,039 |
| *Income* | | | | |
| Less than $25,000 | 2.45 | 1.50 | 0–8 | 601 |
| $25,000–$49,999 | 2.71 | 1.67 | 0–8 | 549 |
| $50,000–$99,999 | 3.27 | 1.89 | 0–8 | 493 |
| $100,000 or more | 3.24 | 1.99 | 0–8 | 402 |

NOTE: In 2000, political knowledge was measured as the number of correct responses a respondent provided to twenty-four factual political questions from the 2000 NAES panel study. In 2004, political knowledge was measured as the number of correct responses a respondent provided to eight factual political questions from the 2004 NAES panel study. Questions are available in Appendix C.

with English-dominant Latinos, although the difference is not quite as large. A similar pattern emerges in examining rates of political knowledge by citizenship status, which has also been used as a benchmark to measure an immigrant's level of political incorporation into the host country (Bloemraad 2006). Noncitizens' mean level of knowledge in 2000 was 2.86, while U.S. citizens' mean level of knowledge was 5.08. In 2004, the level of political knowledge for Latino citizens is only somewhat higher than it is for noncitizen Latinos. One reason why the differences in levels of knowledge are less pronounced in 2004 than they are in 2000 may be due to the fact that the political knowledge scale in 2000 ranged from 0 to 24, whereas in 2004, the scale ranged from 0 to 8.

When examining political knowledge by socioeconomic factors, one can see that an increase in a Latino's educational attainment and income apparently leads to a corresponding increase in his or her rates of knowledge. In the 2000 NAES, Latinos with no high-school degree had a mean level of learning of 3.19, whereas those with some college or beyond had a mean level of learning of 5.67. Higher levels of educational attainment are also associated with greater levels of political knowledge among Latinos in the 2004 survey, albeit at more conservative rates. In both survey years, Latino respondents with a household income of less than $25,000 exhibited lower levels of knowledge than did those in the highest income brackets. Latinos earning a household income between $25,000 and $49,999 also had lower levels of political knowledge than did Latino respondents in the income bracket right above them. These distributions offer some initial insights into Latino political learning in the 2000 and 2004 election seasons. First, Latinos did not all learn at the same rate about politics and the presidential candidates' issue positions; Latinos who were more acculturated and politically incorporated knew more than their less-incorporated counterparts. This pattern remained constant across the different measures of acculturation. Although the findings presented are insightful and reveal variations in political information within the Latino electorate, they leave some unanswered questions. Which of these measures of incorporation best explains their rates of knowledge? More importantly, did exposure to television ads influence political knowledge, and if so, which ads affected Spanish-dominant Latinos' and English-dominant Latinos' knowledge of the candidates?

The first step in addressing these questions is to examine rates of political knowledge based on the types of messages that Latinos were exposed to. In

Figures 6.1a and 6.1b, I present the average rates of learning for Spanish- and English-dominant Latinos as a function of exposure to complex policy, explained policy, simple policy, and targeted Latino ads. Figure 6.1a presents this information for the 2000 campaign, and Figure 6.1b provides it for the 2004 presidential campaign.

Overall, the data shown in these graphs suggest that policy-focused ads contributed to political knowledge to a greater extent than did nonpolicy ads. In both of these presidential election campaigns, English-dominant Latinos exposed to the three different types of policy ads exhibited higher levels of knowledge than those exposed to the targeted Latino ads. Also, the dropoff in political knowledge that occurred when English-dominant Latinos were exposed to targeted Latino ads instead of policy ads was steeper than was the same dropoff for Spanish-dominant Latinos. This suggests that the content of political ads has a more substantive impact on English-dominant Latinos than it does on Spanish-dominant Latinos. Spanish-dominant Latinos exposed to policy ads also exhibited slightly higher rates of political knowledge than those exposed to targeted Latino ads. But note that this difference is much less pronounced than it is for English-dominant Latinos.

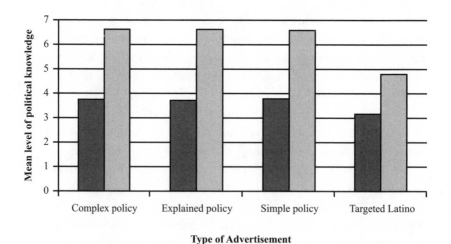

**Type of Advertisement**

■ Spanish-dominant Latinos    ◻ English-dominant Latinos

**Figure 6.1a** Rates of political learning in 2000, by type of advertising exposure. Political learning was measured as the number of correct responses a respondent provides to factual political questions from the 2000 NAES.

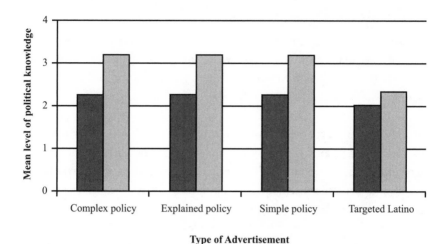

**Figure 6.1b**  Rates of political learning in 2004, by type of advertising exposure. Political learning was measured as the number of correct responses a respondent provides to factual political questions from the 2004 NAES.

## A Model of Voter Knowledge

Aside from exposure to political ads, the distributions presented in Table 6.1 reveal a host of other factors that can contribute to one's knowledge of the issue positions adopted by candidates. For instance, as just discussed, more-educated and higher-income individuals exhibited more political knowledge than did their less-affluent and less-educated counterparts. Also, campaign information is not restricted to televised ads; reading the newspaper or watching television news may contribute to political knowledge too. In addition, being personally contacted by a campaign, which has been found to significantly influence other forms of political behavior, such as the likelihood of voting (Gerber and Green 2000), may also aid in a citizen's knowledge of politics. Contact by a campaign has been found to be particularly effective among Latinos (Michelson et al., forthcoming; de la Garza et al. 2008; Leighley 2001). To account for these different factors, I estimate a multivariate model of voter knowledge.[2] In line with existing research on this subject (Brians and Wattenberg 1996; Patterson and McClure 1976), this model of voter knowledge accounts for an individual's demographic attributes, media-viewing habits, campaign contact, and exposure to political ads.[3]

Demographics takes into account a respondent's level of education, household income, age, marital status, gender, and citizenship status. Given that education and income often serve as proxies for a voter's level of political knowledge, Latinos with more education and higher income levels should have greater issue recall than do those with lower levels of education and income. One's knowledge of politics may also be influenced by age; older individuals will have experienced and witnessed more political events than their younger counterparts. Moreover, respondents who are married may be more likely than single respondents to discuss politics with a partner, and thereby learn more about politics. And, as seen in previous work by García Bedolla (2005) and Pardo (1997), Latino political knowledge may also vary based on gender, so that Latinas may exhibit higher levels of knowledge than Latinos. Finally, the model accounts for acculturation status, one of the key indicators guiding this work. The extent to which individuals are acculturated into American society is captured by their citizenship status, with the expectation that Latino citizens will exhibit higher levels of political knowledge than will noncitizen Latinos.

To capture media effects, I included in the model of voter knowledge a variable that measures the frequency with which a respondent reports reading the newspaper in a given week.[4] Finally, I included several measures of adver-

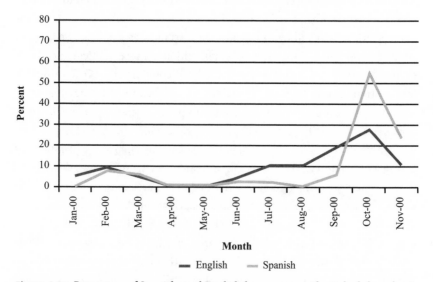

**Figure 6.2a** Percentage of Spanish- and English-language presidential ads broadcast in 2000. *Source:* 2000 CMAG data.

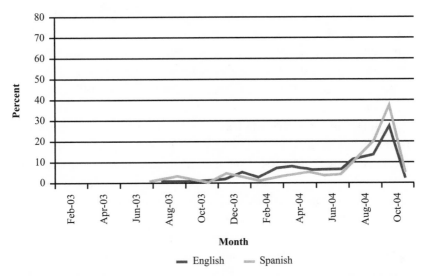

**Figure 6.2b** Percentage of Spanish- and English-language presidential ads broadcast in 2004. *Source:* 2004 CMAG data.

tising exposure—one for the number of simple policy ads that a respondent, for his or her given media market, was exposed to, another for explained policy ads, another for complex policy commercials, and one for targeted Latinos ads.[5] Given the theory of information-based advertising, one can assume that certain policy ads are more informative than others, and so complex policy and explained policy messages aid in learning to a greater extent than do simple policy ads. To understand the impact of Spanish-language ads on political learning for Spanish-dominant Latinos and the impact of both Spanish- and English-language ads on English-dominant Latinos' rates of knowledge, I estimated a separate model of voter knowledge for each group.

Before I delve into this discussion, however, it is important to examine the amount of information available to voters over the course of the 2000 and 2004 campaigns. Figure 6.2a presents the broadcast rate of the English- and Spanish-language advertisements in 2000, broken down by the month of broadcast, and Figure 6.2b shows this information for the 2004 presidential campaign.

In both of these presidential races, the major party candidates decided to broadcast the bulk of their Spanish-language ads just before the general election. Bush and Gore aired a total of 54 percent of their Spanish-language ads in October 2000; in this same month four years later, Kerry and Bush broadcasted 37.2 percent of their Spanish-language ads. Thus, Spanish-dominant Latinos, and bilingual Latinos watching Spanish-language television, were exposed to these political ads rather late in the campaign. Although candidates also aired most of their English-language ads just a month before the election, they did so at a lower rate (approximately 27 percent). The rate of broadcast for English-language ads in general gradually increased from June through October 2000, with 44 percent of English-language ads airing during this time period. By contrast, only 9 percent of the Spanish-language ads were broadcast during these same months. In the 2000 presidential campaign, there seems to be a clear contrast regarding the timing and broadcast rates of Spanish- and English-language ads. The difference suggests that any information Spanish-dominant Latinos gained from political ads was not acquired until the very end of the 2000 campaign season.

The variation in the rates of broadcast between Spanish- and English-language ads during the 2004 presidential campaign is not nearly as skewed as it was in 2000. Consider that in the same period just discussed (June–October), an almost equal percentage of Spanish- and English-language ads were broadcast, approximately 37 percent. Although most of the Spanish-language ads were broadcast in October 2004, Spanish-speaking Latinos in this presidential race were exposed to campaign information over a longer period of time than were Spanish-speaking Latinos in the 2000 race. Whether and how this difference affects their levels of political knowledge remains to be seen. Should it be the case that campaign messages have only short-term effects, then this advertising strategy may actually benefit Spanish-speaking Latinos by helping them increase their levels of information right before the general election.

### Findings from the Model of Voter Knowledge

The empirical results from the models of voter knowledge are presented in Table 6.2 for Spanish-dominant Latinos, and Table 6.3 for English-dominant Latinos. The most striking difference between these two sets of estimates is that exposure to advertising affects only the knowledge levels of English-dominant, and not Spanish-dominant, Latinos. Exposure to complex policy messages—the most sophisticated type of policy message—positively influenced the rates of knowledge for English-dominant Latinos in both 2000 and 2004. In substantive terms, for a one-unit increase in spending on complex policy messages in 2000, English-dominant Latinos were likely to correctly answer one additional political question. The same increase in spending on

**Table 6.2** The impact of Spanish-language ads on the political knowledge of Spanish-dominant Latinos

| Variable | 2000 | | 2004 | |
|---|---|---|---|---|
| | *Estimated coefficient* | *Standard error* | *Estimated coefficient* | *Standard error* |
| Constant | .44 | .19 | 1.25*** | .38 |
| *Demographics* | | | | |
| No high-school degree | −.17 | .11 | −.22 | .17 |
| High-school degree | −.08 | .12 | −.22 | .18 |
| Income | .09*** | .03 | .07 | .04 |
| Age | .00 | .01 | −.01** | .006 |
| Married | −.18 | .08 | −.20 | .14 |
| Women | −.13 | .08 | −.03 | .14 |
| U.S. citizen | −.05 | .08 | .33** | .15 |
| Democrat | .07 | .09 | .12 | .14 |
| Republican | .06 | .11 | .16 | .22 |
| *Media/campaign exposure* | | | | |
| Watch TV news daily | .00 | .02 | .01 | .04 |
| Read newspaper daily | .06* | .02 | −.07 | .07 |
| Contacted by a campaign | 1.47*** | .45 | —ᵃ | —ᵃ |
| *Advertising exposure* | | | | |
| Spanish complex policy | −2.14 | 4.25 | −.35 | 3.83 |
| Spanish explained policy | 1.83 | 3.76 | −2.79 | −2.79 |
| Spanish simple policy | −1.17 | 5.49 | −1.96 | 1.80 |
| Spanish targeted Latino ad | .03 | .14 | 1.87 | 1.73 |
| $N$ | 398 | | 362 | |
| $R^2$ | .13 | | .07 | |

SOURCE: 2000 and 2004 NAES.

NOTE: Cell entries are OLS estimates. The sample is restricted to Latino respondents who interviewed in Spanish. The dependent variable was knowledge of factual political questions.

ᵃ Campaign contact question was asked only in a small portion of the 2004 NAES, and did not include enough Latinos to estimate this model.

*$p < .10$
**$p < .05$
***$p < .01$

complex policy messages in 2004, however, had a more moderate affect on the rates of political knowledge for English-dominant Latinos.

Exposure to simple and explained policy ads also affected the rates of learning for English-dominant Latinos in 2000, but it did so in a negative manner. Exposure to these policy messages reduced political knowledge;

**Table 6.3** The impact of Spanish- and English-language ads on the political knowledge of English-dominant Latinos

| Variable | 2000 | | 2004 | |
|---|---|---|---|---|
| | Estimated coefficient | Standard error | Estimated coefficient | Standard error |
| Constant | 5.45*** | 1.25 | .31 | .46 |
| *Demographics* | | | | |
| No high-school degree | −1.31*** | .74 | −.02 | .34 |
| High-school degree | −1.24*** | .41 | −.30 | .22 |
| Income | .22*** | .10 | .14*** | .05 |
| Age | −.02 | .01 | .02*** | .01 |
| Married | .60*** | .36 | −.44*** | .18 |
| Women | −.37 | .34 | −.13 | .17 |
| U.S. citizen | 1.94* | .49 | −1.11 | .22 |
| Democrat | 1.30*** | .54 | .10 | .19 |
| Republican | .23 | .68 | .14 | .64 |
| *Media/campaign exposure* | | | | |
| Watch TV news daily | .05 | .09 | .02 | .03 |
| Read newspaper daily | .19** | .09 | −.12 | .09 |
| Contacted by a campaign | 1.57 | 1.04 | —ᵃ | —ᵃ |
| *Advertising exposure* | | | | |
| Complex policy | 1.13*** | .39 | .37* | .22 |
| Explained policy | −.53** | .19 | −.38 | .34 |
| Simple policy | −.85** | .29 | −.09 | .29 |
| Targeted Latino ad | 2.98 | 3.04 | 1.13 | .82 |
| | | | | |
| N | 269 | | 548 | |
| $R^2$ | .19 | | .07 | |

SOURCE: 2000 and 2004 NAES.

NOTE: Cell entries are OLS estimates. The sample is restricted to Latino respondents who interviewed in English. The dependent variable was knowledge of factual political questions.

ᵃCampaign contact question was asked only in a small portion of the 2004 NAES, and did not include enough Latinos to estimate this model.

*$p < .10$

**$p < .05$

***$p < .01$

thus, it appears that not all types of policy messages contributed to English-dominant Latinos' knowledge of the candidates. Only those offering detailed and complex information contributed to voter learning. Although explained policy ads should have also served this function, the results suggest otherwise. If one looks at the magnitude of these advertising effects, exposure to simple policy ads led to a greater reduction in political knowledge than did explained policy ads in 2000.

A Latino's personal characteristics and demographics also impact his or her political knowledge. As suggested by the distributions in Table 6.1, one's education level, income, and citizenship status can and does influence one's knowledge of politics. In the estimates from the 2000 NAES, one can see that English-dominant Latinos with a high-school degree or less were not as likely to learn as those who were college educated. The Latinos in the high-income brackets also had greater issue recall than did those in lower income brackets. Citizenship matters too: English-dominant Latinos who are U.S. citizens had a higher likelihood of learning than did noncitizen English-dominant Latinos. Given that Latino citizens are likely to be politically incorporated and therefore more interested in and aware of politics than are Latino noncitizens, one can see why these differences emerge. Note that the magnitude of this effect is quite large; English-dominant Latinos who were U.S. citizens increased by two points on the knowledge scale (meaning that they were able to provide two additional correct answers). English-dominant Latinos who were married also improved their knowledge levels when compared with those who were not married.

Along with advertising exposure and personal traits, the media viewing habits of Latinos in 2000 also emerged as a factor that influenced their rates of political knowledge. Spanish- and English-dominant Latinos who read the newspaper daily had greater issue recall than did those who did not read the newspaper regularly. Watching local television news, however, had no significant impact on Latino political information. This finding is consistent with the previous research by Brians and Wattenberg (1996), who note a positive relationship only between ad exposure and learning, and not between television news-watching and learning.

Finally, the model accounted for the possibility that personal contact from a campaign would aid in Latino political learning. Given the positive association between personal contact and other forms of political behavior, for example, turnout (de la Garza et al. 2008; Gerber and Green 2000), it may be that personal interaction with a campaign worker could provide Latinos with substantive information about the two presidential candidates. The estimates indicate that campaign contact is positively associated with learning only for Spanish-dominant Latinos. The substantive effect of this contact was considerable: Spanish-dominant Latinos who were contacted by a campaign were able to answer one additional political question correctly. Thus, although exposure to Spanish-language advertising contributed little to Spanish-dominant Latinos' rates of political knowledge, personal contact was one aspect of the campaigns that aided in this group's understanding of the candidates' issue positions. This finding reinforces the importance of personal contact during an election season on an individual's political behavior. And while this relationship has focused largely on turnout efforts, it appears that this form of contact can also lead to an increased awareness of the candidates and their policy platforms.

I turn now to the 2004 estimates. Several of the same factors influenced Latino political knowledge in this presidential campaign as in the previous one. Most notably, English-dominant Latinos with high-income levels were more likely to be politically knowledgeable than were those with lower income levels. English-dominant Latinos who were older also had a higher probability of identifying candidates' issue positions than did younger Latinos. Although being married had a positive impact on English-dominant Latinos' knowledge of politics in the 2000 election, it seems to have had the opposite effect in 2004. Why this was so is not immediately apparent, but perhaps it can be attributed to the different types of questions used to construct the measure of political knowledge. Among Spanish-dominant Latinos, only two factors influenced their levels of political knowledge in 2004—age and citizenship status. Age operated in a negative manner, so that Spanish-dominant Latinos who were older exhibited lower levels of political knowledge than did their younger counterparts. And as immigration scholars have noted (for example, Bloemraad 2006), one's level of political incorporation, measured here by citizenship status, should be positively associated with political orientations and dispositions. In this case, Spanish-dominant Latinos who are U.S. citizens were more politically knowledgeable than were Spanish-dominant Latinos who had yet to undergo the citizenship process.

A primary goal of this chapter was to explore the consequences of adopting an information-based theory of advertising. In particular, to what extent did exposure to political ads contribute to Latino political knowledge?

The analyses conducted seem to show that only English-dominant Latinos' knowledge levels benefited from these political ads. Spanish-dominant Latinos did not benefit. This discrepancy can likely be traced back to the types of campaign messages featured in the Spanish-language ads, which provided fewer informative policy messages than did English-language ads. English-dominant Latinos, then, behave like other Americans, in that exposure to advertising influenced their political decisions both directly and indirectly. Chapter 5 demonstrated how certain campaign ads directly affected Latinos by persuading them to cast their ballots in favor of the candidate who sponsored the commercial. The indirect effects of political advertising, such as encouraging individuals to vote and enabling voters to increase their political knowledge, are also at work, but only among the more politically incorporated segment of the Latino electorate.

## Comparing Latino Rates of Knowledge to Other Racial and Ethnic Groups

Another potential consequence of adopting an information-based advertising strategy is that Latinos' rates of political knowledge may not be on par with the rest of the electorate, particularly for Spanish-dominant Latinos. To determine whether this is so, I examined the distributions of answers to several questions pertaining to one's knowledge of the presidential candidates' personal backgrounds and political ideologies using panel data from the National Annenberg Election Panel Survey of 2000 and 2004.[6] This data set differs from the one used in Chapter 5 because this data set contains information for survey respondents who are interviewed before the general election in a pre-election survey and then are reinterviewed following the general election. Thus, if individuals learned anything from the campaign, we should see a difference in their responses to the fact-based political questions from the pre-election to the post-election survey. In 2000, a total of 6,535 respondents were interviewed in these two surveys, of whom 360 respondents identified themselves as Latino, 5,653 as non-Hispanic Anglo, 463 as African American, and 59 as Asian.[7] In 2004, more than 8,600 individuals were involved in the panel study, of whom 492 identified themselves as Hispanic, 7,598 as non-Hispanic Anglo, 484 as African American, and 99 as Asian. A moderate increase from 2000 to 2004 is seen in the number of ethnic and racial minorities interviewed.

Table 6.4 presents the distributions for each group's responses to the following questions from the 2000 survey: (1) Bush or Gore was U.S. senator, (2) Bush or Gore was the son of a former U.S. senator, (3) Bush or Gore was governor, (4) Bush or Gore spoke at Bob Jones University, and (5) Bush or Gore is a born-again Christian. Respondents could have answered *Bush, Gore, both, neither,* or *don't know.* In the 2004 panel study, the political knowledge questions focused primarily on a respondent's familiarity with Bush and Kerry's issue positions. Table 6.5 presents distributions for each ethnic and racial group's responses to questions asking them to identify Bush's and Kerry's policy positions on social security, prescription drugs, and tax cuts.

There are two sets of responses for each racial and ethnic group, one set from the pre-election survey (*pre*) and the other from the post-election survey (*post*). I turn first to Table 6.4. The general pattern from these distributions is that a larger percentage of Anglos than of Spanish- and English-dominant Latinos and African Americans consistently reported the correct answer in both the pre- and post-election surveys. For instance, 63.9 percent of Anglos in the pre-election survey correctly identified Gore as a U.S. senator, whereas 16.9 percent of Spanish-dominant Latinos, 46.8 percent of English-dominant Latinos, and 46.2 percent of African Americans responded in the same manner. Moreover, when asked in the pre-election survey which of the two candidates once served as governor, 90.1 percent of Anglos provided the right answer (*Bush*), compared with 46.8 percent of Spanish-dominant Latinos, 75.4 of English-dominant Latinos and 75.6 percent of African Americans. This same pattern emerges in the responses provided by each group for the other three questions; Anglos were best able to recall the candidates' backgrounds and qualifications both before and after the general election, followed by African Americans and English-dominant Latinos (although the order of these two switched depending on the question) and then Spanish-dominant Latinos, who were always at the bottom. One caveat worth noting is that the number of Spanish-dominant Latinos interviewed in this survey is considerably smaller than the number of Anglos, African Americans, and English-dominant Latinos surveyed.

Another important trend to notice from these distributions is that Spanish-dominant Latinos were much more likely to provide a *don't know/ no answer* response than were the other groups. For example, on the question that asks respondents to identify the candidate whose father was a former U.S. senator, more than one-third of Spanish-dominant Latinos in both of the survey waves provided a nonresponse. In contrast, only 8.9 percent of

**Table 6.4** Knowledge of Bush and Gore's personal backgrounds (2000), by racial or ethnic group

| | Anglos | | Spanish-dominant Latinos | | English-dominant Latinos | | African Americans | |
|---|---|---|---|---|---|---|---|---|
| | Pre | Post | Pre | Post | Pre | Post | Pre | Post |
| *Bush or Gore U.S. senator* | | | | | | | | |
| Bush | 10.6 | 5.6 | 37.7 | 12.7 | 15.7 | 12.3 | 19.6 | 13.0 |
| Gore (correct) | 63.9 | 71.7 | 16.9 | 22.2 | 46.8 | 47.5 | 46.2 | 55.5 |
| Both | 3.6 | 0.5 | 6.5 | 7.9 | 6.5 | 0.9 | 3.7 | 1.0 |
| Neither | 11.3 | 11.5 | 9.1 | 6.4 | 16.3 | 20.3 | 16.3 | 20.3 |
| DK/NA | 10.6 | 10.4 | 29.9 | 50.8 | 14.8 | 19.1 | 14.2 | 10.3 |
| N | 6,729 | 5,195 | 77 | 63 | 338 | 236 | 541 | 409 |
| *Bush or Gore son of former U.S. senator* | | | | | | | | |
| Bush | 30.9 | 18.7 | 37.8 | 28.6 | 34.4 | 39.0 | 35.1 | 33.8 |
| Gore (correct) | 46.2 | 66.4 | 12.2 | 21.4 | 32.4 | 45.0 | 31.3 | 43.1 |
| Both | 8.4 | 4.8 | 4.1 | 0.0 | 9.2 | 3.7 | 4.2 | 8.1 |
| Neither | 5.6 | 2.7 | 6.8 | 15.7 | 9.5 | 3.0 | 10.8 | 11.3 |
| DK/NA | 8.9 | 7.4 | 39.2 | 34.3 | 14.6 | 9.3 | 18.6 | 11.3 |
| N | 6,765 | 5,002 | 74 | 70 | 349 | 269 | 499 | 397 |
| *Bush or Gore governor* | | | | | | | | |
| Bush (correct) | 90.1 | 91.9 | 46.8 | 46.0 | 75.4 | 78.4 | 75.6 | 79.7 |
| Gore | 1.8 | 2.2 | 9.1 | 9.5 | 5.0 | 4.7 | 4.4 | 4.4 |
| Both | 0.7 | 0.4 | 6.5 | 9.5 | 2.4 | 1.3 | 1.9 | 0.5 |
| Neither | 3.5 | 2.3 | 7.8 | 3.2 | 9.5 | 8.5 | 8.7 | 7.7 |
| DK/NA | 3.8 | 3.2 | 29.9 | 31.8 | 7.7 | 7.2 | 9.4 | 7.1 |
| N | 6,729 | 5,195 | 77 | 63 | 338 | 236 | 541 | 409 |
| *Bush or Gore spoke at Bob Jones University* | | | | | | | | |
| Bush (correct) | 51.7 | 50.5 | 11.7 | 9.5 | 32.0 | 33.9 | 35.7 | 41.6 |
| Gore | 9.2 | 10.8 | 16.9 | 7.9 | 13.0 | 8.1 | 12.0 | 12.5 |
| Both | 1.5 | 1.7 | 6.5 | 11.1 | 2.1 | 1.3 | 3.5 | 1.7 |
| Neither | 5.6 | 4 | 13.0 | 11.1 | 11.5 | 14.8 | 10.5 | 9.5 |
| DK/NA | 31.9 | 33.0 | 52.0 | 60.3 | 41.4 | 42.0 | 38.3 | 34.7 |
| N | 6,729 | 5,195 | 77 | 63 | 338 | 236 | 541 | 409 |
| *Bush or Gore is born-again Christian* | | | | | | | | |
| Bush (correct) | 33.2 | 41.4 | 20.3 | 7.1 | 32.4 | 41.3 | 26.9 | 25.9 |
| Gore | 12.1 | 11.3 | 17.6 | 25.7 | 10.9 | 11.2 | 22.9 | 28.2 |
| Both | 17.0 | 14.7 | 12.2 | 12.9 | 12.3 | 8.2 | 17.0 | 17.6 |
| Neither | 18.9 | 12.8 | 14.9 | 12.9 | 21.5 | 15.2 | 16.2 | 13.0 |
| DK/NA | 18.9 | 19.8 | 35.1 | 41.4 | 22.9 | 24.2 | 17.0 | 15.1 |
| N | 6,765 | 5,002 | 74 | 70 | 349 | 269 | 499 | 397 |

SOURCE: 2000 NAES General Election Panel Survey.

NOTE: Cell entries denote column percentages unless otherwise indicated. Columns labeled *pre* are from the pre-election survey and columns labeled *post* are from the post-election survey.

**Table 6.5** Knowledge of Bush and Kerry's policy positions (2004), by racial or ethnic group

| | Anglos | | Spanish-dominant Latinos | | English-dominant Latinos | | African Americans | |
|---|---|---|---|---|---|---|---|---|
| | Pre | Post | Pre | Post | Pre | Post | Pre | Post |
| *Bush or Kerry favors investing Social Security in stock market* | | | | | | | | |
| Bush (correct) | 61.1 | 74.8 | 24.2 | 26.3 | 52.9 | 70.9 | 46.8 | 63.2 |
| Kerry | 13.3 | 10.5 | 26.3 | 26.3 | 16.1 | 12.1 | 20.7 | 16.5 |
| Both | 5.5 | 3.7 | 11.6 | 15.8 | 5.8 | 2.2 | 4.4 | 7.8 |
| Neither | 7.7 | 4.1 | 15.8 | 8.4 | 13.0 | 6.7 | 13.2 | 6.1 |
| DK/NA | 12.4 | 6.9 | 22.1 | 23.2 | 12.1 | 8.1 | 14.9 | 6.4 |
| *N* | 4,898 | 4,898 | 95 | 95 | 223 | 223 | 295 | 295 |
| *Bush or Kerry favors reimporting drugs from Canada* | | | | | | | | |
| Bush | 9.6 | 10.0 | 19.7 | 23.9 | 13.3 | 12.2 | 12.2 | 16.1 |
| Kerry (correct) | 61.9 | 68.2 | 39.4 | 32.4 | 58.3 | 63.3 | 57.0 | 64.8 |
| Both | 5.7 | 5.3 | 16.9 | 16.9 | 3.9 | 6.1 | 5.6 | 2.6 |
| Neither | 10.9 | 7.5 | 7.0 | 5.6 | 13.3 | 8.9 | 12.6 | 7.4 |
| DK/NA | 11.9 | 9.0 | 16.9 | 21.1 | 11.1 | 9.4 | 12.6 | 9.1 |
| *N* | 3,945 | 3,945 | 71 | 71 | 180 | 180 | 230 | 230 |
| *Bush or Kerry favors making tax cuts permanent* | | | | | | | | |
| Bush (correct) | 75.5 | 81.8 | 22.1 | 27.5 | 67.8 | 68.3 | 55.5 | 61.2 |
| Kerry | 7.3 | 6.0 | 29.5 | 22.0 | 10.1 | 15.0 | 19.7 | 20.6 |
| Both | 3.5 | 3.0 | 13.7 | 14.3 | 4.4 | 5.7 | 4.8 | 4.0 |
| Neither | 6.3 | 4.0 | 12.6 | 9.9 | 9.7 | 5.7 | 11.5 | 8.1 |
| DK/NA | 7.4 | 5.2 | 22.1 | 26.4 | 7.9 | 5.3 | 8.5 | 6.1 |
| *N* | 4,898 | 4,898 | 95 | 91 | 227 | 227 | 296 | 296 |

SOURCE: 2004 NAES General Election Panel Survey.

NOTE: Cell entries denote column percentages unless otherwise indicated. Columns labeled *pre* are from the pre-election survey and columns labeled *post* are from the post-election survey.

Anglos in the pre-election survey and 7.4 percent in the post-election survey responded in this fashion, whereas 14.6 of English-dominant Latinos in the pre-election survey and 9.3 percent in the post-election survey offered this answer. In fact, for the question in which respondents are required to identify the presidential candidate who served as a U.S. senator and the one that asks which of the two candidates spoke at Bob Jones University, more than 50 percent of the Spanish-dominant Latinos provided a nonresponse in either the pre- or post-election survey. This high frequency of nonresponses among Spanish-dominant Latinos is problematic for two reasons. As Althaus (1998) notes, because public opinion surveys are biased toward the groups who provide substantive responses, the opinions of Spanish-dominant Latinos may be underrepresented in the surveys. Another potential concern is that those providing nonresponses may not be accurately reflecting their predispositions and beliefs. Elected officials today give considerable weight to public opinion polls when making policy decisions (Althaus 1998), but the issue concerns of the entire Latino community may not be conveyed by these polls.

The final piece of insight from these distributions is that, with few exceptions, an increase occurs in the percentage of respondents from each ethnic and racial group that provided the correct answers from the pre-election to the post-election survey. Although it is indeed encouraging to note that gains were made in political knowledge from one survey to the other, these gains varied across the groups. For example, on the question asking respondents to identify which presidential candidate was the son of a former senator, 46.2 percent of Anglos provided the correct answer (*Gore*) in the pre-election survey, whereas in the post-election survey, the percentage of Anglos with this response increased by approximately 20 percentage points to 66.4 percent. On this same question, African Americans experienced an 11.8 percentage-point increase from the pre-election to the post-election survey, compared with a 12.6 percentage-point gain among English-dominant Latinos and a 9.2 percentage-point gain for Spanish-dominant Latinos. The advances in knowledge on this question are especially high; for other questions that were more difficult (for example, identifying the candidate that spoke at Bob Jones University), these gains were more tempered.

The findings from the 2004 panel study, presented in Table 6.5, reveal similar variations in political knowledge. On all three questions, a larger percentage of Anglos than of African Americans and both groups of Latinos provided the correct response in the pre- and post-election surveys. For example, 61.1 percent of Anglos in the pre-election survey correctly identified Bush as supporting the proposal to invest Social Security funds in the stock market, compared with 52.9 percent of English-dominant Latinos and 46.8 of African Americans. The plurality of Spanish-dominant Latinos, by contrast, incorrectly attributed this policy position to Kerry. Moreover, Anglos improved

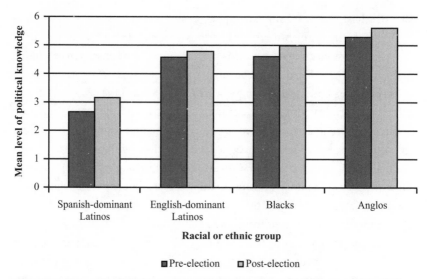

**Figure 6.3** Rates of political learning in 2000, by racial and ethnic group. The difference in means for each racial and ethnic group is statistically significant at the $p <$
.05 level. $N$ (Anglos) = 10,197; $N$ (African Americans) = 591; $N$ (Spanish-dominant
Latinos) = 143; $N$ (English-dominant Latinos) = 505. The political knowledge scale
in 2000 ranged from 0 to 24. *Source:* 2000 NAES General Election Panel Survey.

their knowledge levels on each of the questions, as evidenced by the increase
in the number of correct responses from the pre- to the post-election survey.
Gains in knowledge also occurred for English-dominant Latinos and African
Americans on all three questions, but the percentage of Anglos providing the
correct response in the post-election survey was higher than it was for the
other groups. So, the results from the 2004 panel are identical to the findings
from 2000: Anglos tend to be the most politically knowledgeable ethnic and
racial group both before and after a presidential campaign.

It is also remarkable to note that, in the 2004 survey, on none of the questions did a majority of Spanish-dominant Latinos correctly identify the policy
position of Bush or Kerry; this is true in both the pre- and post-election interviews. In fact, Spanish-dominant Latinos are the only ethnic and racial group
that exhibits such a pattern. These findings further reaffirm just how much
they would benefit from more-informative campaign messages. Furthermore,
a higher percentage of Spanish-dominant Latinos in the 2004 NAES panel
study offered more nonresponses to the political knowledge questions than
did the other ethnic and racial groups, just as was true in the 2000 NAES

panel study. On average, approximately 20 percent of the Spanish-dominant Latinos in each survey wave provided a nonresponse. This is almost double the percentage of nonresponses offered by Anglo, English-dominant Latino, and African American respondents. Among English-dominant Latinos, the greatest gains in knowledge on the 2004 survey occurred on the question pertaining to Social Security. In the pre-election survey 52.9 percent of English-dominant Latinos correctly attributed the proposal to invest Social Security in the stock market to Bush, and the percentage who answered correctly post-election rose to 70.9 percent, an increase of 18 percentage points.

In Figures 6.3 and 6.4, I present an aggregate measure of political knowledge from the 2000 and 2004 panel surveys. Figure 6.3 depicts the mean levels of political knowledge before and after the 2000 presidential campaign, and Figure 6.4 presents the same information for the 2004 presidential campaign. Here, the difference in the mean level of political knowledge from the pre- to the post-election survey is the amount of learning that occurred for each of ethnic and racial groups. Presumably, voters learned something about the candidates over the course of the campaign; the acquisition of campaign

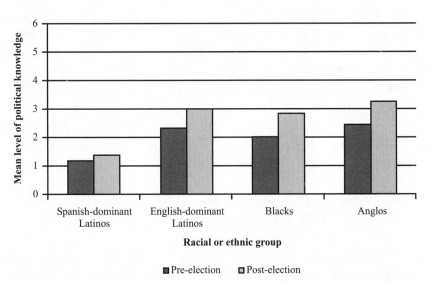

**Figure 6.4** Rates of political learning in 2004, by racial and ethnic group. The difference in means for each racial and ethnic group is statistically significant at the $p <$ .05 level. $N$ (Anglos) = 7472; $N$ (African Americans) = 476; $N$ (Spanish-dominant Latinos) = 151; $N$ (English-dominant Latinos) = 341. The political knowledge scale in 2004 ranged from 0 to 8. *Source:* 2004 NAES General Election Panel Survey.

information should lead to increases in their political knowledge levels following the election. These increases should, in turn, be exhibited in their responses from the post-election survey.

Consistent with the discussion so far, Anglos experienced the greatest amount of learning both before and after the election in the 2000 presidential campaign, followed by African Americans, English-dominant Latinos and, finally, Spanish-dominant Latinos. In 2004, this pattern remains the same, except that English-dominant Latinos learned more than African Americans. Thus, in both this aggregate measure of political knowledge and the individual-level measures discussed earlier, Spanish-dominant Latinos exhibited the lowest levels of political knowledge. These findings are further indication of the negative consequences associated with an information-based strategy of political advertising.

If one looks specifically at each of the campaign cycles, the difference in the levels of knowledge between African Americans and English-dominant Latinos in the 2000 pre- and post-election surveys is quite small, with English-dominant Latinos possessing a mean level of knowledge of 4.59 in the pre-election survey and African Americans a mean level of 4.60. In the post-election survey, English-dominant Latinos' mean level of knowledge was 4.81, and the mean level of knowledge for African Americans was 5.00. Thus, there appears to be very little difference between these two groups in their rates of political knowledge before and after the general election. But as the results thus far suggest, the rates of learning for Spanish-dominant Latinos are significantly different from these two groups. The average level of knowledge for Spanish-dominant Latinos was 2.66 in the pre-election survey and 3.15 in the post-election survey. Clearly, these levels of political knowledge are lower when compared with those of English-dominant Latinos, Anglos, and African Americans. One encouraging observation to note is that Spanish-dominant Latinos experienced the greatest increase in learning, .49, from the pre- to the post-election surveys, compared with .22 for English-dominant Latinos, .34 for Anglos, and .40 for African Americans.

In the 2004 campaign, Anglos possessed the greatest mean levels of political knowledge in the pre-election survey at 2.49, followed by English-dominant Latinos at 2.36, African Americans at 2.08, and Spanish-dominant Latinos at 1.23. As in 2000, the scores of Anglos, African Americans, and English-dominant Latinos are not considerably different. But the gap in levels of political knowledge between these groups and Spanish-dominant Latinos is where the clear distinction lies, in both survey waves. In the post-election survey, Anglos topped the knowledge scale at 3.3, whereas English-dominant Latinos' mean level of knowledge was 3.05. African Americans' mean level of knowledge was slightly lower, at 2.87, and Spanish-dominant Latinos ranked last, with an average political knowledge score of 1.23. Unlike in the 2000 presidential campaign, though, it was not Spanish-dominant Latinos who made the greatest gains in political knowledge. In fact, in the 2004 campaign, this group had the smallest gains in political learning. Instead, Anglos experienced the highest rates of learning, followed closely by African Americans and English-dominant Latinos. Political learning among Spanish-dominant Latinos was .49 in 2000, and .23 in 2004. Thus, although the percentage increase was larger in 2000 than it was in 2004, neither gain is very substantial.

Another way to assess the extent to which individuals learn from a campaign is to explore other factors that contribute to an individual's political dispositions. In particular, one factor that serves as the basis for many of the political decisions that an individual makes is ideology (Converse 1964). This specific predisposition helps individuals to understand the world of government, filter and deal with incoming political information, and structure their civic behavior. Political ideology can incorporate an individual's views on moral traditionalism, authoritarianism, and the role of government. But the political socialization process of many immigrants does not follow the same path that it does for native-born Americans, and the newcomers may conceptualize these ideological terms in a distinct manner (Abrajano and Alvarez, forthcoming).

Given the fundamental role that ideology plays in American political behavior, I examined respondents' evaluations (in both the pre- and post-election interviews) of the major party candidates' political ideologies in 2000 and 2004. Over the course of the campaign, voters could have acquired some knowledge about the candidates' ideological positions through political ads, the media, or contact from the campaigns. Or they could infer ideology through the policy proposals and campaign platforms of the candidates. Thus, there is some possibility that individuals would be able to more precisely identify candidates' ideological positions following the general campaign season.

I turn first to the results from the 2000 panel study. Figures 6.5a and 6.5b

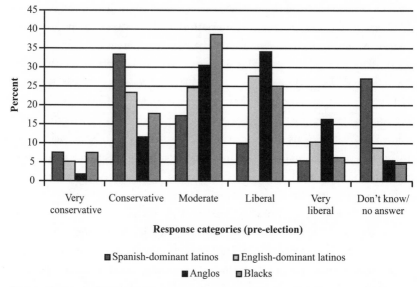

**Figure 6.5a** Evaluations of Gore's political ideology, pre-election survey (2000). *Source:* 2000 NAES General Election Panel Survey

present evaluations of Gore's ideology by racial or ethnic group in both the pre- and post-election survey. Figures 6.6a and 6.6b also show responses grouped by ethnic or racial background and depict individuals' perceptions of Bush's ideology in the pre- and post-election surveys. Respondents were offered a five-point scale on which to identify a candidate's political ideology, with the endpoints being *very conservative* and *very liberal,* and the midpoint being *moderate.* I turn now to each group's placement of Gore's political ideology in the pre-election survey. Most Anglos and English-dominant Latinos considered Gore to be liberal, whereas the bulk of African American respondents perceived Gore as a moderate. The plurality of Spanish-dominant Latinos, however, evaluated Gore's ideology as conservative, which is not the correct characterization of his political orientation. And a larger percentage of Spanish-dominant Latinos provided more nonresponses than did the other racial and ethnic groups, which is consistent with previous patterns.

These patterns do not change very much in the post-election survey. Most Anglos still perceived Gore as liberal, and the bulk of African Americans still considered him to be moderate. Among English-dominant Latinos, a slight shift does seem to appear, with an almost equal number (approximately 30 percent) viewing Gore as moderate versus liberal. Most Latinos who primarily rely on Spanish continued to perceive Gore as being ideologically conservative, suggesting that little learning occurred. Again, because these individuals are newcomers to the political process, they may still be familiarizing themselves with these ideological terms and concepts. These Latinos also may still be deciding how to fit their own values and beliefs into the American ideological spectrum.

Voters were apparently better able to identify Bush's ideological position than they were Gore's. For instance, in the pre-election survey, both Spanish- and English-dominant Latinos viewed Bush's ideology as conservative. Most Anglos and African Americans also considered Bush to be conservative. Note, though, that over a quarter of the Spanish-dominant Latino respondents provided *don't know* responses or nonresponses. In the post-election survey, the distributions remain fairly similar—most Spanish- and English-dominant Latinos considered Bush to be conservative, as did Anglos and African Americans. Although some improvement occurs in English-dominant Latinos' and Anglos' placement of the candidate on the ideological spectrum, the increase is rather modest. And given that more than 20 percent of Spanish-dominant Latinos in both survey waves provided a nonresponse,

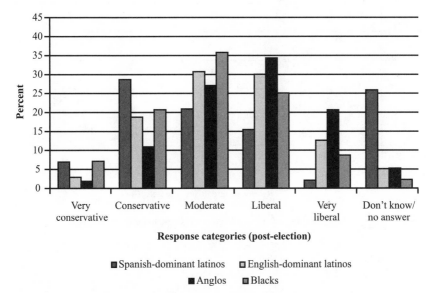

**Figure 6.5b** Evaluations of Gore's political ideology, post-election survey (2000).
*Source:* 2000 NAES General Election Panel Survey

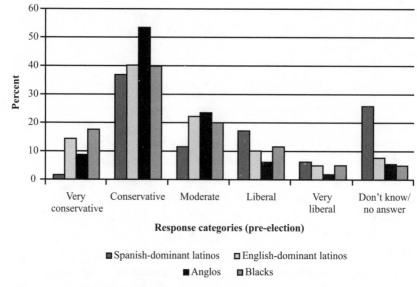

**Figure 6.6a** Evaluations of Bush's political ideology, pre-election survey (2000).
*Source:* 2000 NAES General Election Panel Survey

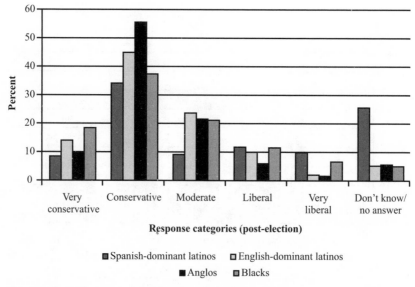

**Figure 6.6b** Evaluations of Bush's political ideology, post-election survey (2000).
*Source:* 2000 NAES General Election Panel Survey

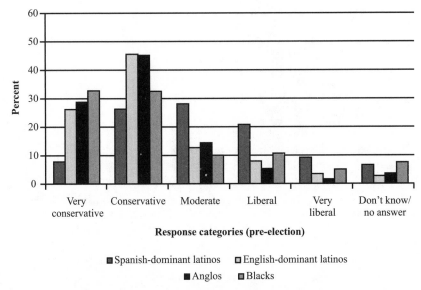

**Figure 6.7a** Evaluations of Bush's political ideology, pre-election survey (2004).
*Source:* 2004 NAES General Election Panel Survey

they seem to have faced some difficulty in identifying Bush's ideological position just as they had had identifying Gore's.

In the 2004 campaign, respondents were also asked to evaluate the political ideology of the two major party presidential candidates. Their responses
are presented in Figures 6.7a, 6.7b, 6.8a, and 6.8b. In the pre-election survey,
the plurality of Spanish-dominant Latinos identified Kerry as being ideologically conservative, which is, of course, an inaccurate depiction of his political
behavior and preferences. Rather interestingly, this evaluation of the Democratic candidate is identical to the one offered by Spanish-dominant Latino
respondents in the 2000 pre-election interview. One reason for this repeated
mischaracterization may be due to how Spanish speakers interpret the terms
*conservative* and *liberal*. For instance, the literal translation of *conservative*
(conservador) in Spanish may lead a respondent to think about his or her cultural and religious values, and unlike this term's meaning in the American
context, in Spanish it carries no economic connotation to it. As such, Kerry
may have been perceived to be *conservative* by Spanish-dominant Latinos,
since he is Roman Catholic.[8]

The plurality of English-dominant Latinos and African Americans considered Kerry to be moderate. Most Anglos (33.3 percent), though, identi-

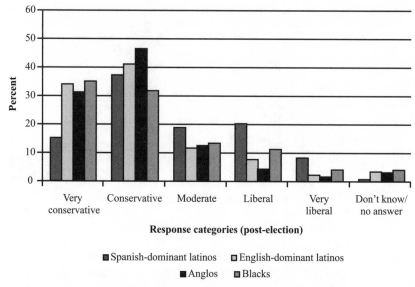

**Figure 6.7b** Evaluations of Bush's political ideology, post-election survey (2004).
*Source:* 2004 NAES General Election Panel Survey

fied Kerry as a liberal. In the post-election survey, the plurality of Spanish-dominant Latinos, 28.9 percent, considered Kerry a liberal, but an almost equal number, 27.6 percent, still continued to identify him as a conservative. English-dominant Latinos shifted their ideological evaluation of Kerry to the left in the post-election survey, because the plurality identified him as a liberal. The majority of Anglos' and African Americans' assessments of Kerry's political ideology remained the same in the post-election survey.

In comparing the rates of political knowledge and learning across ethnic and racial groups, one sees that the largest disparities emerge between our nation's recent newcomers, Spanish-dominant Latinos, and those with a more established presence in the U.S. Possible sources for these newcomers' relatively low levels of political knowledge include a lack of familiarity with the ins and outs of American political practices, customs, and concepts, and the dearth of substantive policy information that they received from the campaigns. Although Spanish-dominant Latinos were fortunate enough to be targeted with political ads during the presidential campaigns, these commercials did not appear to help elevate their rates of political knowledge to the same levels as the rest of the electorate. Low levels of knowledge within the Spanish-dominant Latino population will likely persist if candidates continue to emphasize cultural messages rather than policy-related messages in

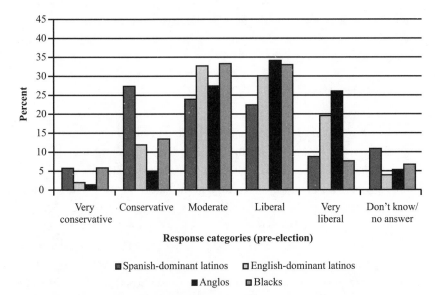

**Figure 6.8a** Evaluations of Kerry's political ideology, pre-election survey (2004).
*Source:* 2004 NAES General Election Panel Survey

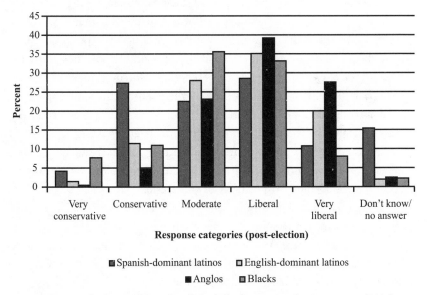

**Figure 6.8b** Evaluations of Kerry's political ideology, post-election survey (2004).
*Source:* 2004 NAES General Election Panel Survey

their Spanish-language ads. The most recent arrivals to the Latino electorate may need to seek other information outlets that could help them learn about politics.

## Latinos as Issue Voters

Another consequence that may result from an information-based theory of advertising is that individuals may be less able to use their issue positions and ideological beliefs when making political decisions (Carmines and Stimson 1980; Jackson 1975; Key 1966; Page and Brody 1972; Page and Jones 1979; Pomper 1972). Several strains of research in the field of political science document the effects that issues and political ideology have on vote choice. The spatial proximity model suggests that voters will choose the candidate closest to their own position on the issues (Downs 1957; Enelow and Hinich 1984; Alvarez and Nagler 1998; Alvarez and Nagler 1995), whereas the directional model of issue voting finds voters supporting candidates who are on the same side of issues that they are on (Rabinowitz and Macdonald 1989). The salience of issues is also believed to affect one's vote intention (Rabinowitz and MacDonald 1989). A key assumption of these theories of issue voting is that individuals possess preexisting values and beliefs that enable them to adopt a position on abortion, school vouchers, and so on. But if voters are relatively new to the political process, as are Spanish-dominant Latinos, they may have yet to formulate precise opinions on these topics. Moreover, their issue positions and political beliefs, as captured by their self-reported ideology, may not be strongly correlated if they have yet to organize their beliefs according to the left-right ideological continuum that characterizes American politics (Abrajano and Alvarez, forthcoming). And as the previous results indicated, Spanish-dominant Latinos had greater difficulty than other Americans in identifying the ideological positions of the presidential candidates in both 2000 and 2004. This difficulty is just one indicator of the challenges that Spanish-dominant Latinos face in using their policy and ideological preferences in their vote choice. As such, it may be the case that issues and ideology will play a less prominent role in the vote decisions of Spanish-dominant Latinos than in those of English-dominant Latinos.

One issue that could have played an important role for Latino voters in these two elections was abortion (Alvarez and Bedolla 2003). The social conservatism that characterizes many Latinos led Bush and the Republicans to emphasize this topic in their campaign, in hopes of making further inroads with this electorate. The issues of school vouchers, federally sponsored health insurance, the economy, and Social Security could have also affected the way Latinos cast their ballots, given the prominence of these four issues in the 2000 and 2004 election cycles. Candidates also held distinct positions on these issues (Abrajano et al. 2008; Abramson et al. 2002). In addition, Latinos' perceptions of their own personal finances can help to shape their vote decisions (Abrajano et al. 2008), just as these concerns can significantly affect the rest of the public's vote intentions (Page and Brody 1972; Carmines and Stimson 1980; Alvarez and Nagler 1995; Alvarez and Nagler 1998; Abramson et al. 2002).

Because the Democratic contender in both 2000 and 2004 favored government assistance in providing health care, Latinos with a similar position should have been more likely to support Gore or Kerry rather than Bush. But Latinos who are in favor of restricting abortion should be less inclined to vote for the Democratic candidate, given that both Gore and Kerry are pro-choice; instead, those holding a pro-life stance should have been supporters of Bush. School vouchers is another issue that would give an advantage to Bush. Because this policy finds favor among Republicans, we should expect Latinos who like the idea of a school-voucher program to cast their ballots for Bush rather than for the Democratic candidate.

As the literature on economic voting finds (Kinder and Kiewiet 1981; Hibbs 1982; Erikson 1989; Alesina et al. 1997), those who view their personal finances and national economic conditions favorably should reward the current presidential administration. As such, individuals who perceived their finances and the economy to have improved would have been more supportive of Bush in 2004 than of Kerry. But individuals who felt that their personal finances and the national economy had worsened should have punished the current administration and lent support to the candidate from the nonincumbent party.

Along with the specific issues that rose to prominence in these two presidential races, the demographic characteristics and political dispositions of Latinos could also have shaped their vote decisions. It is therefore important that the model of vote choice accounts for characteristics such as age, gender, education, income, religious affiliation, and marital status. Finally, no model predicting individual voting would be complete without some measure of party identification and self-reported political ideology, given the critical role that both factors play in one's vote choice (Campbell et al. 1964).

To determine how all these factors influenced Latino voting behavior in the 2000 and 2004 presidential elections, I estimated a multivariate model of vote choice in which the dependent variable is the probability of voting for the Democratic candidate (in 2000, this is the likelihood of voting for Gore, and in 2004, the likelihood of voting for Kerry).[9] The explanatory variables, as described earlier, account for numerous factors that can influence one's vote decision—demographics, political attitudes, and issue positions.[10] To determine whether variations exist in the roles of issues and ideology in Spanish- and English-dominant Latino vote choice, I estimated a separate model of vote choice for each of these Latino groups. The estimates from the 2000 model of presidential vote choice are presented in Table 6.6, and the estimates for 2004 are presented in Table 6.7.[11]

In both of these presidential races, the policy positions and ideological predispositions of English-dominant Latinos played a somewhat larger role in their vote decisions than these factors did for Spanish-dominant Latinos. Note that of the six issue questions in the 2000 model of vote choice, only one affected the vote decision of Spanish-dominant Latinos, but three impacted the vote choice of English-dominant Latinos. Spanish-dominant Latinos in favor of restricting abortion were 23 percent less likely to support Gore.[12] This issue also significantly affected the vote choice of English-dominant Latinos in 2000; those supporting a ban on abortion experienced a 20 percent reduction in their probability of voting for Gore. English-dominant Latinos' attitudes toward federal spending on health care also affected their vote decision. Those who favored greater efforts by the federal government in these two policy domains preferred the Democratic candidate over the Republican candidate. The magnitude of these effects was fairly substantial, ranging from 9 to 23 percent in both elections.

The vote-choice estimates from the 2004 presidential election correspond fairly well to those from 2000. Overall, a greater number of issue attitudes entered into the vote calculus of the more-acculturated Latinos. The national economy was the only issue that influenced the voting behavior of Spanish-dominant Latinos, but health care, school vouchers, and abortion all factored into the decision-making process of English-dominant Latinos. As discussed in Chapter 2, language use among immigrants could be viewed, to some degree, as a proxy for political knowledge. Thus, the fact that Spanish-dominant Latinos' issue positions did not play such an influential role in their vote choice could be attributed to their lower levels of familiarity with American politics in general and with the context of these two elections specifically.

**Table 6.6** Latino vote choice in the 2000 presidential elections

| Variable | English-dominant Latinos | | | Spanish-dominant Latinos | | |
|---|---|---|---|---|---|---|
| | Estimated coefficient | Standard error | Estimated change in probability of vote[a] | Estimated coefficient | Standard error | Estimated change in probability of vote[a] |
| Constant | −.14 | .57 | — | 1.01 | 1.27 | — |
| *Demographics* | | | | | | |
| No high-school degree | −.06 | .25 | −.02 | −.30 | .38 | −.12 |
| High-school degree | −.14 | .18 | −.05 | −.01 | .40 | −.00 |
| Income | −.06 | .05 | .02 | .06 | .10 | .02 |
| Age | .00 | .01 | .00 | −.00 | .09 | −.00 |
| Married | −.23 | .17 | −.07 | −.09 | .26 | −.03 |
| Women | −.06 | .15 | −.01 | .02 | .28 | .01 |
| Catholic | .13 | .20 | .05 | −.68 | .57 | −.26 |
| Protestant | −.00 | .24 | −.00 | −.45 | .63 | −.18 |
| *Political dispositions* | | | | | | |
| Democrat | 1.05*** | .18 | .37*** | 1.00*** | .31 | .37*** |
| Republican | −.89*** | .21 | −.34*** | −.78*** | .34 | −.30*** |
| Liberal | .24*** | .09 | .09*** | −.10 | .13 | −.04 |
| *Issue positions* | | | | | | |
| Economy fair | −.13 | .19 | −.05 | −.36 | .29 | −.14 |
| Economy poor | −.39 | .27 | −.16 | .66 | .50 | .24 |
| Personal finances fair | −.18 | .18 | −.07 | .06 | .33 | .02 |
| Personal finances poor | .45 | .32 | −.16 | −.11 | .41 | −.05 |
| Restrict abortion | −.52*** | .17 | −.20*** | −.58** | .26 | −.23** |
| Pro-vouchers | −.07 | .16 | −.02 | −.40 | .30 | −.16 |
| More/same spending on Social Security | .56* | .30 | −.22* | .53 | .63 | .21 |
| More/same government spending on health care for uninsured | .23* | .13 | .09* | .10 | .33 | .04 |
| | | | | | | |
| N | | 417 | | | 139 | |
| Log-likelihood | | −185.31 | | | −74.71 | |
| Baseline | | 58.77 | | | 50.23 | |
| Percent correctly predicted | | 64.62 | | | 54.09 | |

NOTE: The dependent variable is the probability of voting for Gore.

[a]Reports the change in the probability for an infinitesimal change in each independent, continuous variable and the discrete change in the probability for dummy variables.

*$p < .10$
**$p < .05$
***$p < .01$

**Table 6.7** Latino vote choice in the 2004 presidential elections

| Variable | English-dominant Latinos | | | Spanish-dominant Latinos | | |
|---|---|---|---|---|---|---|
| | Estimated coefficient | Standard error | Estimated change in probability of vote[a] | Estimated coefficient | Standard error | Estimated change in probability of vote[a] |
| Constant | −.83 | .56 | — | −.20 | 1.35 | — |
| *Demographics* | | | | | | |
| No high-school degree | −.19 | .26 | −.07 | −.13 | .34 | −.05 |
| High-school degree | .06 | .17 | .02 | −.23 | .37 | −.09 |
| Income | .01 | .04 | .00 | −.07 | .07 | .02 |
| Age | .00 | .01 | .00 | −.01 | .01 | −.00 |
| Married | −.17 | .16 | −.07 | −.34 | .27 | −.12 |
| Women | .04 | .15 | .02 | −.36 | .23 | −.13 |
| Catholic | −.24 | .18 | −.09 | −.08 | .35 | −.03 |
| Protestant | −.22 | .21 | −.09 | −.48 | .41 | −.18 |
| *Political dispositions* | | | | | | |
| Democrat | .91*** | .16 | .37*** | .72*** | .27 | .25*** |
| Republican | −1.09*** | .21 | −.34*** | −.83** | .33 | −.32** |
| Liberal | .16** | .08 | .09*** | −.02 | .12 | −.01 |
| *Issue positions* | | | | | | |
| Economy fair | .38* | .20 | .15* | .52* | .28 | .18* |
| Economy poor | .49** | .23 | .18** | 1.27*** | .43 | .34*** |
| Personal finances fair | −.09 | .17 | −.04 | .30 | .33 | .11 |
| Personal finances poor | −.18 | .24 | −.07 | −.19 | .41 | −.07 |
| Restrict abortion | −.61*** | .17 | −.24*** | .11 | .24 | .04 |
| Pro-vouchers | −.30** | .15 | −.11** | −.03 | .35 | −.01 |
| Favor investing social security in stock market | .16 | .18 | .07 | .39 | .32 | .13 |
| More/same government spending on health care for uninsured | .58* | .33 | .23* | 1.09 | 1.00 | .41 |
| N | | 484 | | | 179 | |
| Log-likelihood | | −203.88 | | | −89.11 | |
| Baseline | | 56.70 | | | 64.9 | |
| Percent correctly predicted | | 58.19 | | | 67.54 | |

[a]Reports the change in the probability for an infinitesimal change in each independent, continuous variable and the discrete change in the probability for dummy variables. The dependent variable is the probability of voting for Kerry.

*$p < .10$
**$p < .05$
***$p < .01$

**Table 6.8** Descriptive statistics for variables presented in Tables 6.2–6.3 and 6.5–6.6

| | 2000 | | | 2004 | | |
|---|---|---|---|---|---|---|
| | Mean | Standard deviation | Range | Mean | Standard deviation | Range |
| *Political dispositions/media exposure* | | | | | | |
| Liberal ideology | 2.83 | .94 | 1,5 | 2.81 | 1.00 | 1,5 |
| Democrat | .28 | .45 | 0,1 | .32 | .48 | 0,1 |
| Republican | .25 | .43 | 0,1 | .30 | .46 | 0,1 |
| Interested in government | 2.02 | .99 | 1,4 | 1.90 | .91 | 1,4 |
| Watch TV news daily | 4.22 | 2.69 | 0,7 | 4.06 | 2.75 | 0,7 |
| Read newspaper daily | 3.78 | 2.89 | 0,7 | 2.33 | .96 | 1,4 |
| Contacted by a campaign | .06 | .24 | 0,1 | n/a | n/a | n/a |
| *Demographics* | | | | | | |
| No high-school degree | .09 | .28 | 0,1 | .07 | .26 | 0,1 |
| High-school graduate | .26 | .44 | 0,1 | .25 | .44 | 0,1 |
| Some college/beyond | .16 | .36 | 0,1 | .18 | .38 | 0,1 |
| Income | 4.94 | 2.07 | 1,9 | 5.33 | 2.10 | 1,9 |
| Married | .57 | .49 | 0,1 | .57 | .50 | 0,1 |
| Women | .55 | .50 | 0,1 | .55 | .50 | 0,1 |
| Age | 46.09 | 16.57 | 18,96 | 47.99 | 16.59 | 18,97 |
| U.S. citizen | .04 | .20 | 0,1 | .62 | .49 | 0,1 |
| Catholic | .13 | .33 | 0,1 | .28 | .45 | 0,1 |
| Protestant | .27 | .45 | 0,1 | .62 | .49 | 0,1 |
| *Issues* | | | | | | |
| Economy good | .26 | .44 | 0,1 | .25 | .43 | 0,1 |
| Economy fair | .13 | .33 | 0,1 | .43 | .49 | 0,1 |
| Economy poor | .04 | .19 | 0,1 | .28 | .45 | 0,1 |
| Personal finances good | .27 | .44 | 0,1 | .40 | .49 | 0,1 |
| Personal finances fair | .15 | .36 | 0,1 | .35 | .48 | 0,1 |
| Personal finances poor | .04 | .20 | 0,1 | .14 | .35 | 0,1 |
| Restrict abortion | .35 | .48 | 0,1 | 3.59 | 1.66 | 1,5 |
| Pro-vouchers | .22 | .42 | 0,1 | .50 | .50 | 0,1 |
| Social Security | 1.49 | .63 | 1,4 | 2.83 | 1.59 | 1,5 |
| Health insurance | 1.43 | .73 | 1,4 | 1.39 | .75 | 1,4 |
| *Advertising exposure* | | | | | | |
| Complex policy | .17 | 1.43 | 0,117.18 | 2.55 | 7.32 | 0,59.91 |
| Explained policy | .33 | 2.47 | 0,179.28 | 2.31 | 6.47 | 0,51.38 |
| Simple policy | .39 | .77 | 0,2 | 1.48 | 4.20 | 0,35.99 |
| Targeted Latino ad | .001 | .01 | 0,.13 | .02 | .70 | 0,1.13 |

The estimates from the vote-choice models also indicate that political ideology influenced the voting behavior for only one group of Latinos. How one defined oneself on the left-right ideological scale had no bearing on the voting decisions made by Spanish-dominant Latinos in both 2000 and 2004. In contrast, political ideology was a significant predictor of vote choice among English-dominant Latinos for both elections; those identifying with a liberal ideology increased their likelihood of voting for the Democratic candidate by 9 percent in 2000 and 2004. Given that Spanish-dominant Latinos are still in the process of becoming acquainted with American politics, the concept of political ideology, at least in the U.S. context, may still be in its formative stages. This could partly explain why ideology plays a less meaningful role in the vote decisions of Spanish-dominant Latinos.

In addition to one's issue beliefs and political dispositions, these models considered a Latino's demographic characteristics to be potential explanatory factors in their vote decisions. But as the estimates from Tables 6.6 and 6.7 reveal, age, education and income level, religious affiliation, marital status, and gender all failed to have any significant impact on the voting behavior of both English- and Spanish-dominant Latinos. The one other factor that did significantly affect Latino decision making is partisanship. For both groups of Latinos, identifying as a partisan (either Democrat or Republican) influenced voting behavior in the predicted manner. That is, Latino Democrats were more likely to support the Democratic candidate, and Latino Republicans were less likely to vote for the Democratic candidate. In both of these scenarios, the baseline category is Latinos who consider themselves Independents. Partisanship, as expected, has a substantial impact on vote choice; identifying as either a Republican or a Democrat affects one's decision to support the candidate of one's party by about one-third. The fact that party affiliation is such a strong and influential predictor of vote choice for Spanish-dominant Latinos while ideology is not presents a rather interesting puzzle. Earlier, it was suggested that ideology failed to be salient for Spanish-dominant Latinos due to the variation in the political socialization process between this group and the native-born population. But a similar argument could be made about the acquisition of the use of partisan labels in the U.S. It may be that Spanish-dominant Latinos can more easily distinguish the terms *Democrat* and *Republican* because presidential candidates seem to emphasize party labels to a much greater extent than they do political ideologies in their campaign ads, particularly in their Spanish-language ads (Connaughton 2005). Thus, even without a significant degree of familiarity with the American political system, Spanish-dominant Latinos may be able to more easily infer from these campaign messages what it means to be a Democrat or Republican as opposed to liberal or conservative. Although the analysis here cannot determine whether this is the case, subsequent work in this area could reinforce the existing studies on information shortcuts (see Kahneman et al. 1979; Popkin 1994; Lupia and McCubbins 1998). It may also be that because these party labels are identical in meaning whether they are used in a Spanish- or English-language ad, it is unlikely that they will be interpreted differently among Spanish- and English-dominant Latinos. The same cannot be said, however, for terms pertaining to American political ideology.

Understanding the components that factored into the vote decisions of Spanish- and English-dominant Latinos in the 2000 and 2004 presidential elections offers just one glimpse of the effects that different advertising strategies can have on this growing segment of the American electorate. The models of vote choice indicated that political ideology played an insignificant role in determining who Spanish-dominant Latinos supported for president in both of these elections. In contrast, political ideology was a strong and important predictor of vote choice for English-dominant Latinos. Because the relationship between political ideology and voter decision making serves as one of the cornerstones of American political behavior, it is somewhat unsettling to find that such a relationship is absent for many of our recent newcomers. This pattern was also echoed in the difficulty that Spanish-dominant Latinos experienced in correctly identifying the ideological positions of the Democratic candidates and, to a somewhat lesser extent, of Bush. Perhaps candidates need to do a better job of communicating in their Spanish-language ads exactly what political ideology they identify with. By doing so, they could help Spanish-dominant Latinos learn more about the issues, ideals, and values that go along with being liberal and conservative, and this group of Latinos could be more sure that they are casting their ballots for the "right" candidate (that is, the candidate who is most closely aligned with their own beliefs and values). It is important to keep in mind, however, that partisanship was an important predictor of vote choice for Spanish-dominant Latinos in both presidential elections. This finding suggests that partisanship carries more weight than does ideology in the vote decisions of the recently arrived segment of the Latino population. Thus, although it would not be accurate to conclude that political predispositions had no affect on the voting behavior of Spanish-dominant Latinos, only one out of the two key political indicators were significant.

## Summary

This chapter examined the consequences of adopting an information-based strategy of campaign advertising on the political well being of the Latino electorate. I discussed two main effects that could result from candidates advertising less substantively based policy messages in their Spanish-language ads than in their English-language ads. First, although English-dominant Latinos' levels of political learning were positively influenced by exposure to the most sophisticated and informative policy messages, exposure to such ads did not provide the same educational benefits to Spanish-dominant Latinos. In fact, being exposed to political ads had no influence whatsoever on their rates of political knowledge. Instead, in the 2000 presidential election, other information sources available during a campaign, such as newspapers and personal contact from a campaign worker, positively impacted Spanish-dominant Latinos' rates of political knowledge.

In both the 2000 and 2004 presidential races, Spanish-dominant Latinos also knew less about candidates' issue positions, ideological orientations, and personal backgrounds when compared with the rest of the electorate. This was the case both before and immediately after the general election. A more in-depth examination of the responses to the factual political questions also showed that Spanish-dominant Latinos provided a larger percentage of non-responses than did other racial and ethnic groups. Perhaps one reason why so many Spanish-dominant Latinos responded in this manner can be attributed to the types of political ads that they were exposed to. These ads provided little in the way of substantive policy information about the presidential candidates. As a result, it appears that many of the nation's most recent newcomers could not take advantage of the educational benefits associated with televised political ads.

Another consequence associated with these advertising strategies is that Spanish-dominant Latinos are less influenced in their vote decisions by their issue positions and ideological beliefs than are English-dominant Latinos. One implication from this result is that Spanish-dominant Latinos' vote intentions may not entirely reflect their true issue preferences (Lau and Redlawsk 2006). This is of particular concern since one's positions on issues play an integral role in the vote-decision process (Page and Brody 1972; Carmines and Stimson 1980; Alvarez and Nagler 1995; Abramson et al. 2002). Other possible repercussions from adopting an information-based strategy of advertising may include low levels of political interest, trust, and efficacy among Spanish-dominant Latinos, as some might find Spanish-language campaign messages to be much too simplistic and, perhaps, even somewhat condescending. It could even backfire among bilingual Latinos, leading them to react negatively to Spanish-language ads.[13] Although providing such evidence would require further research and analysis, these possibilities highlight the fact that candidates' advertising decisions have a wide range of consequences, some of which may have been unintended or even unexpected on the part of politicians. The way candidates target specific groups influences not only who these groups end up voting for, but also how they behave in a variety of political arenas. Unfortunately, these ramifications happen to disadvantage the political and civic voice of a growing and increasingly influential segment of the American electorate.

# 7  The Future of Ethnically Targeted Campaigns

AS A NATION COMPRISED OF IMMIGRANTS from vastly different cultures and backgrounds, *who* and *wha*t we consider to be the American electorate has constantly been in flux. At the beginning of the twentieth century, those of Irish, Italian, German, and Jewish ancestry made up the majority of entrants to the political process. Most of these people settled in the large urban centers of the American northeast. In the mid-1960s, newcomers arrived from as far as East and Southeast Asia and from nearer locales in Latin America. The rate of immigration from Latin America since then has been so continuous that Latinos are now the largest racial and ethnic group in the U.S.

Although the ethnic composition of our nation's newcomers has fluctuated over the decades, the strategies that politicians have used to appeal to these immigrant groups have remained relatively unchanged. The political machines active at the beginning of the twentieth century won the support of immigrant groups via symbolic gestures and the provision of jobs and social services. Of course, the goal of these efforts was to signal a candidate's interest and concern for these groups, and, in turn, capture their electoral support. At the core of this strategy is the belief that a group's shared ethnic identity translates into shared political beliefs and preferences (Erie 1988). According to this view, an ethnic group should behave as a monolithic voting bloc and therefore care about the same issues and share similar concerns. A key assumption of this belief is that one's ethnic identity is correlated to one's political behavior and actions. Such a perspective has led to the conventional wisdom—that when candidates are campaigning for elected office, they target ethnic minorities in a different way from the rest of the electorate. The strategies used for ethnic minorities could include campaigning to them using ethnic-specific appeals or emphasizing issues that the candidates perceive to be important to these groups. In the current era of ethnic and racial campaigns, presidential candidates spent more than $3 million on Spanish-language media buys in 2000 and more than $8.7 million in 2004 (Segal 2006). In just one presidential election cycle, then, the amount spent on Spanish-language advertising more than doubled.

Because politicians, particularly those competing for the U.S. presidency, cannot afford to reach out to potential supporters individually for lack of time and resources, a more efficient way to campaign to the electorate is to target those who are like-minded, and one way to do this is through group affiliations. A shared culture, race, ethnicity, or to a lesser extent, occupation or gender can closely tie individuals together and can also translate into shared political views and concerns. This is why micro-targeting has become the preferred campaign strategy among today's top political consultants (Shea and Burton 2006). And as Bishin's (2009) subconstituency politics theory points out, politicians intentionally make group appeals in order to activate their group-based identities. The research on consumer-based advertising strategies toward ethnic and racial minorities further documents the benefits of ethnic-based appeals, made through visual images or language, in generating positive reactions to the product being advertised (Whittler 1989; Dimofte et al. 2003/2004).

The goal of this book was to systemically determine whether this conventional wisdom on ethnic and racial campaigns holds true and what repercussions it may have on the political well being of the ethnic or racial group being targeted. Part of the explanation for these distinct campaign strategies is that candidates perceive ethnic identity to be a salient factor in the political decisions that ethnics make; the other primary factor in the explanation pertains to variations in a group's familiarity with politics. That is, the extent to which groups participate in and are interested in politics, and the frequency with which they follow political campaigns and politics in general all play into candidates' advertising strategies. These two factors serve as the basis for the theory of information-based advertising and help to explain the differences in the content of the Spanish- and English-language political ads used in the 2000–2004 election cycles. In examining the primary form of campaign communication used to target the largest immigrant group today, Latinos, one can see how the Spanish-language ads developed for presidential, congressional, and gubernatorial races had a greater tendency to emphasize nonpolicy and simplistic policy messages than did the English-language ads created for these elections. The content of these English-language ads focused on informative policy messages to a greater extent than did that of the Spanish-language ads. For example, the total percentage of Spanish-language ads featuring symbolic and character messages was almost one and a half times the percentage of the ads created in English. But the total number of explained policy and complex policy messages in English-language ads outpaced those in Spanish-language ads by a margin of 5 percent and 11 percent, respectively.

In an additional test of the theory of information-based advertising, I examined on what types of programs these different commercials were broadcast. Based on this theory, candidates would be expected to broadcast the most informative policy messages on television news programs, which have more politically sophisticated audiences that would be likely to respond to them. One would expect simple policy messages, however, to be broadcast on more entertainment-focused programs. Only partial support for this argument emerged, and that support was for candidates' broadcasting decisions about their Spanish-language ads. The bulk of the English-language spots aired on the news regardless of their content. Because candidates spend a much larger amount of their advertising budget on English-language spots than on Spanish-language ones, they have an incentive to air these spots on programs with audiences composed of likely voters, and studies have shown that those who watch the news are also those most likely to vote (Delli Carpini and Keeter 1996).

At the micro level, congressional and statewide candidates also considered the ethnic composition and political knowledge levels of their intended audience. Candidates competing in districts with a large percentage of politically informed Latinos were more likely to advertise policy messages in Spanish than those representing a less politically informed Latino electorate. The competitiveness of the election also played a role in advertising choices; close elections increased the chances that candidates would broadcast policy messages that could differentiate themselves from their competitors. In developing targeted ethnic appeals, candidates once again took into account the demographic composition of the electorate. Candidates were more likely to advertise in Spanish and feature a Latino in their commercials as their share of the Latino electorate increased. The same held true in their decisions to feature other ethnic and racial minorities in their ads; for example, a sizeable

African American electorate resulted in an increased probability of an African American appearing in a commercial. Altogether, these analyses demonstrate how candidates do consider their target audience when crafting their political ads.

As the conventional wisdom predicts, Latinos were affected by these televised campaign ads in their political behavior. But the extent to which a Latino is incorporated into American society determines which types of political ads affect their vote decisions and likelihood of voting. Among Latinos who are still in the process of becoming politically and socially incorporated, only those commercials that tap into their ethnic identity play an important role in deciding which presidential candidate they will support. Politically incorporated Latinos, however, are persuaded in their vote choice more by informative policy ads than by targeted Latino ads. Exposure to these ads also generated an indirect effect—that of encouraging Latinos to vote on election day. But again, this indirect effect varied based on a Latino's level of political incorporation. Only those ads that specifically appealed to Latinos influenced the more-incorporated English-dominant Latinos to turn out and vote. Yet, Spanish-dominant Latinos who were exposed to both Spanish-language ads and general ads were positively influenced to vote.

Although these distinct advertising efforts provided support for the commonly held belief that candidates advertise differently to easily identifiable groups in the electorate, in this case ethnic and racial minorities, this strategy has several negative repercussions for the political well being of our nation's largest immigrant population. Given that one of the benefits associated with political advertising is its ability to assist in voter learning and promote increased levels of knowledge (Geer 2006; Jamieson 1996; Joslyn 1980; Patterson and McClure 1976), can Latinos who are exposed to Spanish-language ads learn anything from them, despite their lack of policy content? Unfortunately, among the Spanish-dominant segment of the Latino community, the answer to this question is no. Exposure to political ads did not contribute to the political knowledge of Spanish-dominant Latinos. English-dominant Latinos did learn from these ads, but only from the ones containing informative policy messages. Spanish-dominant Latinos had to rely on other information sources, such as newspapers and personal contact by a campaign worker, to learn about the candidates and their policy positions.

It was also the case that both during and after the campaign, Spanish-dominant Latinos knew less about candidates' issue positions, ideological orientations, and personal backgrounds when compared with other ethnic and racial groups. A more-detailed examination of the responses to the factual political questions also revealed a greater tendency among less politically incorporated Latinos than among other racial and ethnic groups to provide nonresponses. Spanish-dominant Latinos also exhibited some difficulty identifying the ideological positions of the 2000 and 2004 presidential candidates. As this group is already disadvantaged in their familiarity with and knowledge of politics when compared with other Americans, they would stand to gain the most from the educational benefits that come from exposure to political ads. But given that the content in Spanish-language policy ads favored style over substance, it is not surprising that these ads provided no assistance in political learning.

Another potential consequence of these different advertising strategies concerns the role that a person's issue and political beliefs play in his or her vote intention. Perhaps one reason why political ideology failed to factor into the vote decision of Spanish-dominant Latinos is because of the types of political ads that they were exposed to. Although the issues of abortion and the national economy mattered to all Latinos, the topic of government-sponsored health insurance factored into the vote decisions only for English-dominant Latinos.

## Research Implications

Political strategists who believe that campaign ads impact the Latino electorate equally may wish to reevaluate this belief. Although all Latinos are influenced by targeted ethnic appeals in their vote intentions, exposure to informative policy ads plays a larger role in the vote decision of those who have incorporated into American society and politics than does exposure to targeted Latino ads. But less-incorporated Latinos are persuaded only by ethnic-specific appeals when casting their ballots. Assuming that all Latinos will respond equally to these cultural messages implies that personal ideological and issue stances and candidates' issue positions have no bearing on their decision-making process. Such an assumption incorrectly depicts Latinos as a cohesive and homogenous political group, but as this research and previous research on Latino political behavior demonstrates (Abrajano and Alvarez, forthcoming; Alvarez and García Bedolla 2003; de la Garza and DeSipio 1992), this ethnic group is highly heterogeneous in their political preferences and behaviors. Strategists are not incorrect to create campaign messages that are culturally and symbolically based, because Latinos do respond to them. But it is important to note that the vote intentions of English-dominant Latinos, who constitute the segment of the Latino electorate most likely to vote, are guided to a greater degree by substantive, policy-oriented messages and less so by cultural ones.

Moreover, because candidates are targeting Spanish-dominant Latinos primarily with simple policy appeals and nonpolicy messages, these Latinos are less likely to behave as "completely informed" issue voters when compared with the rest of electorate (Lupia 1994). In deciding which candidate to support, Spanish-dominant Latinos may be limited in their capacity to evaluate the contenders based on the contenders' policy positions and proposals. After all, how can voters differentiate between two candidates from simple policy messages promising "better schools" or "a stronger economy"? Such messages not only fail to reveal how candidates plan to effect improvements but also fail to provide voters with enough information about the candidates' specific positions on important issues. The dearth of informative policy messages in Spanish-language ads also means that Spanish-dominant Latinos may lack the necessary information to participate in the political arena in an influential way (for example, by letter writing or lobbying). In turn, Spanish-dominant Latinos may be less able to hold their elected representatives accountable. This concern is especially relevant for a socioeconomically disadvantaged group such as Latinos, given that the costs associated with interest group participation are fairly high (Bishin 2009). Also note that partisanship was more important for Spanish-dominant Latinos than was ideology.

As it stands now, Spanish-dominant Latinos' lack of familiarity with politics is likely to persist because of the structural inequalities that plague the educational opportunities of many ethnic and racial minorities in the United States (Orfield and Lee 2006). Changes in the high-school curriculum could help alleviate this problem (Niemi and Junn 1998). If public high schools systematically incorporated a greater number of civics and current events classes into their curricula, African American and Latino students could learn more about politics and increase their stored levels of political knowledge. Of course, implementing this kind of change would require more funding from the government at both the federal and state levels. The passage of the No Child Left Behind Act makes the chances for such reform seem slim, because public schools nationwide must now focus their efforts on adequately preparing students for national achievement tests that emphasize reading and math proficiency if they wish to retain their funding. As Wong (2006) and others (Bloemraad 2006; DeSipio 2001; Wong et al. 2008) have documented, churches, community groups, labor unions, homeland associations, and ethnic businesses are alternative avenues through which immigrants can become incorporated into the political process. Although many of these groups are not political in nature, they can still serve as important resources from which immigrants can develop valuable political skills and gain exposure to the different functions of government. Bloemraad (2006) also notes the importance of family and friends in teaching newcomers about the ins and outs of their newly adopted country and encouraging them to become politically involved.

Candidates and their respective parties may also want to reconsider their current advertising strategies if they wish to build party loyalty among Spanish-speaking Latinos and potentially win the votes of this highly coveted segment of the American electorate. This is by far the most pressing concern that Democrats and Republicans have today, as Latinos continue to be an important—perhaps the most important—swing group in the nation. Capturing the support of these Latinos would translate into winning the allegiance of almost a quarter of the population nationwide, and of an even greater number in the next several decades. In addition, recall that when Latinos are compared with the rest of the American electorate, more of them see themselves as Independents or "don't know" their party affiliation (Abrajano and Alvarez, forthcoming; Hajnal and Lee 2008). This lack of strong partisan rootedness can likely be attributed to Spanish-dominant Latinos' uncertainty about the ideological positions of the major party candidates, and to their lack of familiarity regarding American politics. Candidates could reduce this uncertainty by communicating their issue positions and ideological beliefs as clearly as possible in their political advertisements. Candidates should also be careful how they translate these ideological concepts in their Spanish-language ads, and do a better job of linking issue positions with political ideology.

If future presidential campaigns follow the current pattern of broadcasting mainly targeted Latino appeals to Spanish-dominant Latinos, this group will have little choice but to search for other avenues of information. The responsibility of providing substantive and relevant information during an election year may shift to independent organizations and advocacy groups, because the content of television ads as it is currently conceived will not help to reduce the information gap that exists between Spanish-dominant Latinos and the rest of the electorate.

The lessons learned from the campaigns of the 2000–2004 elections also have important implications for the second largest immigrant group in the nation—Asian Americans. Their steady rates of immigration to the United States over the past thirty years have increased their share of the total U.S. population to 4.5 percent (U.S. Census Bureau 2000b). By 2050, Asian Americans are projected to make up 8 percent of the U.S. population (U.S. Census Bureau 2000b). As in the Latino population, high levels of socioeconomic, cultural, and generational heterogeneity exist within the Asian American community (Lien et al. 2004; Espiritu 1992). Asian Americans' political interests and orientation to politics thus vary significantly from one ethnic subgroup to another (Lien et al. 2004). Moreover, a large share of the Asian American population is foreign born, which means that their political socialization takes place outside the United States. But unlike Latinos, Asian Americans do not share a common language. So if candidates and politicians intend to target Asian Americans through specialized media outlets, they will not be able to communicate to the entire community as easily as they can to Latinos.

How, then, should candidates and politicians communicate to racial and ethnic groups? This study has shown that emotional and affective appeals based on Latino culture influence the voting behavior of Latinos but do not contribute to the political learning and political knowledge levels of Spanish-dominant Latinos. Candidates may therefore be better off advertising both ethnic appeals and more-informative policy messages in their Spanish-language ads. The same may also be said of the advertising decisions directed toward other immigrant groups, such as Asian Americans. Because many immigrants are newcomers to the American political process (Lien et al. 2004), they should also benefit from ads containing both types of messages. The findings in this book thus have implications not just for Latinos but also for immigrant groups more broadly.

As mentioned earlier, another reform that candidates ought to consider is advertising a greater number of campaign messages that clearly state their policy positions. They should also pay special attention to distinguishing their positions from those of the opposition candidate. Such a shift could help Latinos learn which issues Democrats "own" and which ones Republicans "own" and how this relates to political ideology. Furthermore, if candidates want to gain the allegiance of Latinos, they have to start taking the necessary steps to encourage party loyalty based on shared issue and policy concerns. Like other Americans, Latinos are concerned about the issues that impact their daily lives: health insurance, jobs and the economy, and education. Latinos generally tend to be fiscally liberal but socially conservative (DeSipio 1996), which makes it difficult to categorize them as solidly liberal or conservative. Candidates need to take a definitive and concrete stand on the issues, however, if they want to win Latinos' support and allegiance not just for one election, but also for years to come.

Exposure to more-informative political ads in Spanish would also enable Spanish-dominant Latinos to learn something substantive about the candidates, the political parties, and the greater U.S. political system. This would make the latest newcomers feel welcomed by the political parties, and such feelings may motivate Latinos and other immigrants who have not yet naturalized to do so. A shift in candidates' Spanish-language advertising strategies could also increase Spanish-dominant Latinos' levels of political efficacy, rates of participation, and overall levels of political knowledge. Whether or not current and aspiring politicians have fully realized it, Latinos and other racial and ethnic minorities will become a sizable part of the American electorate, so it is in candidates' best interest, and in the interest of concerned citizens, to enable Latinos to become active and informed participants in an essential part of the democratic process.

# 8 Epilogue: The 2008 Campaigns

*"Nobody can make it to the White House without Univision."*
**—Jorge Ramos, anchorman for *Noticiero* Univision**[1]

THE QUOTE FROM LONG-TIME NEWS ANCHOR JORGE RAMOS succinctly captures one of the central arguments of this book. As America's most watched Spanish-language broadcast television network, Univision is the gateway through which politicians can communicate to the millions of Spanish-speaking voters in the United States. This form of political communication enables candidates to tailor very specific messages to this group of voters, with very little risk that non-Spanish speakers will be exposed to them. Without such a medium, candidates would miss out on the opportunity to target an increasingly important segment of the nation's electorate. To be sure, the 2008 presidential campaigns took full advantage of this media outlet. Univision Communications estimated sales of approximately $37 million on paid political advertising.[2] Moreover, then-Democratic-candidate and now-president Barack Obama is estimated to have spent approximately $20 million on Latino outreach efforts, which is more than twice the combined amount spent by Kerry and Bush in 2004.[3] These resources were used primarily to broadcast Spanish-language ads in the battleground states with sizeable Latino populations—Colorado, Florida, New Mexico, and Nevada. Some of these funds were also directed at the grassroots level; Obama's team emulated outreach efforts created by John F. Kennedy's 1960 presidential campaign and established "Viva Obama!" clubs across the country. The goal of these organizations was to provide information about the candidate and, of course, to get Latinos to the polls in November.

Such strategies proved to be a wise move on the part of Obama and the Democrats; he not only secured two-thirds of the Latino vote but also won more than a majority of the popular vote (53 percent). Obama's share of the popular vote translated into 365 electoral votes, which is considerably more than the 270 electoral votes needed to win the presidency. According to most media reports, the fact that the crucial swing states of Florida, Nevada, Colorado, and New Mexico all went from "red" in 2004 to "blue" in 2008 can be attributed largely to the Latino vote (Preston 2008). Indeed, with Latinos in Florida constituting 11 percent of registered voters and those in Nevada and Colorado constituting 9 percent of registered voters in each state, they had the numbers that could have tipped the election in either direction. As Chapter 1 discussed, a Democratic victory in Florida is no small feat, as only two other Democrats had managed it since 1968.[4] Although in 2004 the majority of Florida's Latino population cast their ballots in favor of Bush, in 2008 the majority (57 percent) supported the Democratic candidate. Thus, it is likely that Obama's campaign efforts played some role in the shifts in political preferences among Latinos in Florida and other states. This epilogue briefly reviews the campaign tactics used to target Latino voters in the primaries and caucuses as well as in the general election. Comprehensive advertising data, akin to that used throughout this book, is yet to be available for the 2008 elections. As such, the following discussion is unable to compare the content of Spanish- and English-language ads in a manner consistent with the analysis presented in Chapter 4. Nonetheless, information does exist on the Spanish-language ads created by the 2008 presidential candidates, which makes it possible to draw some inferences about any overarching themes or messages.

## The Primary Elections

The importance of the Latino electorate was understood from the onset of the presidential campaign season, particularly among the Democratic contenders. September 9, 2007, marked the seventh in a series of nineteen Democratic Party debates, and the first ever nationally televised bilingual debate. The questions and answers of each of the participants were instantly translated from English to Spanish.[5] The fact that this debate was broadcast in both languages is likely due to one of its sponsors, Univision. Many political observers viewed this debate as a historic moment, and according to Maria Elena Salinas, Univision anchor and co-moderator of the debate, the format of the debate was a "a sign of respect" to the Latino electorate (Garvin 2007, A1).

Although it is not new for presidential contenders to begin their Spanish-language ad buys during the primaries and caucuses, the 2008 campaigns witnessed a significant increase in the resources devoted to such efforts. According to Segal (2008), more than $4 million went toward Spanish-language advertising in the 2008 primaries and caucuses. This figure exceeds the amount allocated to televised Spanish-language advertising in the past two presidential primaries combined. One key reason for this increased attention is that many states with large Latino populations decided to hold their primary elections earlier on in the season. It was Obama and former Democratic contender Bill Richardson who aired the first Spanish-language ads in the summer of 2007. These political spots were intended for Latino voters participating in the Nevada caucuses scheduled for January 19, 2008, because that was the first state on the primary and caucus calendar with a sizeable Latino population. In December 2007, then-senator Hillary Clinton launched her Spanish-language campaign by airing a radio spot in both Iowa and New Hampshire. Clinton also reached out to Spanish speakers before the Nevada caucus with a Spanish-language televised ad titled "La Voz de los Que No Tienen Voz" (The Voice of the Voiceless), in which she is depicted as an advocate and friend of Latinos. She is portrayed as someone who has "worked in favor of the interests of [their] community for decades and she always delivers." [6] Republican candidates also began their Spanish-language campaigns early in the primary and caucus season. Three of the contenders vying for the Republican nomination, Rudy Giuliani, John McCain, and Mitt Romney, produced Spanish-language television or radio ads aimed at Latino voters in Florida, which had its primary election scheduled for January 29, 2008. Because the majority of Latinos in Florida supported Bush in 2004, the decision to target this group very early on in the campaign seemed quite reasonable.

As mentioned before, several states with sizeable Latino populations, including Arizona, California, Connecticut, Colorado, and New Mexico, were holding their primaries on Super Tuesday, which was moved up a month earlier in that election year, from March to February. In light of the fierce competition between Clinton and Obama for the Democratic Party's nomination, their Spanish-language ad buys increased considerably. Clinton's Spanish-language ad "Nuestra Amiga" (Our Friend) was broadcast in Arizona, California, Connecticut, and New York. As in the ad broadcast in Nevada, "Nuestra Amiga" portrays Clinton as someone who understands Latinos and "respects [their] culture and understands the problems that affect [their] community."[7] This particular ad would fit squarely within the framework of identification theory (Connaughton 2005; Connaughton and Jarvis 2004; Benoit 2000).

Recall that this theory expects that candidates will craft their political messages by associating themselves, either through symbols or personal experiences, with the group in question. But as the main findings from Chapter 6 highlight, a downside to such ads is that many Spanish-speaking Latinos do not learn much from them, especially compared with how much voters learn from policy-focused ads.

Based on the best information available when this book went to press, Obama produced three Spanish-language ads for the Super Tuesday primaries, "Hope," "El Nos Entiende" (He Understands Us), and "Gutierrez." In the ad titled "Gutierrez," Illinois congressman Luis Gutierrez, who is of Latino origin, speaks about Obama's involvement as a community activist in Chicago and of his participation in the immigration rallies of May 2006. The congressman goes on to mention Obama's commitment to immigration reform. The "Hope" ad also featured an endorsement from an elected official very prominent in the Latino community, Massachusetts senator Edward Kennedy. In "El Nos Entiende" (He Understands Us), Obama attempts to connect to Latinos based on their shared minority status. The ad states that Latinos "know what it feels like being used as a scapegoat just because of [their] background and last name. And no one understands this better than Barack Obama!"[8] These ads are further reflective of identification theory, because the messages in Obama's ads emphasize the commonalities between him and the Latino community.

An independent effort aside from the official campaign also emerged in support of Obama. Particularly successful in its reach, a web music video titled "Viva Obama" featured a mariachi band singing about Obama's background as a community organizer and about his proposed health care plan. The video, produced by Nueva Vista Media, Inc., gained immediate popularity on YouTube and was viewed approximately 500,000 times by February 2008 (Segal 2008).[9] The creator of the video, Miguel Orozco, wanted to produce a video that was "well thought out" and contained an "uplifting message [as well as one mentioning] issues." Orozco also aimed to develop an ad that differed from the typical Spanish-language campaign, which he described as "sterile," with a "deliberate strategy to play it safe" and that does "just enough to show [that candidates] care."[10]

The outcomes from the Super Tuesday primaries and caucuses produced no outright winner for the Democratic nomination, so the next big battle, especially for the Latino vote, was the primary election in Texas, held on

March 4, 2008. It is estimated that the Clinton campaign spent approximately $730,000 and that Obama allocated $970,000 for Spanish-language ad buys in Texas. Obama's campaign produced the Spanish-language ads "Oportunidad" (Opportunity), "Demostro Caracter" (Showed Character), and "Como un Padre" (Like a Father) for this election.[11] The ad "Como un Padre" begins with the statement, "As a father, his thoughts, naturally, are focused on the future," and continues that he therefore intends to open doors for the future of Latino children. The ad goes on to mention some pertinent issues for families—health care for all children, financial aid for students, and a new law that will enable families to retain their homes. Although the ad does include policy-related messages, in no way does it actually reveal how Obama would provide all children access to health care or specify the manner in which the federal government would assist in the housing crisis. As such, these policy messages can be characterized more as simple policy statements than as explained or complex policy messages. Even in the final days of the Democratic primary and caucus season, Latinos remained a visible and important voting group to the presidential contenders. The fact that Puerto Rico was scheduled second to last on the Democratic primary and caucus calendar is the likely reason for this sustained interest. Thus, both contenders for the Democratic party nomination made several campaign stops in Puerto Rico and targeted Spanish-speakers there with television and radio ads (Grunwald 2008). Although Puerto Ricans overwhelmingly supported Clinton by a margin of more than 2 to 1, Clinton was still short of the necessary 2,118 delegate votes. In the end, it was the last two primary races that ultimately decided the 2008 Democratic presidential nominee. On June 3, 2008, Obama clinched the party's nomination by winning in South Dakota and Montana.

## The General Election

The best information available as this book went to press shows that Obama and the Democratic National Committee produced six Spanish-language ads for the general election, whereas John McCain, the Republican presidential nominee, and the Republican National Committee created thirteen Spanish-language ads.[12] Independent groups, such as the National Rifle Association (NRA), Born Alive Truth Organization, and the Service Employees International Union (SEIU), also joined in the efforts to target the Spanish-speaking electorate. McCain took advantage of both Spanish-language radio and television ads, broadcasting them in the battleground states of Nevada, New

Mexico, and Colorado. The content of these ads included information about immigration, Latino service in the armed forces, and the Colombia Free Trade Agreement. The ads presented biographical information about McCain as well. Several of these commercials also featured Frank Gamboa, who is Latino and was McCain's Naval Academy roommate. McCain also produced several attack ads, one of which questioned Obama's experience and another that accused Obama and the Democrats of supporting a tax on small business. The second negative ad goes on to accuse Obama of voting against immigration reform efforts that included a guest-worker program, a pathway to citizenship, and securing the nation's borders.[13] The use of negative ads is relatively new to Spanish-language advertising, as most previous presidential candidates opted to convey their messages in a positive manner. Several recurring themes emerged among the positive ads used in the 2008 presidential campaign—military service, families, children, and the issues of immigration and education.

Obama's two television ads, "No Hay Mayor Obligacion" (There is No Greater Obligation) and "Dos Caras" (Two Faces), were also crafted in a negative fashion. The former attacked McCain for claiming that the "fundamentals of [the] economy are strong" and criticized him for making such a statement in light of the current economic hardships that faced the nation.[14] The latter, a response to McCain's attack ad, has Obama finding fault with McCain's decision to abandon immigration reform. The ad also contains a visual image of conservative radio talk show host Rush Limbaugh expressing the following sentiments: "Mexicans are stupid and unqualified" and "shut your mouth or get out" (O'Keefe 2008). Obama's other ad, "Un Mensaje de Barack Obama" (A Message from Barack Obama), focused on the theme of the American dream, which, according to the commercial, voters would be one step closer to achieving if they cast their ballots for him.[15]

In the final days of the campaign, Obama aired his 30-minute infomercial, "Barack Obama: American Stories," not only on several network television stations (CBS, NBC, and FOX) but also on the largest Spanish-language network, Univision. The decision to broadcast this ad on Univision speaks to the importance of Latinos in this election. As Manny Diaz, Democratic mayor of Miami, expressed, "This ad buy is historical. The fact that it will air on Univision is a testament [to] the campaign's outreach to the Hispanic community" (O'Keefe 2008). Overall, the content of both candidates' Spanish-language ads strayed little from that of those used by previous presidential contenders, although the use of negative and untruthful advertising was more prominent in their Spanish-language campaigns

In addition to these advertising efforts, McCain and Obama reached out to Latinos by participating in several Latino-specific events. The two presidential contenders addressed the nation's Latino political leaders at the National Association for Latino Elected Officials (NALEO) conference in June 2008. Obama's opening and closing remarks emphasized his immigrant background and his experience working with the Mexican-American Legal Defense and Education Fund (MALDEF) and other Latino leaders as a civil rights attorney in Chicago. Obama also spoke about the need to reform immigration policies so that they will "secure our borders, and punish employers who exploit immigrant labor; reform [will] finally [bring] the twelve million people who are here illegally out of the shadows by requiring them to take steps to become legal citizens . . . that is a priority that I will pursue from my very first day."[16] Moreover, Obama discussed the need to end the housing crisis, create new jobs, improve schools, and provide health insurance to millions of uninsured Latinos. Finally, he emphasized the critical role of the Latino vote, stating that "this election could well come down to how many Latinos turn out to vote." In McCain's speech at the NALEO conference, he too recognized the importance of Latinos, but only in terms of their military service and their contributions "to the culture, economy and security of the country."[17] Unlike Obama, McCain did not talk about the significance of Latinos in the political arena. McCain also discussed tax policy, and the business tax rate in particular, because there are "two million Latino-owned businesses in America." In addition, he mentioned the need for reforming education, lowering barriers to trade, and decreasing the nation's dependence on foreign oil. Regarding comprehensive immigration reform, McCain recognized the need to "secure our borders first, while respecting the dignity and rights of citizens and legal residents of the United States." He made no mention, however, of immigration reform being a priority in his administration, which sharply contrasted with Obama's position.

Both candidates also spoke at the annual conferences of the League of United Latin American Citizens (LULAC), the nation's largest and oldest Latino organization, and the National Council of La Raza (NCLR), which is the largest Latino civil rights group in the U.S. Obama's speech at each of these conferences reverberated many of the themes from his NALEO address— making immigration reform a main priority in his first year in office, providing affordable health care, reforming the education system, and addressing the mortgage crisis. He also introduced his small-business plan that would provide a tax credit to employers who offered health insurance to their employees. Moreover, Obama reemphasized the importance of the Latino vote in the upcoming election. In his NCLR speech, he stated, "If you have any doubt about whether you can make a difference, just remember how, back in 2004, 40,000 registered Latino voters in New Mexico didn't turn out on election day. Senator Kerry lost that state by fewer than 6,000 votes . . . In 2008, an estimated 170,000 Latinos in New Mexico aren't registered to vote. I know how powerful this community is. Just think how powerful you could be on November 4th if you translate your numbers into votes."[18]

McCain's address at the NCLR conference also overlapped with the speech he gave at the NALEO conference. He once again emphasized the need to create more jobs, offering economic incentives to small businesses, and he proposed a health-care plan that would provide households with a $5,000 tax credit in order to make their own health-care decisions. McCain also outlined his "HOME" plan that "allows families who need help to apply—either at their local post office or online—for a new, guaranteed, fixed-rate, thirty-year mortgage that will allow them to remain in their home and raise their family with dignity."[19] Although these speeches included the policy plans and proposals of both candidates, they were not being communicated to the vast majority of the Latino electorate. Instead, those attending these events were mostly members of the media and community and business leaders.[20] Nonetheless, the candidates' appearances at the conferences of the major Latino civil rights organizations further demonstrates the importance of the Latino vote. In the last days of the campaign, in what has become a tradition for presidential nominees, Obama and McCain appeared on Univision's longest-running variety program, *Sabado Gigante*. Both candidates provided pre-taped interviews that aired on November 1, just days before the election.

Much like the outreach efforts we saw in the 2000 and 2004 presidential campaigns, both Obama and McCain focused on several symbolic and nonpolicy messages in their ads as a means to connect with Latinos. Among McCain's and Obama's Spanish-language ads that are publicly available, a total of approximately 54 percent feature a Latino. Moreover, 29 percent of these ads focused on the favored candidate's personal qualities, whereas a significantly larger number (54 percent) chose to emphasize the qualities of the opposing candidate. McCain emphasized his service in the military as the common thread between him and the many Latinos who serve in the armed forces. Recall that this strategy is much like the one developed by Kerry in his Spanish-language ads. Obama also highlighted part of his personal background as a way to connect with Latinos. Along with his shared status as a racial and ethnic minority, he emphasized in several of his Spanish-language ads that his father was an immigrant from Kenya. Obviously, the fact that Latinos are largely an immigrant population makes this particular theme salient and relevant to them. Symbols such as the American dream and themes related to it (that is, opportunity and hope) were, as in past elections, key fixtures in the presidential candidates' political ads. And consistent with the Spanish-language ads used in presidential, congressional, and gubernatorial races from 2000 to 2004, McCain's and Obama's ads included endorsements from prominent Latino elected officials.

Education, health care, and jobs appear to be the topics most frequently mentioned in the candidates' Spanish-language ads. How these messages were expressed and the extent to which they conform to the theory of information-based advertising cannot be determined without a complete content analysis of both Spanish- and English-language ads.[21] One notable trend in this campaign, however, was the number of fraudulent claims made by the two candidates in their televised Spanish-language ads. Recall that one of Mc-Cain's negative ads criticized Obama and the Democrats for not passing the immigration reform bill proposed in 2006. This statement was false, because Obama favored immigration reform and a pathway to citizenship, which was one aspect of the reforms that McCain did not support. Obama was guilty of the same crime; his attack ad, "Dos Caras," falsely links Rush Limbaugh with McCain. In reality, Limbaugh berated McCain for supporting a less restrictive immigration bill. Although both the print and television media alerted the public to these inaccuracies, candidates may nonetheless continue to use this strategy in their Spanish-language ads.

As the Latino electorate has solidified its role as a key constituency in American politics, candidates and political leaders must decide whether they want to continue to appeal to this electorate based primarily on the ethnic and cultural identity of its members, or whether they will incorporate into their political ads more-informative messages about their policy proposals. A decision by politicians to expound on their policies in their Spanish-language ads would contribute to the political well being of a significant portion of the Latino population. From a broader perspective, such a decision would also help to uphold the democratic values that we as a nation hold so dear.

# Appendix A: Coding the Advertisements

## Method

Four undergraduate research assistants coded the advertisements using the questions that follow (in the next section) and the storyboards provided by the Wisconsin Advertising Project for 2000 and 2002 (Goldstein et al. 2002; Goldstein and Rivlin 2005, 2007a, 2007b). Three graduate assistants coded the 2004 ads. Each storyboard was compiled as a pdf (portable document format) file. Intercoder reliability was calculated using Cohen's κ test statistic, which has a scale that ranges from 0 to 1, with 1 indicating perfect reliability and 0 indicating almost no agreement (Stemler 2001). This measure accounts for the probability that agreements between the coders occurred intentionally and by chance. I coded 10 percent of the sample in order to calculate the κ score. This technique is considered standard practice to determine reliability (Stemler 2001). The following equation was used to calculate Cohen's κ test statistic:

$$\kappa = \frac{P_a - P_c}{1 - P_c}$$

where

$P_a$ is the proportion of stories in which there is agreement between the coders, and

$P_c$ is the proportion of stories in which there is agreement by chance.

For the advertising data, $\kappa = .66$. Landis and Koch's (1977, 165) scale to interpret this test statistic is as follows: 0.0–0.20 indicates slight agreement,

0.21–0.40 fair agreement, 0.41–0.60 moderate agreement, 0.61–0.80 substantial agreement, and 0.81–1.00 almost perfect agreement. Because a κ test statistic reveals that the strength of agreement is substantial, I am confident in the reliability of the data and the coding scheme used.

Research assistants were asked to go through each question and code it as a *1* if the ad contains the item and *0* if not. They were also told that an ad could contain more than one of the items from the questionnaire. Moreover, they were informed that an ad could be coded as a *1* for question 2, parts a–d. These questions are not mutually exclusive, so they were told that an ad could contain multiple types of policy content. If they were unsure or unclear about whether an ad contained the item, they were asked to code it as missing data.

## Codebook Used for Content Analysis of Ads

1. Does the ad contain any policy/issue statements? If yes, go to question 2; if not, go to question 3.
2. If so, how are the policy/issues discussed in the ad?
    a. Policy/issue is phrased so that it requires the viewer of the ad to know what the status quo (current legislation or the current status of an issue) is in order to have an opinion on the issue (e.g., Candidate X favors an increase in minimum wage, Candidate X supports prayer in schools).
    b. Policy/issue is explained or described in the ad, so the viewer knows what the issue is about from the text in the ad (e.g., natural gas is safe, effective, and more cost efficient than electricity).
    c. Policy/issue is one that the viewer would immediately be familiar with; it would be considered a "simple" policy message (e.g., Candidate X is pro-life, believes in safe schools).
    d. Policy/issue is stated in way that would benefit everyone. Policy/issue is stated in a normative, positive way (e.g., Candidate X is fighting for smaller class sizes, clean schools, better education, protecting Medicare, reduced crime, cutting unemployment, increased jobs).
3. Does the ad make any references to specific bills or pieces of legislation (e.g., HR 463, The Sarbanes-Oxley Act, The Patients' Bill of Rights)?
4. The ad discusses the favored candidate's personal qualities (a list of qualities was provided based on those used in the Wisconsin Advertising Project codebook).

5. The ad discusses the opposing candidate's personal qualities (refer to list below).

6. Latino in the ad, no speaking role

6a. Latino in the ad, speaking role

7. African American in the ad, no speaking role

7a. African American in the ad, speaking role

8. Asian American in the ad, no speaking role

8a. Asian American in the ad, speaking role

9. Rural images / farmers in the ad, no speaking role

9a. Rural images / farmers in the ad, speaking role

10. Someone carrying a gun in the ad

11. Ad mentions the phrase "American Dream"

12. Senior citizen in the ad, no speaking role

12a. Senior citizen in the ad, speaking role

13. Disabled individual in the ad, no speaking role

13a. Disabled individual in the ad, speaking role

14. Military images/anything relating to war in the ad

15. Students (in a classroom setting) featured in the ad, no speaking role

15a. Students (in a classroom setting) featured in the ad, no speaking role

16. Blue-collar workers in the ad (e.g., construction workers, factory workers, maintenance workers), no speaking role

16a. Blue-collar workers in the ad (e.g., construction workers, factory workers, maintenance workers), speaking role

17. Sports images in the ad (e.g., children playing soccer)

18. Children in the ad

19. A woman in the ad, no speaking role

19a. A woman in the ad, speaking role

Examples of issues/policies (based on the 2000 Wisconsin Advertising Project codebook: Taxes; Deficit/surplus/budget/debt; Minimum wage; Other economic reference; Suicide; Gun control; Other reference to social issues; Attendance record; Crime; Drugs; Death penalty; Other reference to law and order; Ideology; Education; Lottery for education; Child care; Other child-related issues; Personal values; Defense; Veterans; Foreign policy; Bosnia; Other defense/foreign policy; Special interests; Environment; Immigration; Health care; Social Security; Medicare; Welfare; Civil rights/race relations; Campaign finance reform; Government ethics; Tobacco; Affirmative action; Gambling; Farming; Business; Employment/jobs; Poverty; Trade/NAFTA; Political record; Abortion; Homosexuality; Moral values.

**Table A.1** Descriptive statistics for variables presented in Tables 4.4–4.8

|  | Mean | Standard deviation | Range |
|---|---|---|---|
| *District characteristics* |  |  |  |
| Percent with a high-school degree | 81.48 | 6.55 | 29.1, 94.1 |
| Percent Latino | 6.29 | 13.18 | .01, 77.7 |
| Percent Black | 5.81 | 10.52 | .003, 65.9 |
| Percent Asian American | 1.08 | 1.77 | 0.01, 28.8 |
| South | 0.37 | 0.48 | 0, 1 |
| Competitiveness | 22.89 | 23.85 | .28, 94 |
| Distance | 0.31 | .17 | 0, .90 |
| *Candidate specific* |  |  |  |
| Democrat | .51 | .50 | 0, 1 |

# Appendix B: Constructing the Ad Exposure Variable

$$(\text{Ad\_Exposure}_m) = \sum_{a=1}^{a,m} \text{CostPH}_{a,m}$$

where

$\text{Ad\_Exposure}_m$: a measure that indicates the number of advertisements a respondent in the $m^{th}$ media market was exposed to.

$\text{CostPH}_{a,m}$: cost per television household of airing the $a^{th}$ ad in the $m^{th}$ media market.

$_{a,m}$: Number of advertisements aired in the $m^{th}$ media market.

The cost per household of airing an ad serves as a proxy for the likelihood that a given household watched the ad when it aired, because television stations usually charge based on audience size. The cost of broadcasting each ad should be directly proportional to the number of people who saw each ad. I calculated the per household cost to advertise an ad by taking the estimated cost of broadcasting each ad, which is provided in the CMAG data set, and dividing it by the number of television households for the particular media market.

CMAG estimated the cost of airing an ad by relying on the media market in which the ad aired and the average cost of airing an ad in a particular time slot. I then merged this ad exposure variable with each observation in the NAES, based on the respondent's media market. I was able to determine which media market the respondent belonged to because the data set includes the county in which the respondent resides.

I then merge this measure of ad exposure with the NAES data by matching the respondent with advertisements that were broadcast in his or her media market. The respondent's media market was determined by the county that the respondent lived in, represented by the FIPS code. It is likely that some measurement error exists, because this measure does not capture the actual number of advertisements a respondent was exposed to. All measures of ad exposure, however, suffer from shortcomings and measurement errors.

## Details of the 2000 and 2004
## National Annenberg Election Survey (NAES)

The Annenberg School of Communication and the Annenberg Public Policy Center at the University of Pennsylvania conducted the NAES. Schulman, Ronca and Bucuvalas, Inc. and Princeton Survey Research conducted the data processing. The interviews were conducted in the continental United States and Washington, D.C. Each interview lasted for approximately 30 minutes. The following questions were used in the construction of the variables for the probit model.

> *Vote choice.* For president, did you vote [in the general election] for George W. Bush, the Republican; Al Gore, the Democrat; Pat Buchanan of the Reform Party; Ralph Nader of the Green Party; or someone else? 1 Bush; 2 Gore; 3 Buchanan; 4 Nader; 5 Other; 6 Did not vote for president; 998 Don't know; 999 No answer.
>
> *Education.* What is the last grade or class you completed in school? 1 Grade eight or lower; 2 Some high school, no diploma; 3 High-school diploma or equivalent; 4 Technical or vocational school after high school; 5 Some college, no degree; 6 Associates or two-year college degree; 7 Four-year college degree; 8 Graduate or professional school after college, no degree; 9 Graduate or professional degree; 998 Don't know; 999 No answer.
>
> *Party ID.* Generally speaking, do you usually think of yourself as a Republican, a Democrat, an independent, or something else? 1 Republican; 2 Democrat; 3 Independent; 4 Verbatim; 998 Don't know; 999 No answer. My measure of partisanship is captured by two dummy variables, one indicating Democrats and the other Republicans. They are coded as a *1* if the respondent identifies with his or her respective party, and *0* otherwise. The baseline category is respondents who are Independents.

*Political ideology.* Generally speaking, would you describe your political views as very conservative, conservative, moderate, liberal, or very liberal? 1 Very conservative; 2 Conservative; 3 Moderate; 4 Liberal; 5 Very liberal; 998 Don't know; 999 No answer.

*Restrict abortion.* Make it harder for a woman to get an abortion—should the federal government do this or not? 1 Yes; 2 No; 998 Don't Know; 999 No answer.

*Social Security.* Social Security benefits—should the federal government spend more money on this, the same as now, less, or no money at all? 1 More; 2 Same; 3 Less; 4 None; 998 Don't Know; 999 No answer.

*Watch news.* How many days in the past week did you watch the national network news on TV—by national network news, I mean Peter Jennings on ABC, Dan Rather on CBS, Tom Brokaw on NBC, Fox News, or UPN News? Range 0–7; 998 Don't Know; 999 No answer.

*Government interest.* Some people seem to follow what is going on in government and public affairs most of the time, whether there is an election or not. Others are not that interested. Would you say you follow what is going on in government and public affairs most of the time, some of the time, only now and then, or hardly at all? 1 Most of the time; 2 Some of the time; 3 Now and then; 4 Hardly at all; 998 Don't Know; 999 No answer.

Following is how I coded the variables used in the vote choice and turnout models. Demographics: Gender is coded as a dichotomous variable, with a *1* indicating that the respondent is a woman, *0* indicating that the respondent is a man. The same is true for one's marital status, with a *1* indicating that the respondent is married, and *0* otherwise. Income is a categorical variable, ranging from those who make less than $10,000 annually to those who earn $150,000 or more annually. A respondent's age is a continuous variable, ranging from 18 to 96 years of age in 2000 and 18 to 97 years of age in 2004. Finally, education is measured as two dummy variables, one denoting those with a high-school degree and the other those with less than a high-school education. Education at the college level and beyond is the omitted category. The three variables that capture a respondent's ethnicity are all treated as dichotomous variables. Each ethnicity variable is coded as *1* if the respondent is from that ethnic group (for example, Mexican), and *0* otherwise. The baseline category comprises respondents from South or Central America.

## Appendix C: Voter Learning and Vote-Choice Model Specification

See Tables 6.2, 6.3, 6.6, and 6.7 for more information.

### Dependent Variable

*Vote Choice*: I created a dummy variable that is coded as *1* if the respondent voted for Gore, and *0* if they voted for Bush.

*Political Knowledge in 2000*: I created an index of political learning and relied on responses to twenty-four factual political questions from the 2000 NAES. For all the questions, with the exception of questions 15–19, the answers available to respondents were *Bush, Gore, both, neither, don't know,* or *no answer.* The more questions that a respondent identified correctly, the higher his or her level of political knowledge. Following are the questions used to construct the political knowledge variable: (1) Bush or Gore favors biggest tax cut; (2) Bush or Gore favors paying down debt most; (3) Bush or Gore favors using Medicare surplus to cut taxes; (4) Bush or Gore favors biggest increase for Social Security; (5) Bush or Gore favors investing Social Security into the stock market; (6) Bush or Gore favors school vouchers; (7) Bush or Gore favors universal health care for children; (8) Bush or Gore favors right to sue HMOs; (9) Bush or Gore favors restricting abortion; (10) Bush or Gore favors death penalty; (11) Bush or Gore supported concealed handgun law; (12) Bush or Gore favors soft-money ban; (13) Bush or Gore favors gays in military; (14) Bush or Gore favors $3,000 tax credit for health care; (15) Does Bush favor selling strategic oil reserve for winter heating? (16) Does Bush favor a soft-money ban?

(17) Does Gore favor a soft-money ban? (18) Does Bush favor handgun licenses? (19) Does Gore favor handgun licenses? (20) Bush or Gore is governor; (21) Bush or Gore is a senator; (22) Bush or Gore is the son of a former senator; (23) Bush or Gore is a born-again Christian; and (24) Bush or Gore spoke at Bob Jones University.

*Political Knowledge in 2004*: The political knowledge variable in 2004 is based on a respondent's ability to correctly identify the presidential candidate's issue position on eleven questions. Respondents were asked whether Kerry or Bush favors (1) reducing the number of frivolous law suits; (2) an assault weapons ban; (3) making abortion more difficult; (4) investing Social Security in the stock market; (5) reimporting drugs from Canada; (6) eliminating overseas tax breaks to cut taxes for companies that create jobs; (7) eliminating the estate tax; and (8) making Bush tax cuts permanent. They were also asked (9) whether Bush or Kerry was a former prosecutor. Finally, interviewees were asked whether Bush or Kerry favors (10) government health insurance for children and workers, and (11) cutting the deficit in half. The responses available were *Bush, Kerry, both, neither, don't know,* or *no answer*.

## Independent Variables

*Political Dispositions*: Two dummy variables were created to measure partisanship. For the Democrat variable, a *1* indicates respondents who identified as Democrats, and *0* otherwise. The Republican variable was coded in the same manner, with a *1* indicating that a respondent identified with the Republican party and *0* otherwise. The omitted category is respondents who identified as Independents. Ideology is treated as a continuous variable, with a *1* denoting those respondents who are very liberal and a *5* those respondents who are very conservative.

*Issue Variables*: Abortion is treated as a dichotomous variable, with a *1* indicating respondents who are in favor of restricting abortion and a *0* indicating respondents who are against restricting abortion. School vouchers is also coded as a dummy variable, with a *1* indicating those respondents who support the use of school vouchers, and a *0* denoting respondents who are against school vouchers. The variable on federally sponsored health insurance is a categorical variable, ranging from *more, some, less, or no government spending on health care for the uninsured*. The variable for Social Security was coded as a dummy variable, with *1* indicating those favoring more or the same amount of spending on Social Security, and *0* indicating those favoring less to no government spending. The three variables measuring national economic indicators are dichotomous, with the omitted category being those respondents who perceive the national economy as excellent. The variables capturing evaluations of one's personal finances are also dichotomous, with the baseline category being those individuals who perceive their personal finances as excellent.

*Demographics*: Two dichotomous variables measure a respondent's level of education. The first education variable was coded as *1* if a respondent has no high-school degree, and *0* otherwise. The other education variable was coded as *1* if the respondent has a high-school degree, and *0* otherwise. The baseline category is respondents with some college education or beyond. Income was treated as a categorical variable, ranging from those who earn less than $10,000 to those earning $150,000 or more. Age was also treated as a continuous variable, and ranges from 18–97. Two dummy variables capture a respondent's religious affiliation. The first was coded as a *1* if the respondent identified as a Catholic, and *0* otherwise. The other religion variable was coded as a *1* if the respondent identified as a Protestant, and *0* otherwise. A respondent's citizenship was treated as a dichotomous variable, with a *1* indicating that the respondent is a U.S. citizen, and *0* otherwise.

*Media/Campaign Exposure*: There were two variables capturing a respondent's self-reported levels of media exposure (watching local television news and reading the newspaper) in a given week. Thus, the variables range from 0–7, so that *0* means the respondent did not watch television news or read the newspaper in a given week, and *7* means the respondent watched television news and read the newspaper on a daily basis. The campaign contact variable is treated as a dichotomous variable, with a *1* indicating that the respondent was personally contacted by a campaign, and *0* otherwise.

*Advertising Exposure*: The variables measuring a respondent's exposure to political ads were constructed in the same manner as the political advertising variables in the models of vote choice and turnout.

# Notes

## Chapter 1

1. This quote is from Adam J. Segal's 2002 report, "The Hispanic Priority: The Spanish-Language Television Battle for the Hispanic Vote in the 2000 U.S Presidential Election."

2. This is especially true considering that Clinton won Florida in 1996, marking only the second time that a Democrat has won that state. Part of the victory was attributed to the inroads that Clinton had made with the Latino electorate.

3. Moreover, as Adam J. Segal, director of the Hispanic Voter Project at Johns Hopkins University, notes, the insufficient advertising funds spent on the Miami Latino community was "an error that surely cost more than 537 votes there and the entire national election" (2006, 2). Likewise, Stephan Dinan made the following observation in a July 24, 2008, article in the *Washington Times*, "It's become almost axiomatic among campaign consultants that if Democrat Al Gore had put more effort into Hispanic vote outreach in Florida in the 2000 presidential race, he would have won the presidency."

4. The terms *Latino* and *Hispanic* can be used interchangeably; throughout this book, I will use the term *Latino*.

5. Puerto Rico is a protectorate of the United States.

6. As a point of comparison, from 1992 to 2006 African Americans consistently supported the Democratic candidate in both presidential and midterm elections at rates of 80 percent or more, according to national election poll estimates.

7. These exit poll estimates have been disputed by the William C. Velasquez Institute, which conducted its own exit poll in 2004. The institute estimates the Latino vote for Bush to have been much lower, at 35.1 percent. The *Los Angeles Times* also conducted an independent exit poll, finding that 45 percent of Latino voters supported Bush. Finally, the National Annenberg Election Survey estimates that 41 per-

cent of Latinos supported Bush in 2004. Regardless of the precise numbers, the exit polls demonstrate a considerable shift to the Republican Party.

8. It is important to keep in mind that the term *Latino* is a panethnic label that encompasses a diverse group of individuals who vary based on national origin, culture, region, and reasons for immigrating to the U.S. Thus, these socioeconomic and political indicators are reported for the total Latino population, although variations certainly exist by ethnic groups, generational status, language proficiency, and so on.

9. Refer to West (2001), page 52, for a detailed breakdown of the content of advertisements from 1952 to 2000.

10. This strain of research is discussed in greater detail in Chapter 4.

11. Latino surname lists are more accurate than relying on census bureau data alone.

12. According to U.S. Census Bureau estimates (2007), *Garcia* and *Rodriguez* are the eighth and ninth most common surnames in the U.S.

13. The number of Spanish speakers is based on Census 2000 estimates (Guzman 2001) of the Latino population (35.3 million).

14. The storyboard of the ad is available from the University of Wisconsin Advertising Project dataset (2000). File name: gore_national_anthem_spanish.pdf.

15. The storyboard of the ad is available from the University of Wisconsin Advertising Project dataset (2000). File name: gore_veteran.pdf.

16. The advertising data is from the University of Wisconsin Advertising Project (Goldstein et al. 2002; Goldstein and Rivlin 2005, 2007a, 2007b). Each advertisement is compiled as a storyboard, such that its visual images and corresponding text are presented. Advertising data from 2002 and 2004 was obtained from the University of Wisconsin Advertising Project and includes media tracking data from TNSMI/Campaign Media Analysis Group in Washington, DC. The University of Wisconsin Advertising Project was sponsored by a grant from The Pew Charitable Trusts. For the 2000 ads, the data was obtained from a joint project of the Brennan Center for Justice at New York University School of Law and Professor Kenneth Goldstein of the University of Wisconsin–Madison. The Brennan Center–Wisconsin project was sponsored by a grant from The Pew Charitable Trusts. The opinions expressed in this book are those of the author and do not necessarily reflect the views of the University of Wisconsin Advertising Project or The Pew Charitable Trusts.

## Chapter 2

1. The percentage of the foreign-born population has continually increased from 1970 to 2000. In 1970, 19.9 percent of the Latino population was foreign born. The figure was 28.6 percent in 1980 and 35.8 percent in 1990.

2. Although the percentage of foreign-born Asians in the U.S. is also quite high, their economic indicators are much higher than those for Latinos.

3. The amount of political interest and knowledge in the foreign-born population may be lower than it is for Latinos born in the U.S., but since the foreign-born population makes up almost half of the U.S. Latino population, they also drive down the political knowledge rates of the entire group.

4. For the specific questions, see Niemi and Junn (1998, 111).

5. Even when Niemi and Junn controlled for a student's home environment (e.g., structure of household and parents' education level) and individual achievement (e.g., plans of going to a four-year college), the school's civics curriculum remains the most robust predictor of political knowledge.

6. Of course, these are the average rates for Latinos, with variations based on generational status, ethnicity, and so on (Telles and Ortiz 2008).

7. U.S. Census Bureau 2007 estimates.

8. Although I have focused only on the structural inequalities that I believe are most significant in influencing Latinos' rates of political knowledge, other structural factors, such as differences in household configuration, levels of wealth, and occupation, also exist. These factors are important but are closely linked to education levels and nativity.

9. For the exact questions used, refer to Verba and colleagues (1995, 553–556).

10. These percentages are consistent with past presidential voting patterns broken down by ethnic and racial groups (DeSipio 1996).

11. Noncitizens are allowed to vote in several cities and towns across the U.S. (e.g., Takoma Park, Maryland). See Hayduk (2006) for an in-depth discussion of this issue.

12. This type of ad would be considered a policy ad, not a character ad.

13. Based on author's analysis using the 2000–2004 Wisconsin Advertising Project data.

## Chapter 3

1. Television advertising was first used in the presidential election of 1948 (Jamieson 1996). Congressional ads followed two years later in the 1950 campaign of Senator William Benton of Connecticut. Thus, the creation of televised ads that cater to minority groups is a relatively novel practice.

2. This ad is titled "Mrs. JFK" and is available at http://www.livingroomcandidate .org/commercials/1960.

3. ABC Evening News, November 5, 1984.

4. CBS Evening News, November 4, 1984.

5. Television News Archive, Vanderbilt University.

6. ABC Evening News devoted 2 minutes and 10 seconds to discussing the Latino vote on June 29, 1996.

7. Pew Hispanic Survey, "Changing Channels and Crisscrossing Cultures: A Survey of Latinos on the News Media," April 19, 2004, http://www.pewhispanic.org.

8. The title of this ad is "BUSH/I'm a Young Latino" and is available in the University of Wisconsin Advertising Project dataset (2000). File name: BUSH_I'm_A _Young_Latino.pdf.

9. The title of this ad is "Bush/Speech Spanish" and is available in the University of Wisconsin Advertising Project dataset (2000). File name: BUSH_Speech_Spanish .pdf.

10. The Latino population in these cities is 65 percent in Miami, 19.3 percent in Tampa, 39.9 percent in Albuquerque, and 23.6 percent in Las Vegas (U.S. Census Bureau 2007). Media markets are designated based on the county one lives in. For more information about media markets, refer to http://www.nielsenmedia.com.

11. Some of Kerry's Spanish-language ads were "Oportunidades" (Opportunities), "Cultures," "Honor," "Hospital," and "Memorial Day Ad." Examples of Bush Spanish-language ads are "Más Seguros, Más Fuertes" (Safer, Stronger), "Diferencias" (Differences), "Aceptar Responsabilidad" (Accountability), "Prioridades" (Priorities), "Nuestro Pais, Nuestro Presidente" (Our Country, Our President), "Agenda Nacional" (National Agenda), "Dos Planes" (Two Plans), and "Plan Más Trabajos" (Plan for More Jobs).

12. This ad is available in the University of Wisconsin Advertising Project dataset (2004). File name: PRES_KERRY_HUSBAND_AND_FATHER_SPANISH.pdf.

13. This ad is available in the University of Wisconsin Advertising Project dataset (2004). File name: PRES_KERRY_CULTURE_SPANISH.pdf.

14. This ad is available in the University of Wisconsin Advertising Project dataset (2004). File name: PRES_BUSH_ACCOUNTABILITY.pdf.

15. This ad is available in the University of Wisconsin Advertising Project dataset (2004). File name: PRES_BUSH_OUR_COUNTRY_OUR_PRESIDENT.pdf.

16. Keep in mind, though, that the Latino voting eligible population (VEP) for a given state is lower than the state's total Latino population.

17. In "Nuestra Comunidad" (Our Community), the current Los Angeles mayor, Antonio Villaraigosa, is speaking on behalf of Davis, emphasizing Davis's efforts to improve education in California by providing "more resources to keep the best teachers teaching in our neighborhood schools" (Kinnard 2002).

18. The Wisconsin Advertising Project data set contains no information about the content of this ad.

19. *The Almanac of American Politics* (2000–2004), by Michael Barone and Richard Cohen (2004), considered this district to be competitive in each of these election cycles. In 2000, the vote share was 50 percent to 43 percent. In 2002, the vote share was 55 percent to 45 percent. And in 2004, the vote share was 54 percent to 46 percent.

## Chapter 4

1. See Chapter 3 for a more in-depth discussion of the advertising expenditures associated with this election.

2. The difference is statistically significant at the $p = .01$ level.

3. These percentages are also from the Wisconsin Advertising Project dataset, but they are not presented in Table 4.2.

4. While the Wisconsin Advertising Project data includes which show each ad was broadcast on, it does not include a category for the type of show. It was therefore necessary to conduct separate coding for these categories. Nielsen does not make the data on the demographics of a show publicly available, so these categorizations of show types were the next best alternative.

5. In particular, Markus finds that the personal traits of honesty, trustworthiness, and morality are the most important to voters.

6. The universe of cases used for the multivariate analyses are all non-open-seat congressional elections in 2000–2004, including cases in which candidates broadcast Spanish-language ads and those in which they did not. To be sure that there are no systematic differences between races that advertise in Spanish and those that do not, I also estimated a model that included a dummy variable coded as $1$ for those races in which neither of the candidates advertised in Spanish and $0$ for those races in which one or both of the candidates advertised in Spanish. The results remain unchanged.

7. Each of these variables is coded as $1$ if the ad contains the specific policy of interest, and $0$ otherwise.

8. For character ads, the variable is coded as $1$ if either the favored or opposing candidate's personal qualities are mentioned, and $0$ otherwise.

9. Descriptive statistics and the coding of these variables are available in Appendix A, Table A.1.

10. Although this measure does not fully encapsulate all the factors that make up political familiarity, this is the best available data at the congressional and statewide levels.

11. These education statistics are from the U.S. Census Bureau. Even though education is regressed as a function of the distance measure, education and the distance measure are not highly correlated when I control for both variables in the multivariate model.

12. I used Nominate scores to measure candidate ideology (Poole and Rosenthal 1997). To estimate the distance between a candidate's ideological position and that of the median voter in his or her district, I first estimated a predicted Nominate score for each district as a function of the Democratic share of the two-party vote in the 1996 presidential election, the household median income of the district, the percentage of the district's voters with a high-school degree, and whether the district is in a Southern state. I then took the absolute value of the predicted value of each estimate and subtracted it from the candidate's actual DW-Nominate score. This results in the distance measure. The variable ranged from 0–.90, with a mean of .32 and a standard deviation of .17.

13. To capture the percentage of Latinos, Asian Americans, and African Ameri-

cans in a district, I use population data from the U.S. Census Bureau. Although the advertising images from the Wisconsin Advertising Project are still shots taken every 3 to 4 seconds, thus allowing for the possibility that some individuals pictured in an advertisement may be omitted from the screen captures, the researchers involved in the Project included numerous variables pertaining to the visual images in the ads. Thus, I follow the coding practice of the Wisconsin Advertising Project, keeping in mind that some individuals may be omitted.

14. This variable is coded as *1* if it is a Southern district, *0* otherwise.

15. I present these predicted probabilities as first difference estimates and compute them by holding the independent variables at their mean or mode and shifting the variable of interest from its mean to its maximum level for the district characteristics (King et al. 2001). For a candidate's personal attributes, I calculate a hypothetical scenario in which the candidate changes from being a Republican to a Democrat.

16. Estimates of senate and gubernatorial candidates' English-language advertising decisions are similar to House candidates' English-language advertising decisions and are available, by request, from the author.

17. These estimates were computed in the same manner as the predicted probabilities presented in Table 4.7. Estimates are available, by request, from the author.

## Chapter 5

1. See Goldstein and Ridout (2004) for a comprehensive review of this literature.

2. At least 50 interviews were conducted daily, and as many as 300 interviews took place each day at important points in the campaign, such as the days just before and after presidential debates. In 2004, an average of 150 and 300 interviews were conducted daily.

3. For a detailed explanation of how the exposure variable was estimated, refer to Appendix B.

4. For more detailed information on this data set, refer to Chapter 4.

5. Unfortunately, I was unable to estimate a vote-choice model that specifies the particular type of policy in the Spanish-language ads because there was too much collinearity among these policy message variables. In other words, there was not enough variation in the policy messages contained in the Spanish-language presidential ads to allow me to account for the specific type of message.

6. All individuals in the United States live in a designated market area (DMA). The respondents' media market was determined by the county that the respondent lived in, represented by the FIPS code. For a more detailed explanation of media markets and DMAs, refer to http://www.neilsenmedia.com.

7. In the models that look at the impact of Spanish-language advertising on vote choice and turnout, I interact the language in which the respondent took the survey with the advertising exposure variables. Since the interview language variable is

coded as *1* if the respondent took the survey in Spanish, and *0* if he or she took the interview in English, the interaction terms can be interpreted as the impact of the specific ad in question on the likelihood of voting for Gore or Bush among Spanish-dominant Latinos.

8. In 2000, respondents who voted for Nader were excluded from the sample because they constituted only 3 percent of the sample. Given the dichotomous nature of the independent variables, I estimated the vote-choice and turnout models using probit analysis.

9. These estimates are presented in Table 5.3 and were calculated based on a hypothetical respondent (one that contains mean or modal characteristics from the set of explanatory variables) who goes from being exposed to the mean number of the particular ad of interest to an increased number of that particular ad equal to a one-standard-deviation increase in spending.

10. I calculated several counterfactual scenarios in which the amount of advertising exposure is varied, from its mean level to a one-standard-deviation increase, for a hypothetical Latino voter. The hypothetical Latino voter possesses the modal or mean characteristics on each of the independent variables. The calculations were performed with the CLARIFY package in STATA. See King and colleagues (2001) for details.

## Chapter 6

1. The questions used to construct this variable are available in Appendix C.

2. Given that the dependent variable, voter learning, is coded as continuous, I use ordinary-least squares (OLS) regression to estimate this model.

3. The model specification and coding of these variables are available in Appendix C.

4. I constructed a similar variable to measure self-reports on television news-watching. Both of these measures ranged from *0*, meaning that a person does not watch any television news or read the newspaper in a given week, to *7*, indicating that the respondent watched the news or read the newspaper daily.

5. These measures of advertising exposure were calculated in the same manner as in Chapter 4.

6. The 2000 and 2004 NAES are national, rolling cross-sectional (RCS) surveys. Because the surveys were rolling, the pre- and post-interviews did not all take place on the same date. In 2000, the pre-interview surveys were conducted from January 3 to November 6, and the post-interview surveys took place anywhere from November 11 to December 7. In 2004, the pre-election poll took place from July 15 to November 1, and the post-election poll was conducted from November 4 to December 28.

7. Given that the sample of Asian respondents is so small, I did not include them in my analysis.

8. Of course, the ideal situation would be for interviews that are conducted in

Spanish to avoid having literal translations of political terms that are likely to be more meaningful to native-born Americans than they are for the foreign born. See Abrajano and Alvarez (forthcoming) for more discussion on this subject matter.

9. Because the dependent variable is a binary outcome, I estimated the model using probit analysis.

10. I estimated the vote-choice model using survey data from the 2000 and 2004 NAES to remain consistent with the analyses presented in this chapter and those presented in Chapter 4.

11. The descriptive statistics of the variables used in this model are presented in Table 6.8.

12. In 2004, the impact of abortion on the voting behavior of English-dominant Latinos was nearly identical, at 24 percent.

13. Dimofte and colleagues (2004) found this effect on consumer-based ads, but such an effect has yet to be found for political ads.

## Chapter 8

1. *Noticiero* is the news program for Univision. The quote is from "Sabado Gigante for Obama, McCain," by John Eggerton, *Broadcasting & Cable*, October 30, 2008.

2. "Politics pays off for Spanish TV," by Daniel Roth, *McClatchy Newspapers*, October 27, 2008.

3. "Democrats to Spend $20 Million to Woo Latino Voters," by Michael Falcone, *The New York Times, The Caucus: The Politics and Government Blog of the Times*, July 29, 2008. http://thecaucus.blogs.nytimes.com/2008/07/29/democrats-to-spend-20-million-to-woo-latino-voters/.

4. Bill Clinton won Florida in 1996 (48 percent versus 42 percent) and Jimmy Carter won it in 1976 (51.9 percent versus 46.6 percent).

5. Candidates were not allowed to speak in Spanish, even though New Mexico governor Bill Richardson was fluent in Spanish. He was required to adhere to the format.

6. The ad and its script are available at the Political Advertising Resource Center, a program of the Center for Political Communication and Civic Leadership at the University of Maryland, http://www.parc.umd.edu/Campaign2008ProjectDems .htm.

7. The ad can be viewed at http://www.parc.umd.edu/Campaign2008Project Dems.htm.

8. The ad is available at the Political Advertising Resource Center, a program of the Center for Political Communication and Civic Leadership at the University of Maryland, http://www.parc.umd.edu/Campaign2008ProjectDems.htm.

9. Orozco also produced another Spanish-language song, "Come Se Dice," which was used at campaign events targeting Hispanics (Jordan 2008).

10. Phone interview with Miguel Orozco, October 19, 2009.

11. The ads, "Demostro Character" and "Como Padre," are available at http://www.parc.umd.edu/Campaign2008ProjectDems.htm.

12. These estimates are based on the campaign advertising database of Stanford University's Political Communication Lab, http://pcl.stanford.edu/.

13. This ad is titled "Which Side Are They On?" and was aired on 9/12/08.

14. The ad is available at http://pcl.stanford.edu/campaigns/2008/bogen.html.

15. The ad is available at http://pcl.stanford.edu/campaigns/2008/bogen.html.

16. The transcript of Obama's speech is available at http://www.realclearpolitics.com/articles/2008/06/obamas_remarks_to_naleo.html.

17. The transcript of McCain's speech is available at http://www.realclearpolitics.com/articles/2008/06/mccains_speech_to_naleo.html.

18. The transcript of the speech is speech is available at http://www.nclr.org/content/viewpoints/detail/52978.

19. The transcript of the speech is speech is available at http://www.nclr.org/content/viewpoints/detail/52978.

20. In addition, these events were not free of charge and therefore not open to the public.

21. 2008 campaign data from the Wisconsin Advertising Project was not publicly available at the time this book went to press.

# References

Abrajano, Marisa A. 2005. "Who Evaluates a Presidential Candidate by Using Non-Policy Campaign Messages?" *Political Research Quarterly* 58: 55–67.

Abrajano, Marisa A., and R. Michael Alvarez. Forthcoming. *New Faces, New Voices: The Hispanic Electorate in America.* Princeton University Press, Princeton, NJ.

Abrajano, Marisa A., R. Michael Alvarez, and Jonathan Nagler. 2008. "The 2004 Hispanic Vote: Insecurity and Moral Concerns." *Journal of Politics* 70(2): 368–382.

Abramson, Paul R., John H. Aldrich, and David W. Rohde. 2002. *Change and Continuity in the 2000 Elections.* CQ Press, Washington DC.

Agranoff, Robert. 1972. *The New Style in Election Campaigns.* Holbrook, Boston.

Alesina, Alberto, Nouriel Roubini, and Gerald D. Cohen. 1997. *Political Cycles and the Macroeconomy.* MIT Press, Cambridge, MA.

Althaus, Scott L. 1998. "Information Effects in Collective Preferences." *American Political Science Review* 92: 545–558.

Alvarez, R. Michael. 1997. *Information and Elections.* University of Michigan Press, Ann Arbor.

Alvarez, R. Michael, and Lisa García Bedolla. 2003. "Similar Yet Different? Latino and Anglo Party Identification." *Journal of Politics* 63: 31–49.

Alvarez, R. Michael, and Jonathan Nagler. 1995. "Economics, Issues, and the Perot Candidacy: Voter Choice in the 1992 Election." *American Journal of Political Science* 39: 714–744.

Alvarez, R. Michael, and Jonathan Nagler. 1998. "Economics, Entitlements, and Social Issues: Voter Choice in the 1996 Election." *American Journal of Political Science* 42: 1349–1363.

Ansolabehere, Stephen, and Shanto Iyengar. 1995. *Going Negative: How Political Advertisements Shrink and Polarize the Electorate.* Free Press, New York.

Ansolabehere, Stephen, Shanto Iyengar, Adam Simon, and Nicholas Valentino. 1994.

"Does Attack Advertising Demobilize the Electorate?" *The American Political Science Review* 88: 829–838.

Atkin, Charles, Lawrence Bowen, Oguz B. Nayman, and Kenneth G. Sheinkopf. 1973. "Quality versus Quantity in Televised Political Ads." *Public Opinion Quarterly* 37: 209–224.

Barreto, Matt. 2007. "Si Se Puede! Candidates and the Mobilization of Latino Voters." *American Political Science Review* 101(3): 425–441.

Bartels, Larry M. 1993. "Messages Received: The Political Impact of Media Exposure." *American Political Science Review* 87: 267–285.

Baum, Matthew. 2003. *Soft News Goes to War: Public Opinion and American Foreign Policy in the New Media Age.* Princeton University Press, Princeton, NJ.

Benoit, William L. 2000. "Comparing the Clinton and Dole Advertising Campaigns: Identification and Division in 1996 Presidential Television Spots." *Communication Research Reports* 17: 39–48.

Berelson, Bernard, Paul Lazarsfeld, and William McPhee. 1954. *Voting.* The University of Chicago Press, Chicago.

Bishin, Benjamin G. 2009. *Tyranny of the Minority: The Subconstituency Politics Theory of Representation.* Temple University Press, Philadelphia.

Bloemraad, Irene. 2006 *Becoming a Citizen: Incorporating Immigrants and Refugees in the United States and Canada.* University of California Press, Berkeley.

Brader, Ted. 2006. *Campaigning for the Hearts and Minds: How Emotional Appeals in Political Ads Work.* University of Chicago Press, Chicago.

Branton, Regina P. 2007. "Latino Attitudes Toward Various Areas of Public Policy." *Political Research Quarterly* 60(2): 293–303.

Bradshaw, Joel C. 2004. "Who Will Vote for You and Why: Designing Campaign Strategy and Message." In *Campaigns and Elections American Style: Transforming American Politics*, pp. 37–56, eds. James A. Thurber and Candice J. Nelson. Westview, Boulder, CO.

Brasher, Holly. 2003. "Capitalizing on Contention: Issue Agendas in U.S. Senate Campaigns." *Political Communication* 20: 453–471.

Brians, Craig Leonard, and Martin P. Wattenberg. 1996. "Campaign Issue Knowledge and Salience: Comparing Reception from TV Commercials, TV News and Newspapers." *American Journal of Political Science* 40: 172–193.

Cain, Bruce, D. Roderick Kiewiet, and Carole J. Uhlaner. 1991. "The Acquisition of Partisanship by Latinos and Asian Americans." *American Journal of Political Science* 35: 390–422.

Campbell, Angus, Philip Converse, W. Miller, and D. Stokes. 1964. *The American Voter.* John Wiley & Sons, Inc., New York.

Campbell, J. Gibson, and Emily Lennon. 1999. "Census Statistics on the Foreign-Born Population of the United States: 1850–1990." Population Division Working Paper No. 29.

Carmines, Edward, and James Stimson. 1980. "The Two Faces of Issue Voting." *American Political Science Review* 74: 78–91.

Clinton, Joshua, and John S. Lapinski. 2004. "'Targeted Advertising' and Voter Turnout: An Experimental Study of the 2000 Presidential Election." *Journal of Politics* 66: 69–96.

Cohen, Bernard. 1963. *The Press and Foreign Policy*. Princeton University Press, Princeton, NJ.

Connaughton, Stacey L. 2005. *Inviting Latino Voters: Party Messages and Latino Party Identification*. Routledge, New York.

Connaughton, Stacey L., and Sharon E. Jarvis. 2004. "Invitations for Partisan Identification: Attempts to Court Latino Voters Through Televised Latino-Oriented Political Advertisements, 1984–2000." *Journal of Communication* 54(1): 38–54.

Conover, Pamela, and Stanley Feldman. 1989. "Candidate Perception in an Ambiguous World: Campaigns, Cues, and Inference Processes." *The American Journal of Political Science* 33: 912–939.

Converse, Philip E. 1964. "The Nature of Belief Systems in Mass Publics." In *Ideology and Discontent*, pp. 206–261, ed. David Apter. The Free Press of Glencoe, London.

Cothran, Dan A. 1994. *Political Stability and Democracy in Mexico*. Praeger, Westport, CT.

Craig, Stephen C., James G. Kane, and Jason Gainous. 2005. "Issue-Related Learning in a Gubernatorial Campaign: A Panel Study." *Political Communication* 22: 483–503.

Dahl, Robert A. 1961. *Who Governs? Democracy and Power in an American City*. Yale University Press, New Haven, CT.

Dawson, Michael. 1994. *Behind the Mule: Race and Class in African-American Politics*. Princeton University Press, Princeton, NJ.

DeFrancesco Soto, Victoria, and Jennifer Merolla. 2008. "Spanish Language Political Advertising and Latino Voters." In *New Race Politics: Understanding Minority and Immigrant Politics*, pp. 114–129, eds. Jane Junn and Kerry Haynie. Cambridge University Press, New York.

de la Garza, M. F.-O., M. D. Newcomb, and H. F. Myers. 1995. "A Multidimensional Measure for Cultural Identity for Latino and Latina Adolescents." In *Hispanic Psychology: Critical Issues in Theory and Research*, pp. 26–42, ed. A. M. Padilla. Sage, London.

de la Garza, Rodolfo O., and Louis DeSipio. 1992. *From Rhetoric to Reality: Latino Politics in the 1988 Elections*. Westview Press, Boulder, CO.

de la Garza, Rodolfo O., Marisa Abrajano, and Jeronimo Cortina. 2008. "Get Me to the Polls on Time: Latino Mobilization and Turnout in the 2000 Election." In *New Race Politics: Understanding Minority and Immigrant Politics*, pp. 95–113, eds. Jane Junn and Kerry Haynie. Cambridge University Press, New York.

Delli Carpini, Michael, and Scott Keeter. 1996. *What Americans Know About Politics and Why It Matters.* Yale University Press, New Haven, CT.

DeSipio, Louis. 1996. *Counting on the Latino Vote: Latinos as a New Electorate.* University Press of Virginia, Charlottesville.

DeSipio, Louis. 2001. "Building America, One Person at a Time: Naturalization and the Political Behavior of the Naturalized in Contemporary American Politics." In *E Pluribus Unum? Contemporary and Historical Perspectives on Immigrant Political Incorporation*, pp. 67–108, eds. G. Gerstle and J. Mollenkopf. Russell Sage, New York.

Dimofte, Claudia V., Mark R. Forehand, and Rohit Deshpanade. 2003/2004. "Ad Schema Incongruity as Elicitor of Ethnic Self-Awareness and Differential Advertising Response." *Journal of Advertising* 32(4): 7–17.

Dinan, Stephen. 2008. "Obama Launches Spanish Ad; Touts Family and 'Values.'" *The Washington Times*, July 24: A6.

Downs, Anthony. 1957. *An Economic Theory of Democracy.* Harper and Row, New York.

Druckman, James. 2004. "Political Preference Formation: Competition, Deliberation, and the (Ir)relevance of Framing Effects." *American Political Science Review* 98(4): 671–686.

Easton, David, and Jack Dennis. 1969. *Children in the Political System: Origins of Political Legitimacy.* McGraw-Hill, New York.

Enelow, James M., and Melvin J. Hinich. 1984. *The Spatial Theory of Voting.* Cambridge University Press, New York.

Entman, Robert M. 1993. "Framing: Toward a Clarification of a Fractured Paradigm." *Journal of Communication* 43: 51–58.

Erie, Steven P. 1990. *Rainbow's End: Irish-Americans and the Dilemmas of Urban Machine Politics, 1840–1985.* University of California Press, Berkeley.

Erikson, Robert S. 1989. "Economic Conditions and the Presidential Vote: The American Case." *American Political Science Review* 83: 567–573.

Espiritu, Yen Le. 1992. *Asian American Panethnicity, Bridging Institutions and Identity.* Temple University Press, Philadelphia.

Faber R. J., and C. Storey. 1984. "Recall of Information from Political Advertising." *Journal of Advertising* 13: 39–44.

Fraga, Luis R., John A. Garcia, Rodney Hero, Michael Jones-Correa, Valerie Martinez-Ebers, and Gary M. Segura. 2006. LATINO NATIONAL SURVEY (LNS), 2006 [Computer file]. ICPSR20862-v1. Miami, FL: Geoscape International [producer], 2006. Ann Arbor, MI: Inter-university Consortium for Political and Social Research [distributor], 2008-05-27.

Freedman, Paul, and Kenneth Goldstein. 1999. "Measuring Media Exposure and the Effects of Negative Campaign Ads." *American Journal of Political Science* 43: 1189–1208.

Freedman, Paul, Michael M. Franz, and Kenneth Goldstein. 2004. "Campaign Advertising and Democratic Citizenship." *American Journal of Political Science* 48: 723–741.

Fry, Richard. 2007. "The Changing Ethnic Composition of U.S. Public Schools." Report. Pew Hispanic Center. Washington, DC.

Frymer, Paul. 1999. *Uneasy Alliances: Race and Party Competition in America.* Princeton University Press, Princeton, NJ.

Garcia, Ignacio M. 2000. *Viva Kennedy: Mexican Americans in Search of Camelot.* Texas A&M University Press, College Station.

García Bedolla, Lisa. 2005. *Fluid Borders: Latino Power, Identity and Politics in Los Angeles.* University of California Press, Berkeley.

Garvin, Glenn. 2007. "Dems' Bilingual Debate a Historic Moment." *Miami Herald,* September 9: 1A.

Geer, John G. 2006. *In Defense of Negativity: Attack Ads in Presidential Campaigns.* University of Chicago Press, Chicago.

Gerber, Alan, and Donald P. Green. 2000. "The Effects of Canvassing, Direct Mail, and Telephone Contact on Voter Turnout: A Field Experiment." *American Political Science Review* 94: 653–663.

Goldstein, Kenneth, and Travis Ridout. 2004. "Measuring the Effects of Televised Political Advertising in the United States." *Annual Review of Political Science* 7: 205–226.

Goldstein, Kenneth, and Joel Rivlin. 2005. "Political Advertising in 2002." Combined File [dataset]. Final release. Madison, WI: The Wisconsin Advertising Project, The Department of Political Science at The University of Wisconsin–Madison.

Goldstein, Kenneth, and Joel Rivlin. 2007a. "Presidential Advertising, 2003-2004." Combined File [dataset]. Final release. Madison, WI: The Wisconsin Advertising Project, The Department of Political Science at The University of Wisconsin–Madison.

Goldstein, Kenneth, and Joel Rivlin. 2007b. "Congressional and Gubernatorial Advertising, 2003–2004." Combined File [dataset]. Final release. Madison, WI: The Wisconsin Advertising Project, The Department of Political Science at The University of Wisconsin–Madison.

Goldstein, Kenneth, Michael Franz, and Travis Ridout. 2002. "Political Advertising in 2000." Combined File [dataset]. Final release. Madison, WI: The Department of Political Science at The University of Wisconsin–Madison and the Brennan Center for Justice at New York University.

Gordon, Milton. 1964. *Assimilation in American Life: The Role of Race, Religion, and National Origins.* Oxford University Press, New York.

Greenstein, Fred I. 1965. *Children and Politics.* Yale University Press, New Haven, CT.

Groenendyk, Eric W., and Nicholas A. Valentino. 2002. "Of Dark Clouds and Silver Linings: Effects of Exposure to Issue Versus Candidate Advertising on Persuasion, Information Retention, and Issue Salience." *Communication Research* 26: 201–225.

Grunwald, Michael. 2008. "The Campaign for Puerto Rico." *Time Magazine*, May 23. http://www.time.com/time/politics/article/0,8599,1809168,00.html.

Guzman, Betsy. 2001. "The Hispanic Population." Census 2000 Brief (C2KBR/01-3). May. www.census.gov/prod/2001pubs/c2kbr01-3.pdf.

Hajnal, Zoltan L., and Taeku Lee. 2008. "Race, Immigration, and Political Independents in America." Unpublished book manuscript.

Hayduk, Ronald. 2006. *Democracy for All: Restoring Immigrant Voting Rights in the United States*. Routledge, New York.

Herrnson, Paul S., and Kelly D. Patterson. 2000. "Agenda Setting and Campaign Advertising in Congressional Elections." In *Crowded Airwaves: Campaign Advertising in Elections*, ed. James A. Thurber, Candice J. Nelson, and David A. Dulio. Brookings Institution, Washington, DC.

Hibbs, Douglas A. 1982. "The Dynamics of Political Support for American Presidents Among Occupational and Partisan Groups." *American Journal of Political Science* 26: 312–332.

Hill, Kevin, and Dario Moreno. 2005. "Battleground Florida." In *Muted Voices: Hispanics and the 2000 Elections*, pp. 213–227, eds. Rodolfo O. de la Garza and Louis DeSipio. Rowman and Littlefield, Lanham, MD.

Hitchon, J. C., and C. Chang. 1995. "Effects of Gender Schematic Processing on the Reception of Political Commercials for Men and Women Candidates." *Communication Research* 22: 430–458.

Hofstetter, Richard, and Cliff Zukin. 1979. "TV Network News and Advertising in the Nixon and McGovern Campaigns." *Journalism Quarterly* 39: 640–652.

Hood, M. V., III, Irwin Morris, and Kurt Shirkley. 1997. "Quedete or Vete: Unraveling the Determinants of Hispanic Public Opinion Toward Immigration." *Political Research Quarterly* 50: 627–647.

Horton, John. 1995. *The Politics of Diversity: Immigration, Resistance and Change in Monterey Park, California*. Temple University Press, Philadelphia.

Hyman, Herbert H. 1959. *Political Socialization*. Free Press, Glencoe, IL.

Iyengar, Shanto. 1991. *Is Anyone Responsible? How Television Frames Political Issues*. University of Chicago Press, Chicago.

Iyengar, Shanto. 1996. "Issue Frames and Group-Centrism in American Public Opinion." *Annals of the American Academy of Political and Social Science* 546: 59–70.

Iyengar, Shanto, and Donald R. Kinder. 1987. *News That Matters: Television and American Opinion*. University of Chicago Press, Chicago.

Jackman, Simon, and Lynn Vavreck. 2009. "The Magic of the Battleground: Uncertainty, Learning and Changing Information Environments in the 2008 Presidential Campaign." Paper prepared for presentation at UCSD American Politics Seminar, May 16.

Jackson, John E. 1975. "Issues, Party Choice, and Presidential Votes." *American Journal of Political Science* 18: 161–185.

Jacoby, William. 2000. "Issue Framing and Public Opinion on Government Spending." *American Journal of Political Science* 44: 750–767.

Jamieson, Kathleen Hall. 1992. *Dirty Politics: Deception, Distraction and Democracy*. Oxford University Press, New York.

Jamieson, Kathleen Hall. 1996. *Packaging the Presidency: A History and Criticism of Presidential Campaign Advertising*. Oxford University Press, New York.

Jiménez, Tomás. 2007. "Weighing the Costs and Benefits of Mexican Immigration: The Mexican-American Perspective." *Social Sciences Quarterly* 88(3): 599–618.

Jordan, Miriam. 2008. "Obama Inspires a Latin Rhythm: Amateur Songwriter Helps Bridge the Gap with Hispanic Voters." *The Wall Street Journal*, March 10. http://online.wsj.com/article/SB120510381813923081.html.

Joslyn, Richard. 1980. "The Content of Political Spot Ads." *Journalism Quarterly* 57: 97.

Just, Marion R., Ann N. Crigler, Dean E. Alger, and Timothy E. Cook. 1996. *Crosstalk: Citizens, Candidates, and the Media in a Presidential Campaign*. University of Chicago Press, Chicago.

Kahn, Kim F., and Patrick J. Kenney. 1999. *The Spectacle of U.S. Senate Campaigns*. Princeton University Press, Princeton, NJ.

Kahneman, Daniel, Paul Slovic, and Amos Tversky. 1979. "Prospect Theory of Decisions Under Risk." *Econometrica* 47(2): 263–291.

Kahneman, Daniel, Paul Slovic, and Amos Tversky. 1982. *Judgment Under Uncertainty: Heuristics and Biases*. Cambridge University Press, New York.

Kasinitz, Philip, John Mollenkopf, Mary Waters, and Jennifer Holdaway. 2008. *Inheriting the City: The Children of Immigrants Come of Age*. Russell Sage Foundation, New York.

Katznelson, Ira. 1981. *City Trenches: Urban Politics and the Patterning of Class in the United States*. Pantheon Press, New York.

Kaufman, Karen. 2003. *The Urban Voter: Group Conflict and Mayoral Voting Behavior in American Cities*. University of Michigan Press, Ann Arbor.

Key, V. O., Jr. 1966. *The Responsible Electorate: Rationality in Presidential Voting, 1936–1960*. Harvard University Press, Cambridge, MA.

Kinder, Donald R., and D. Roderick Kiewiet. 1981. "Sociotropic Politics: The American Case." *British Journal of Political Science* 11: 129–161.

King, Gary, Michael Tomz, and Jason Wittenberg. 2001. "CLARIFY: Software for Interpreting and Presenting Statistical Results." Version 2.0. Harvard University, Cambridge, MA. June 1. http://gking.harvard.edu.

Kinnard, Meg. 2002. "Davis Woos Latinos, Hits Simon." *National Journal*, October 1. http://www.nationaljournal.com/members/adspotlight/2002/10/1001gdca1.htm.

Kochhar, Rakesh, Roberto Suro, and Sonya Tafoya. 2005. "The New Latino South: The

Context and Consequences of Rapid Population Growth." Report. Pew Hispanic Center. Washington, DC.

Koslow, Scott, Prem N. Shamdasani, and Ellen Touchstone. 1994. "Exploring Language Effects in Ethnic Advertising: A Sociolinguistic Perspective." *The Journal of Consumer Research* 20(4): 575–585.

Kozol, Jonathan. 2005. *Shame of the Nation: The Restoration of Apartheid Schooling in America*. Three Rivers Press, New York.

Landis, Richard, and Gary Koch. 1977. "The Measurement of Observer Agreement for Categorical Data." *Biometrics* 33: 159–174.

Lau, Richard R., and Gerald M. Pomper. 2004. "Effects of Negative Campaigning on Turnout in U.S. Senate Elections, 1988–1998." *Journal of Politics* 63(3): 804–819.

Lau, Richard R., and David P. Redlawsk. 2006. *How Voters Decide: Information Processing During Election Campaigns*. Cambridge University Press, New York.

Lau, Richard R., and Lee Sigelman. 2000. "Effectiveness of Negative Political Advertising." In *Crowded Airwaves: Campaign Advertising in Elections*, pp. 10–43, eds. James A. Thurber, Candice J. Nelson, and David A. Dulio. Brookings Institution, Washington, DC.

Leighley, Jan E. 2001. *Strength in Numbers? The Political Mobilization of Racial and Ethnic Minorities*. Princeton University Press, Princeton, NJ.

Lien, Pei-Te, Margaret Conway, and Janelle Wong. 2004. *The Politics of Asian Americans: Diversity and Community*. Taylor and Francis, New York.

Lupia, Arthur. 1994. "Shortcuts Versus Encyclopedias: Information and Voting in California Insurance Reform Elections." *The American Political Science Review* 88: 63–76.

Lupia, Arthur, and Matthew D. McCubbins. 1998. *The Democratic Dilemma: Can Citizens Learn What They Need to Know?* Cambridge University Press, New York.

Markus, Gregory B. 1982. "Political Attitudes During an Election Year: A Report on the 1980 NES Panel Study." *American Political Science Review* 76: 538–560.

McClain, Paula D., and Albert K. Karnig. 1990. "Black and Hispanic Socioeconomic and Political Competition." *The American Political Science Review* 84(2): 535–545.

McNickle, Chris. 1993. *To Be Mayor of New York: Ethnic Politics in the City*. Columbia University Press, New York.

Mendelberg, Tali. 2001. *The Race Card: Campaign Strategy, Implicit Messages, and the Norm of Equality*. Princeton University Press, Princeton, NJ.

Michelson, Melissa, Lisa García Bedolla, and Margaret A. McConnell. Forthcoming. "Heeding the Call: The Effect of Targeted Two-Round Phonebanks on Voter Turnout." *Journal of Politics*.

Nagler, Jonathan, and Jan Leighley. 1992. "Presidential Campaign Expenditures: Evidence of Allocations and Effect." *Public Choice* 73: 319–333.

Nelson, Thomas E., and Donald R. Kinder. 1996. "Issue Frames and Group-Centrism in American Public Opinion." *The Journal of Politics* 58: 1055–1078.

Nelson, Thomas E., Zoe M. Oxley, and Rosalee Clawson. 1997. "Toward a Psychology of Framing Effects." *Political Behavior* 19: 221–246.

Nie, Norman H., Jane Junn, and Kenneth Stehlik-Barry. 1996. *Education and Democratic Citizenship in America.* University of Chicago Press, Chicago.

Niemi, Richard G., and Jane Junn. 1998. *Civic Education: What Makes Students Learn?* Yale University Press, New Haven, CT. ⸱

Nir, Lilach, and James N. Druckman. 2008. "Campaign Mixed-Message Flows and Timing of Vote Decision." *International Journal of Public Opinion Research* 20(3): 326–346.

Oberfield, Zachary, and Adam Segal. 2008. "Pluralism Examined: Party Television Expenditures Focused on the Latino Vote in Presidential Elections." In *The Mass Media and Latino Politics: Studies of U.S. Media Content, Campaign Strategies and Survey Research: 1984–2004*, pp. 291–308, ed. Federico Subervi-Velez. Taylor and Francis, New York.

O'Keefe, Ed. 2008. "Obama Invokes Rush Limbaugh in New Spanish-Language Ads." *The Washington Post*, September 17. http://voices.washingtonpost.com/44/2008/09/17/obama_invokes_rush_limbaugh_in.html#more.

Orfield, Gary, and Chungmei Lee. 2004. "Brown at 50: King's Dream or Plessy's Nightmare?" Report. The Civil Rights Project at Harvard University, Cambridge, MA. January.

Orfield, Gary, and Chungmei Lee. 2006. "Racial Transformation and the Changing Nature of Segregation." Report. The Civil Rights Project at Harvard University, Cambridge, MA. January.

Page, Benjamin I. 1978. *Choices and Echoes in Presidential Elections.* The University of Chicago Press, Chicago.

Page, Benjamin I., and Richard A. Brody. 1972. "Policy Voting and the Electoral Process: The Vietnam War Issue." *American Political Science Review* 66: 979–995.

Page, Benjamin I., and Calvin C. Jones. 1979. "Reciprocal Effects of Policy Preferences, Party Loyalties and the Vote." *American Political Science Review* 73: 1071–1089.

Page, Benjamin I., and Robert Shapiro. 1992. *The Rational Public: Fifty Years of Trends in Americans' Policy Preferences.* The University of Chicago Press, Chicago.

Pardo, Mary. 1997. "Mexican American Women Grassroots Community Activists: Mothers of East Los Angeles." In *Pursuing Power: Latinos and the Political System*, pp. 151–168, ed. F. Chris Garcia. University of Illinois Press, Urbana.

Park, Robert E. 1928. "Human Migration and the Marginal Man." *American Journal of Sociology* 33: 881–893.

Patterson, Thomas, and Robert McClure. 1976. *The Unseeing Eye.* G. P. Putnam, New York.

Petrocik, John. 1996. "Issue Ownership in Presidential Elections, With a 1980 Case Study." *American Journal of Political Science* 40: 825–850.

Pew Hispanic Center. 2007. "Changing Faiths: Latinos and the Transformation of

American Religion." Report. Pew Hispanic Center and Pew Forum on Religion & Public Life. Washington, DC.

Pfau, M., R. L. Holbert, E. A. Szabo, and K. Kaminski. 2002. "Issue-Advocacy Versus Candidate Advertising: Effects on Candidate Preferences and Democratic Process." *Journal of Communication* 52: 301–315.

Pomper, Gerald. 1972. "From Confusion to Clarity: Issues and American Voters, 1956–1968." *American Political Science Review* 66(2): 415–428.

Poole, Keith T., and Howard Rosenthal. 1997. *Congress: A Political-Economic History of Roll Call Voting.* Oxford University Press, New York.

Popkin, Samuel. 1994. *The Reasoning Voter: Communication and Persuasion in Presidential Campaigns.* University of Chicago Press, Chicago.

Popkin, Samuel, and Michael A. Dimock. 1999. "Political Knowledge and Citizen Competence." In *Citizen Competence and Democratic Institutions*, eds. Stephen L. Elkin and Karol Edward Soltan. Pennsylvania State Press, University Park.

Portes, Alejandro, and Ruben G. Rumbaut. 1992. *Immigrant America: A Portrait.* University of California Press, Berkeley.

Preston, Julia. 2008. "In Big Shift, Latino Vote Was Heavily for Obama." *New York Times*, November 7: A24.

Pycior, Julie L. 1997. *LBJ and Mexican Americans: The Paradox of Power.* The University of Texas Press, Austin.

Rabinowitz, George, and Stuart Elaine Macdonald. 1989. "A Directional Theory of Issue Voting." *American Political Science Review* 83: 93–121.

Ridout, Travis, Dhavan V. Shah, Kenneth M. Goldstein, and Michael M. Franz. 2004. "Evaluating Measures of Campaign Advertising Exposure on Political Learning." *Political Behavior* 26: 201–225.

Rosenstone, Steven J., and John M. Hansen. 1993. *Mobilization, Participation, and Democracy in America.* MacMillan, New York.

Schmal, John P. 2004. "Electing the President: The Latino Electorate (1960–2000)." *La Prensa*, April 30. http://www.laprensa-sandiego.org/archieve/april30-04/elect.htm.

Segal, Adam J. 2003. "The Hispanic Priority: The Spanish-Language Television Battle for the Hispanic Vote in the 2000 U.S Presidential Election." Report. Hispanic Voter Project, Washington Center for the Study of American Government, Johns Hopkins University, Washington, DC. January.

Segal, Adam J. 2004. "Bikini Politics: The 2004 Presidential Campaigns' Hispanic Media Efforts Cover Only Essential Parts of the Body Politic: A Select Group of Voters in Few Battleground States." Report. Hispanic Voter Project, Washington Center for the Study of American Government, Johns Hopkins University, Washington, DC. September.

Segal, Adam J. 2006. "Total 2004 Spanish-Language TV Ad Spending by Market and

Campaign." Report. Hispanic Voter Project, Washington Center for the Study of American Government, Johns Hopkins University, Washington, DC. February.

Segal, Adam. J. 2008. "Democratic Candidates Spent Millions of Dollars on Univision, Telemundo Stations This Year. Initial Findings: Spanish-Language Advertising in the 2008 Presidential Campaign." Report. Hispanic Voter Project, Washington Center for the Study of American Government, Johns Hopkins University, Washington, DC. April 9.

Shaw, Daron. 1999. "The Effect of TV Ads and Candidate Appearances on Statewide Presidential Vote, 1988–1996." *American Political Science Review* 93: 345–361.

Shaw, Daron, Rodolfo O. de la Garza, and Jongho Lee. 2000. "Examining Latino Turnout in 1996: A Three-State, Validated Survey Approach." *American Journal of Political Science* 44: 338–346.

Shea, Daniel M., and Michael J. Burton. 2006. *Campaign Craft: The Strategies, Tactics, and Art of Political Campaign Management.* Praeger, Westport, CT.

Shepsle, Kenneth. 1972. "The Strategy of Ambiguity: Uncertainty and Electoral Competition." *American Political Science Review* 66: 555– 568.

Shin, Hyon, and Rosalind Bruno. 2003. "Language Use and English-Speaking Ability: 2000." Census 2000 Brief (C2KBR-29). October. www.census.gov/prod/2003pubs/c2kbr-29.pdf.

Simon, Adam. 2002. *The Winning Message: Candidate Behavior, Campaign Discourse, and Democracy.* Cambridge University Press, New York.

Skerry, Peter. 1997. "E Pluribus Hispanic?" In *Pursuing Power: Latinos and the Political System*, pp. 16–30, ed. F. Chris Garcia. University of Illinois Press, Urbana.

Spilliotes, Constantine J., and Lynn Vavreck. 2002. "Campaign Advertising: Partisan Convergence or Divergence." *Journal of Politics* 64: 249–261.

Steinhorn, Leonard. 2004. "Ads Are Us: Political Advertising in a Mass Media Culture." In *Campaigns and Elections American Style*, pp. 109–128, eds. James A. Thurber and Candice J . Nelson. Westview Press, Boulder, CO.

Stemler, Steve. 2001. "An Overview of Content Analysis." *Practical Assessment, Research, and Evaluation* 7(17). Available from http://edresearch.org.

Subervi-Velez, Federico A., and Stacey L. Connaughton. 2008. "Democratic and Republican Mass Communication Campaign Strategies: A Historical Overview." In *The Mass Media and Latino Politics: Studies of U.S. Media Content, Campaign Strategies and Survey Research: 1984–2004*, pp. 273–290, ed. Federico Subervi-Velez. Routledge, New York.

Telles, Edward, and Vilma Ortiz. 2008. *Generations of Exclusions: Mexican-Americans, Assimilation and Race.* Russell Sage Foundation Publications, New York.

Tversky, Amos, and Daniel Kahneman. 1981. "The Framing of Decisions and the Psychology of Choice." *Science* 2111(4481): 453–458.

U.S. Census Bureau. 2000a. "United States Foreign-Born Population." Population Division. March. http://www.census.gov/population/www/socdemo/foreign/cps2000 .html.

U.S. Census Bureau. 2000b. "U.S. Interim Projections by Age, Sex, Race, and Hispanic Origin: 2000–2050." Population Division. http://www.census.gov/popula tion/www/projections/usinterimproj/.

U.S. Census Bureau. 2007. "The American Community—Hispanics 2004." American Community Survey Reports (ACS-03). February. http://www.census.gov/prod/ 2007pubs/acs-03.pdf.

U.S. Census Bureau. 2009. "Current Population Survey, November 2008." Population Division. February.

Vaillancourt, Pauline. 1973. "Stability of Children's Survey Responses." *Public Opinion Quarterly* 37: 373–387.

Valentino, Nicholas A., and David O. Sears. 1998. "Event-Driven Political Communication and the Preadult Socialization of Partisanship." *Political Behavior* 20: 127–154.

Valentino, Nicholas A., Vincent L. Hutchings, and Ismail K. White. 2002. "Cues that Matter: How Political Ads Prime Racial Attitudes During Campaigns." *American Political Science Review* 96: 75–90.

Vavreck, Lynn. 2009. *The Message Matters: The Economy and Presidential Campaigns.* Princeton University Press, Princeton, NJ.

Verba, Sidney, Kay L. Schlozman, and Henry Brady. 1995. *Voice and Equality: Civic Voluntarism in American Politics.* Harvard University Press, Cambridge, MA.

West, Darrell. 2001. *Air Wars: Television Advertising in Election Campaigns, 1952–2000.* Congressional Quarterly Press, Washington, DC.

Whittler, Tommy E. 1989. "Viewer's Processing of Source and Message Cues in Advertising Stimuli." *Psychology and Marketing* 6: 287–309.

Winter, Nicholas J. G. 2008. *Dangerous Frames: How Ideas About Race and Gender Shape Public Opinion.* University of Chicago Press, Chicago.

Wolfinger, Raymond, and Steven Rosenstone. 1980. *Who Votes?* Yale University Press, New Haven, CT.

Wong, Janelle. 2006. *Democracy's Promise: Immigrants and American Civic Institutions.* University of Michigan Press, Ann Arbor.

Wong, Janelle, Kathy Rim, and Haven Perez. 2008. "Latino and Asian Protestant Churches and Conservative Politics in the United States." In *Civic Hopes and Political Realities: Immigrants, Community Organizations and Political Engagement,* pp. 271–299, eds. S. Karthick Ramakrishnan and Irene Bloemraad. Russell Sage Foundation Press, New York.

Zaller, John. 1992. *The Nature and Origins of Mass Opinion.* Cambridge University Press, New York.

Zhao, Xinshu, and Steven H. Chaffee. 1995. "Campaign Advertisements Versus Television News as Sources of Political Issue Information." *Public Opinion Quarterly* 59: 41–64.

# Index

Italic page numbers indicate material in tables or figures.